Political Change in a West African State

A *Study of the Modernization Process*

in SIERRA LEONE

Martin Kilson

Harvard University Press

Cambridge, Massachusetts

1966

AFFECTIONATELY DEDICATED
TO RUPERT EMERSON

Preface

In this book I undertake a description of the political institutions and processes that have characterized modern political change in African societies. Sierra Leone is used as a case study exemplifying this change. I focus attention particularly upon those political changes that modern colonialism created in local or rural African society. Rural society, after all, is where most Africans reside. It is there, not in urban areas, where the average African—or in our case the average Sierra Leonean—obtains daily experience with modern government and politics.

Many people have aided me in my work. Rupert Emerson, Professor of Government at Harvard, to whom this book is affectionately dedicated, read several drafts in manuscript and gave criticisms of inestimable value. He is, in fact, fundamentally responsible for the publication of this book. He, so to speak, found me and gave me the encouragement and opportunities without which I would have never been in position to undertake this book. My debt to him is immense.

The book has also benefited from comments by Thomas Hodgkin, Balliol College; Stanley Hoffmann and Samuel P. Huntington, Harvard University; and Immanuel Wallerstein, Columbia University. I am particularly indebted to Robert Erwin, Harvard Center for International Affairs, for his keen editorial advice, Linda Jean Harsh, Secretary to the Fellows Program of the Harvard Center for International Affairs, kindly typed several drafts of the manuscript.

My wife, Marion Dusser de Barenne Kilson, assisted in the research upon which this book is based. With enviable efficiency, she recorded documents and figures while simultaneously pursuing her own research, and negotiated thousands of miles of difficult driving through the Sierra Leone hinterland at a time when I did not myself operate a motor vehicle. She also helped me to grasp the theoretical relevance of my materials.

In Britain and Sierra Leone a number of persons lent a helping hand. Sally Chilvers, former Director of the Institute of Commonwealth Studies at Oxford, sheltered me at her commodious institution during my six-month stay at Oxford in 1959. Two other Englishmen who have been associated with Sierra Leone gave me benefit of their advice; Kenneth Little, Edinburgh University, told me how to get along with the Mende, and Bryan Keith-Lucas, University of Kent, aided my early effort to understand African local administration.

Davidson Nicol, Principal of the University College of Sierra Leone, allowed me to reside at the College during my stay in Sierra Leone. Richard Birkett, librarian to the College while I was there and now at Chatham House, London, provided me a collection of Sierra Leonean newspapers dating back to the late nineteenth century and helped me locate some rare copies of government reports. The late Sir Milton Margai, first Prime Minister of Sierra Leone, met every request I put to him for assistance. So did members of the Colonial Service, especially G. R. B. Blake, John Watson, W. Greenwood, and Michael Westcott, to whom I am quite grateful. I am also grateful to a number of Sierra Leoneans who helped me locate the pulse of their country's politics; I have in mind especially Gershon Collier, Constance Cummings-John, Nancy Koroma, the late I. T. A. Wallace Johnson, Issac Ndanema, S. M. Kone, Harrison Tucker, A. Wurie, Arthur Porter, Claude Nelson-Williams, John Nelson-Williams, A. H. Kabia, Maigore Kallon, and Sir Albert Margai, now Prime Minister.

I owe special gratitude to Franklin Ford, Dean of the Faculty of Arts and Sciences, Harvard University, and to Arthur Maass, Chairman of the Department of Government, for their encouragement.

I am indebted to the Ford Foundation Foreign Area Training

PREFACE

Program for a postdoctoral fellowship that enabled me to do research in Sierra Leone from December 1959 to February 1961. I have a related debt to Robert R. Bowie, Director of the Harvard Center for International Affairs, for financing a visit to Sierra Leone in the summer of 1962. I also thank him for running a research establishment that permits its participants to get on with their work, free of a lot of phony scholarly "togetherness."

Martin Kilson

Peterborough, New Hampshire
May 1966

Contents

Part V · Party Politics

Maps

Illustrations following page 176

Sir Milton Margai
Sir Albert Margai
Sir Milton Campaigning in Freetown
I. T. A. Wallace-Johnson and Stella James
Paramount Chief Julius Gulama
H. C. Bankole-Bright
John Karefa-Smart
Siaka Stevens
Paramount Chiefs Fula Koro II and Ella Gulama
Constance Cummings-John
Home of a Paramount Chief
Party Official Stumping for UPP
Madame Nancy Koroma
Tamba S. Mbriwa

Tables

Political Change in
a West African State

Introduction

Sierra Leone is situated in the southwestern portion of the West African bulge, between 7° to 10° north latitude and 10°15′ to 13°15′ west longitude. It is bounded to the north and east by Guinea and to the south by Liberia.

Portuguese voyagers were the first Europeans to make prolonged contact with this area, beginning in the mid-fifteenth century. As Christopher Fyfe has noted, they originally named the peninsula area of the Sierra Leone coast "Serra Lyoa from its wild-looking, leonine mountains . . . Corrupted through the centuries into many variants—as Serra Lyonne, Sierra Leona, Serre-Lions, Sierraleon, Serrillioon—the form Sierra Leone . . . has eventually prevailed."[1] Through trade in European goods, African slaves, and ivory, the Portuguese brought all the peoples around the peninsula under the influence of the Western world. This intercourse was expanded during the succeeding three centuries through British and Dutch slave trading, the human cargo of which went to the plantation economies of the Caribbean Islands and North America.

At the end of the eighteenth century the first step was taken toward establishing a modern governmental system capable of sustaining both commercial and cultural relations with the Western world. In 1787 a group of British businessmen, philanthropists, and missionaries, concerned partly with ending the slave trade and with removing impoverished freed slaves from the streets of London, arranged for the settlement of several hundred freed slaves in the peninsula area of Sierra Leone. By the 1790's

[1] C. H. Fyfe, A History of Sierra Leone (London, 1962), p. 1.

1

the area of settlement had been purchased from local tribal rulers, and, through the formation of the Sierra Leone Company under act of charter from the British government in 1791, it was placed under a limited system of modern government.[2]

In 1808 the area of settlement governed by the Sierra Leone Company was transferred to the British government and became thereby a full-fledged Crown Colony. Throughout the nineteenth century the hinterland experienced only fitful contact with the Colony's government as such. There were, however, more or less frequent economic and cultural contacts between the Colony and the hinterland. These were effected largely through the manifold trading activities of the Creole community of repatriated slaves.[3] The Creoles also assisted European missionaries who worked in the hinterland and were occasionally agents of the Colony's government as well. The combination of these functions gave the Creoles a preferred, caste-like status in relation to the indigenous Africans who resided in the Colony, and this status was supported by the Colony's government throughout the nineteenth century.[4] Moreover, after a British Protectorate was declared over some 27,669 square miles of the Colony's hinterland in 1896, those Creoles living in the Protectorate secured something of the privileged status held by Creoles in the Colony. Subsequent political change, however, worked to reverse this situation in both the Protectorate and the Colony.

Since the establishment of the Protectorate in 1896, the population of Sierra Leone has been comprised of some fifteen tribal or ethnic groups. The largest group today are the Mende (815,000), who inhabit the southern areas of the hinterland. The Temne, who reside in the northern area, are the second largest group

[2] The best account of the history of the settlement of Sierra Leone in 1787 and its subsequent development until the establishment of a Protectorate over its hinterland in 1896 is found in Fyfe, *A History of Sierra Leone.*

[3] The term "Creole" was used to designate the former Negro slaves who settled the coastal area of Sierra Leone, irrespective of whether their origin was as Settlers from Britain and North America or as Liberated Africans from slave ships headed for the New World. See Arthur T. Porter, *Creoledom: A Study of the Development of Freetown Society* (London, 1963), pp. 3–16.

[4] Cf. K. L. Little, "The Significance of the West African Creole for Africanist and Afro-American Studies," *African Affairs* (October 1950), pp. 308–319; Porter, *Creoledom;* Roy Lewis, *Sierra Leone* (London, 1954), pp. 31–40.

2

(620,000). The remaining groups each number less than 200,000 people and reside in the areas designated in Map I.

The total population of the Protectorate in 1960 was estimated at 2,150,000, as against a population of 100,000 for the Colony.[5] The average population density for the twelve administrative Districts of the Protectorate was eighty-five persons per square mile; the northwestern, southwestern, southern, and southeastern areas had the greatest density, ranging from 101 to 500 persons per square mile, while the northern and northeastern areas had a density of 76–100 per square mile and 51–75 per square mile, respectively. There were fifteen towns with 2,000 persons or more; the largest of these were Bo (15,610), Bonthe (7,554), Makeni (7,500), Magburaka (4,500), Kenema (4,000), and Port Loko (3,950). The Colony had a population density of 101–500 persons per square mile, and Freetown, the capital city and largest town, with 64,576 population, had a density above 500 persons per square mile.[6]

The overwhelming majority of Sierra Leone's people (perhaps 85 per cent) live in rural areas and labor mainly in subsistence agriculture, producing the staple crops of rice, cassava, yams, maize, as well as such subsidiary crops as okra, beans, pepper, and tomatoes. Some part of these crops also enter the domestic money market developed under colonialism, though the precise measure is unknown.[7] Cash-crop agriculture is primarily centered on palm oil, palm kernels, coffee, cocoa, piassava, groundnuts, and ginger, all of which enter the world market. In 1957 these crops constituted the bulk of agricultural exports from Sierra Leone (especially palm oil and palm kernels), representing 26 per cent of the value of all domestic exports.[8] Seven years earlier these exports represented 54 per cent of the value of domestic exports, but by the mid-1950's mineral exports had overtaken agricultural exports in this regard.

[5] Population estimates are found in *Sierra Leone Government Provinces Handbook, 1961* (Freetown, 1962)—hereafter cited as *Provinces Handbook* by year.

[6] *Atlas of Sierra Leone* (Freetown, 1953), Appendix, p. III.

[7] E. A. Waldock, E. S. Capstick, and A. J. Browning, *Soil Conservation and Land Use in Sierra Leone, Sessional Paper No. 1 of 1951* (Freetown, 1951), pp. 20–21—hereafter cited as *Soil Conservation*.

[8] D. T. Jack, *Economic Survey of Sierra Leone* (Freetown, 1958), p. 12.

3

MAP I

SIERRA LEONE AND WEST AFRICA

The bulk of subsistence agricultural production occurs in the upland and swamp areas of the southwestern and southern portions of the hinterland. The main cash crops, palm oil and palm kernels, are produced in both the southern and northern areas, the latter ranging from 250 feet above sea level in the northwest to a plateau of 1,000–2,000 feet in the northeast, with scattered outcroppings as high as 4,000 feet. The small amount of cattle raising in Sierra Leone's agriculture (there were 150,000–200,000 cattle in 1957) is carried on in the northern areas, where it is an extension of a larger animal husbandry centered in the highlands of Guinea.

The methods of agricultural production are markedly primitive, characterized by shifting cultivation, slash-and-burn field preparation, and a limited use of fertilizer. Instruments of production are equally primitive, with iron tools in short supply. As a government report observed in 1951: "For an estimated farming population of over a million adult men and women, there were imported (in 1948) 882 axes, 2,254 hoes and 33,214 matchets. When it is considered that few matchets last more than two farming seasons, it can be seen that the average farmer is poorly supplied indeed. In addition the supply of iron for the manufacture of tools locally is very limited."[9] Since 1952, however, mechanical ploughing has been applied to rice growing in some 15,623 acres of swamp grassland; in 1957 mechanically cultivated rice represented nearly 5 per cent of the total rice production.[10]

The organization of agricultural production is also rather undeveloped, based as it is upon a communal land tenure system and centered around the peasant family.[11] In 1950 there were only 29 Cooperative Societies in the agricultural sphere.[12] By 1957 the number of such Societies increased to 283, and there were over 500 in 1961. Of the 283 Cooperative Societies in 1957, some 199

[9] Waldock *et al.*, *Soil Conservation*, p. 13.
[10] Jack, *Economic Survey of Sierra Leone*, p. 14; Waldock *et al.*, *Soil Conservation*, p. 55.
[11] K. L. Little, *The Mende of Sierra Leone* (London, 1951), pp. 77 ff.; Merran McCulloch, *The Peoples of the Sierra Leone Protectorate* (London, 1950).
[12] K. A. L. Hill, *Report on Co-operation in Sierra Leone* (Freetown, 1949), pp. 13–18.

were producers' societies concerned with marketing crops; 108 of these were located in the southeastern area (70 in Kailahun District and 37 in Kenema District), 71 in the southwestern area, and only 19 in the north. The value of produce handled by these 199 producers' societies amounted to £239,180 in 1957.[13] Besides the Cooperative Societies, the other main form of modern agricultural organization is the Sierra Leone Produce Marketing Board, a government statutory body established in 1949. The Produce Marketing Board is responsible for organizing most of Sierra Leone's agricultural export; it sets the quality for cash crops exported and assists in preparing the export of palm oil through the purchase and operation of oil-cracking mills.[14]

Outside of agriculture, the number of persons actively or partially employed for wages or salaries has seldom exceeded 100,000 in recent years. Most of these are employed in government service of one kind or other; in 1960 the Sierra Leone Department of Labour had some 48,740 persons registered as employed for wages or salaries, of whom 26,034 were in government employment and 22,299 in private employment.[15] The majority of government employees worked in administration, transportation, and construction, while the private employees were in commerce, construction, and mining. In the hinterland, the iron and diamond industries, centered in the northern and southeastern areas, respectively, employ a major part of the private employees. In 1959 these industries employed some 7,000 laborers, and in 1957 they paid total wages of £728,000, as compared to £87,000 total wages for laborers in agriculture, £83,000 in forestry, and £629,000 in the building and construction industry.[16] The iron and diamond mining industries, moreover, earned some £7,660,000 through export in 1956, a figure representing 64 per cent of Sierra Leone's exports by value.

[13] Jack, *Economic Survey of Sierra Leone*, p. 59; *Provinces Handbook, 1961*, pp. 72–82; N. A. Cox-George, *Report on African Participation in the Commerce of Sierra Leone* (Freetown, 1958), pp. 19–21—hereafter cited as *African Participation in Commerce*.
[14] *Sierra Leone Produce Marketing Board First Annual Report* (Freetown, 1950).
[15] *Annual Report of the Labour Department, 1960* (Freetown, 1962), p. 17.
[16] Jack, *Economic Survey of Sierra Leone*, p. 7.

In April 1961, Sierra Leone gained its independence from British colonial rule, and an indigenous political elite formed a government. The political change and the modernization process that produced this elite, as well as the governmental institutions it now controls, are the main concerns of this study.[17] The context of this study is historical, and it is conceived in terms of the comparative analysis of African political change. The importance of placing such an analysis in its historical context cannot be over-emphasized. As Merle Fainsod has insisted, in commenting on the analysis of the modernizing role of bureaucracies: "Unless one is prepared to try to come to grips with historical experience in all its complexity and time dimensions, one runs the very real danger that any comparative treatment of the modernizing role of bureaucracies will be shallow, narrowly time-bound, and reflective of little more than contemporary melioristic concerns. Comparisons can be significant, not merely cross-culturally, but as they embrace the sweep of history within a single culture, and, indeed, it is when they combine both that they yield their richest fruits."[18]

Finally, a word about what "modernization" means in the context of this study. The term "modernization" refers to that complex of changes resulting from the contact of Western technological, industrial societies with the largely pre-literate (primitive) and pre-industrial societies of tropical Africa. These changes entail new patterns of social stratification centered on an impersonal market economy rather than the subsistence economy of indigenous African societies. Moreover, political institutions, norms, and power configurations come to extend far beyond the former family, clan, lineage, and tribal structures. The political changes attendant upon the modernization process in colonial Africa are of

[17] For the conception of the modernization process used in this study, see chapter 17 below. See also Martin Kilson, "African Political Change and the Modernization Process," *Journal of Modern African Studies* (December 1963), pp. 425–440.

[18] Merle Fainsod, "Bureaucracy and Modernization: The Russian and Soviet Case," in Joseph LaPalombara, ed., *Bureaucracy and Political Development* (Princeton, 1963), p. 239. Cf. Edward Shils, "On the Comparative Study of the New States," in Clifford Geertz, ed., *Old Societies and New States* (New York, 1963), pp. 10–11. Like Fainsod, Professor Shils insists that "temporal depth is necessary in all social science studies; but the need is more obvious in the study of the new states . . ."

special concern in this study; and the particular features of colonial political change that render it "modern" in the context of indigenous African societies are (1) the process of rationalization and (2) the increase in access to political authority and power on the part of the average person.[19]

[19] Cf. S. N. Eisenstadt, "Modernization and Conditions of Sustained Growth," *World Politics* (July 1964), pp. 576–594. See below, pp. 281–282.

Part 1-

The Establishment of Colonial Rule

CHAPTER I

Modern Colonialism and British Rule in Sierra Leone, 1896-1937

A. NATURE OF THE COLONIAL SITUATION

Stripped to its essentials, modern colonialism, as a social and political system, is a *relationship of dependence* established between the imported European oligarchy and the subject majority. This relationship represents the hub of what Georges Balandier has termed the "colonial situation"; all features of this situation revolve ultimately around the relationship of dependence whose existence rests upon the colonial state and the monopoly of force that it commands.[1]

Apart from the maintenance of the relationship of dependence between the imported oligarchy and the subject majority, the colonial state is concerned to govern this relationship in a manner conducive to the rise and spread of the market economy and related institutions.[2] It is equally concerned that the benefits derived from the market economy shall accrue in favor of the imported oligarchy. Any benefits received by the subject majority come mainly as a by-product of the former's gain.

Although Balandier was responsible for formulating this conception of colonialism in the postwar period, the salient features of it were evident in the work of Rupert Emerson on Southeast

[1] Georges Balandier, "La Situation coloniale: Approche théorique," *Cahiers internationaux de sociologie,* XI (1951), 44–79; Balandier, "Contribution à une sociologie de la dépendance," *ibid.,* XII (1952), 47–69, esp. 52–54.

[2] Balandier, *Sociologie actuelle de l'Afrique noire* (Paris, 1955), pp. 12–15.

11

Asia during the mid-1930's. Concluding his study of British and Dutch rule in Malaysia, Emerson observed that the material consequences of modern colonial transformation "are benefits handed down from on high by an alien master caste to an inferior society . . ."

At worst they are benefits in which the share of the general native public is essentially accidental since they were introduced exclusively or almost exclusively in the interest of the alien superiors . . . Every extension of benefits is conditioned by the existence of a superior caste which knows what is good for the subordinate peoples it rules and which resents and fights off any attempt on the part of its subjects to participate in the creative realm of ultimate decision. For the bulk even of the most enlightened and sympathetic colonial civil servants the fact is ever present that they are rulers of a dependency: their role is to govern while that of the people is to obey. This conception does not in the least exclude sincere efforts to improve the conditions of the natives and to lead them into a happier and more secure existence, but it does exclude the acceptance of the natives as equal collaborators in this work. The mark of the good citizen in a dependency is his readiness to accept and to honor the leadership which has happily been taken from his own incompetent hands by a wiser, stronger, and abler race . . . Socially, economically, and politically the European is a superior being whose superiority must not be called in question.[3]

The writings of the administrators and entrepreneurs who established modern colonialism bear testament to the extent to which this conception of colonialism was operative. In 1916 a British entrepreneur in Sierra Leone remarked that "West Africa must be worked by the African, but guided and ruled by the European."[4] Sir Harry Johnston, by far the most brilliant of the founders of Britain's African empire, proferred a similar observation in a letter to Cecil Rhodes in October, 1893: "This . . . expression, 'From the Cape to Cairo,' though often credited to you, is of my invention and was one of the first phrases I uttered on the

[3] Rupert Emerson, *Malaysia: A Study of Direct and Indirect Rule* (New York, 1937), pp. 484–485. Cf. J. S. Furnivall, *Colonial Policy and Practice* (Cambridge, 1948).

[4] H. Osman Newland, *Sierra Leone: Its People, Products, and Secret Societies* (London, 1916), p. 189.

12

earliest occasion of my meeting you in 1889 which attracted your attention . . . The Foreign Office and the Colonial Office then and now entertained much the same ideas that you and I held about the necessity of extending the British Empire within reasonable limits over countries not yet taken up by other European powers, to provide new markets for our manufactures and afford further scope for British enterprise."[5]

Another variant of the phenomenon which Balandier and Emerson categorized was the view that a colonized people's worth or "civilized quality" was to be measured by their contribution to the world's productive wealth. Sir (later Lord) Frederick Lugard produced perhaps the major treatise in colonial policy based upon this proposition.[6] However there were earlier proponents, among them a Captain Stigand who put the position as follows in 1914: "The real 'worth as a man' of a great number of Central Africans is, from the point of view of Empire, practically *nil*. Many of these live in their own sphere, neither supplying raw, or any other kind of, material to the rest of the world, nor receiving much from it. It seems to me, therefore, that one of the first things to attempt with such as these is to bring them up to the state of a producer; only when they arrive at this state can they claim the right of consideration as useful units of a great empire which is held together by the mutual support of all its component parts . . . The black man who is absolutely self-contained, neither producing for export nor receiving any import, has no place in the world's work."[7] Again, Sir Harry Johnston adumbrated the salient features of this proposition in a report to the Foreign Office on the problem of African labor recruitment in 1895: "All that needs now to be done is for the Administration to act as friends of both sides, and introduce the native labourer to the European capitalist. A gentle insistence that the native should contribute his fair share to the revenue of the country by paying

---

[5] Quoted in Roland Oliver, *Sir Harry Johnston and the Scramble for Africa* (London, 1957), p. 153—cited hereafter as *Scramble for Africa*.

[6] Sir F. D. Lugard, *The Dual Mandate in British Tropical Africa* (Edinburgh, 1922), esp. pp. 60–63.

[7] Captain C. H. Stigand, *Administration in Tropical Africa* (London, 1914), p. 3.

his hut-tax, is all that is necessary on our part to secure his taking that share of life's labour which no human being should evade."[8]

There was of course no necessary connection between the European's conception of what the colonial relationship of dependence should be and do and what was actually obtained in the way of material and other benefits. So many factors could intervene and produce quite different results from those expected. Nevertheless, there was a rather close coincidence between the European's expectations of the colonial relationship of dependence and the manner in which the apparatus of the colonial state evolved and was employed to help fulfill these expectations. When events turned out differently from what had been expected, Europeans seldom questioned the colonial state and administration as instruments of the modernization process.

B. FOUNDATION OF THE SIERRA LEONE PROTECTORATE

The British declared a Protectorate over the Sierra Leone hinterland in 1896. Apart from the strategic requirements of the competition with France to partition West Africa, the British were concerned to obtain access to the exploitable resources, agricultural, material, and human, of the area.

To some extent the Creole community in the Colony settlement had rendered parts of the hinterland commercially exploitable through petty trade carried on since the late eighteenth century.[9] The commercializing, and thus modernizing, effect of this Creole activity upon the institutions and peoples of the hinterland, however, was slight. More extensive and intensive modernization, in all its variants, could be obtained only through direct action of British colonial authority.

[8] Quoted in Oliver, *Scramble for Africa*, p. 270. Two years later Sir Harry remarked that "but for the enterprise and capital of . . . rough and ready pioneers Central Africa would be of no value and the natives would receive no payment for the products of their land, would in fact relapse into their almost ape-like existence of fighting, feeding and breeding." H. H. Johnston, *British Central Africa* (New York, 1897), p. 183.

[9] C. H. Fyfe, "European and Creole Influence in the Hinterland of Sierra Leone before 1896," *Sierra Leone Studies* (June 1956), pp. 113–123.

What was required above all else was a system of rational administration that was capable of protecting and advancing trade, private enterprise, and capital. This requirement of the market economy was quite apparent to the British administrators who established the Protectorate in 1896, as the testimony of T. J. Alldridge, the Travelling District Commissioner who negotiated the treaties of protection with the traditional rulers, makes clear. Writing four years after the promulgation of the Protectorate, Alldridge remarked: "There is now ample scope for the safe introduction of capital into the Protectorate. Formerly there was no means of recovering debts outside the Colony proper; today, under the Protectorate Ordinance, debts as well as crimes can be dealt with by the District Commissioner; there is consequently legal security for all property, whether European or native."[10]

The British penetration of the Sierra Leone hinterland was not, however, conceived solely as an economic proposition. Placed in a broader context of modernization which included all the trappings of the developed Western societies, including Christianity, the economic calculation was seen by British colonial authorities as, in Alldridge's apt words, "the thin edge of the wedge of civilisation." Other forces of civilization were to Alldridge and other British empire builders of much significance for its advance in Africa, but the economic factor had a special status all its own. "I am a great admirer of missionary efforts," wrote Alldridge in 1900, "but I believe primarily in showing to the people the need of individual work and of working to a paying end. With greater comforts about them, procured by their own labour, we may certainly hope that higher ends will be attained, and that the obstacles which encompass missionary enterprise and retard civilisation will be materially modified and more successful results obtained."

This conception of the colonial situation necessarily resulted in a certain type of administrative and judicial system. In general, it meant that British rather than traditional or indigenous author-

[10] This and the two following quotations are taken from T. J. Alldridge, *The Sherbro and Its Hinterland* (London, 1901), pp. 340, 340–341, 343.

ity must govern the behavior of persons not bound by customary rules. Such persons were, of course, foreigners (Europeans or Lebanese), though the Creoles were also partially included. More specifically, this conception of the colonial situation meant that matters affecting the economic activity of foreigners such as land rights, mineral or agricultural concessions, commercial contracts, and debts were invariably subject to British colonial authority. The traditional system of government and law could hardly be permitted jurisdiction over such matters, for, as Lord Hailey has put it, "the African's inexperience of all the contractual relations, involved in commercial transactions based on money economy, have made him (and his juridical system) a stranger to the legal methods in which a modern individualistic and industrialized society has expressed its needs."[11]

Thus, in the Protectorate Ordinance of 1896 which established British authority over the Sierra Leone hinterland, three types of courts were instituted: The Court of the Native Chiefs, the Court of the District Commissioner and Native Chiefs, and the Court of the District Commissioner. To the latter court was granted jurisdiction under the Ordinance in "all cases between persons not natives or between a person not a native and a native and all cases involving a question of title to land although arising exclusively between natives."[12] The District Commissioner's Court was also given jurisdiction in criminal cases involving offenses by natives that were construed as inimical to modern development; among these offenses were "Pretended Witchcraft, slave raiding, dealing in slaves or cases arising out of a faction or tribal fights . . . and such other cases as the Governor-in-Council may from time to time deem expedient." Other criminal offenses by natives such as murder, culpable homicide, rape, cannibalism, and ritual murder connected with secret societies (e.g., Human Leopard

---

[11] Lord Hailey, *An African Survey* (London, 1938), p. 296.

[12] *An Ordinance to Determine the Mode of Exercising Her Majesty's Jurisdiction in the Territories Adjacent to the Colony of Sierra Leone, No. 20 of 1896*, sec. 4 —cited hereafter as *Protectorate Ordinance of 1896*.

Similar provisions prevailed elsewhere in British West Africa. Cf. J. Aitken, *Memorandum on the Constitution, Jurisdiction and Procedure of Native Courts in Nigeria, the Gold Coast and the Gambia* (Freetown, 1930), pp. 1–4.

Society, Alligator Society, Poro Society) were likewise placed under the jurisdiction of the Court of the District Commissioner and Native Chiefs, in which court the Chiefs acted as assessors to the District Commissioner.[13] Finally, the Court of the Native Chiefs, commonly called Native Court, was given jurisdiction mainly in cases not covered by the other courts and involving exclusively natives. The Native Court also had jurisdiction in certain civil disputes involving African traders; but in 1937, as the number of African traders augmented, this jurisdiction was transferred to the District Commissioner's Court.

There is little doubt, then, that the legal system of the early Protectorate administration was related to the colonial authorities' conception of the colonial situation. The changes expected of this situation, especially the rise of the market economy and related institutions, could hardly be obtained with relative efficiency without the type of judicial arrangements established under the Protectorate Ordinance of 1896. Expatriates undertook a major part of these changes, and the legal system provided by the Ordinance endeavored to serve their needs. It was also attentive to the needs of those Africans who increasingly entered the emergent market economy in the post-World War I period.

C. COLONIAL CHANGE AND LOCAL ADMINISTRATION, 1900–1937

By the third decade of the twentieth century basic socio-economic change had necessitated modification of the Protectorate system of law and administration laid down in 1896. Whereas in 1898 Sierra Leone's exports and imports amounted to £290,991 and £606,348, respectively, by 1937 their value increased to £2,843,540 and £1,839,582, respectively.[14] The increased participation of Africans in the market economy was a concomitant feature of this economic advance; this meant in turn a greater measure of contact between Africans and expatriate groups and

---

[13] *Protectorate Ordinance of 1896*, sec. 10 for disruptive offenses, sec. 5 for land tenure.

[14] *Sierra Leone—Report for 1898*, Cmd. 9498 (London, 1899), pp. 6–7; *Trade Report for the Year 1937* (Freetown, 1938), pp. 5–9.

Creoles. New problems accordingly confronted the administrative system. As Lord Hailey remarked in a confidential report to the Colonial Office in 1940: "The problem created by the penetration of Syrian and other traders in the Protectorate is one of growing difficulty."[15]

The system of Protectorate administration established at the turn of the twentieth century was not suited to handle the new and more complex burdens of change. In particular, the role given to traditional authorities was too limited; they were organized mainly to handle problems of law and order, with their main responsibility for direct assistance to modern socio-economic change being limited to labor recruitment for public works and tax collection. These were essentially "extractive" functions, while the socio-economic changes that asserted themselves by the 1930's increasingly required that traditional authorities take on the "regulatory" and "distributive" functions as well.[16]

The new changes did not, of course, render the role of traditional authorities in maintaining law and order redundant; the majority of Africans were still dependent upon traditional arrangements for resolving issues arising from marriage, divorce, rituals, and property inheritance, and the resolution of these was not unrelated to the over-all maintenance of law and order in rural African society. But social change did require further limitations upon the jurisdiction of Native Courts in relation to those Africans increasingly entering the market economy. Thus, as already noted, the original jurisdiction of Native Courts in commercial disputes involving only Africans was denied in 1937 and given to the District Commissioner's Court. Another category of commercial disputes, those involving debts and breach of contract

[15] Lord Hailey, "Native Administration and Political Development in British Tropical Africa, 1940–42" (confidential report; London, *ca.* 1944), p. 73—hereafter cited as "Administration and Political Development."

[16] Myron Weiner, "Traditional Role Performance and the Development of Modern Political Parties: Reflections on the Indian Case" (unpublished MS, 1963), pp. 12–13. For Weiner the regulatory functions "involve placing limits upon what individuals can or cannot do without administrative approval . . ." The distributive functions entail "the distribution of goods and services to the population . . . the construction of roads, schools, electrification, irrigation schemes and the distribution of agricultural credit and fertilizers . . ."

between Africans and expatriates in the Protectorate, was placed under the jurisdiction of a new court called the Combined Court, composed of representatives of expatriate firms and Paramount Chiefs.[17] Furthermore, the whole caliber of the administration of justice in Protectorate was raised by the establishment of the Magistrate Court to be manned by a qualified lawyer, whereas the District Commissioner who manned his own court was rarely a person of full-fledged legal training. The jurisdiction of the Magistrate Court also surpassed that of all other courts in the Protectorate; the Magistrate could "on application of any party concerned or of his own motion (a) suspend, reduce or otherwise modify any sentence or decision of any [Protectorate] court; (b) transfer any cause or matter, either before trial or at any stage of the proceedings, whether before or after sentence passed or judgment given, to the Magistrate's Court."[18] The establishment of the Magistrate Court was accompanied by a reorganization of the earlier Protectorate police system, known as the Court Messenger Force. This force had virtually no central direction, being mainly the personal police arm of the District Commissioner and recruited largely by him, and was quite unsuited for the problems of security and order that began to arise in the 1930's. As the Governor, Sir Douglas Jardine, observed in his report to the Colonial Office in 1939 on the reorganization of the Court Messenger Force: "On my arrival in Sierra Leone . . . it was generally appreciated that the changing conditions of the Protectorate, the tendency towards industrialisation in the mining areas, and the increased sophistication of the natives in the larger towns were all combining to demand an increased standard of efficiency in police work—a standard which the Court Messenger Force under present conditions cannot hope to attain . . ."[19] The Court Messenger Force, thus, was first upgraded by new methods of recruitment and subsequently integrated into the central police force.

---

[17] *The Native Courts Ordinance, Cap. 149*, sec. 23; N. J. Brooke, *Report on the Native Court System in Sierra Leone* (Freetown, 1953), pp. 31–32. See also *Protectorate Courts Jurisdiction (Amendment) Ordinance, No. 9 of 1937.*

[18] *The Native Courts Ordinance, Cap. 149*, sec. 27.

[19] *A Scheme for the Reorganisation of the Court Messenger Force, Sessional Paper No. 7 of 1939* (Freetown, 1939), p. 1.

More significant than these alterations in the Protectorate judicial and police systems were the changes in the role and functions of traditional authorities. Apart from the new problems confronting Protectorate administration by the 1930's such as sanitation, water supply, and general social welfare, new factors affecting the relations between Chiefs and the peasantry and hinterland town-dwellers were also important in causing the colonial government to institute new functions, both regulatory and distributive, for traditional authorities. The rural populace was particularly experiencing change in its pattern of allegiance toward Chiefs, especially with regard to customary labor and tribute payment. By the 1920's these exactions, especially tribute, had undergone a transformation from exactions in kind to exactions expressed in monetary terms; this in turn caused peasants and town-dwellers to question the legitimacy of such customary claims and to seek ways of opposing or escaping them. The instability in the local political structure resulting from this situation increasingly became a matter of concern to the colonial government. As the Provincial Commissioner in the Southern Province observed in 1921: "[It is] evident that closer scrutiny into the relation of the chiefs and their people has become necessary, particularly concerning the levying of tribute. Complaints hitherto inarticulate are . . . gaining force and volume . . . The future points to fields for great improvement and development in the administrative system of the chiefs . . . which it is now possible to submit to closer scrutiny."[20] Related to the peasantry's changing perception of its relationship to chiefly rulers were a variety of new forces which brought the peasantry into touch with new ideas and modes of life. In a report by the Senior District Commissioner, J. S. Fenton, in 1935, which laid down the framework for reorganizing the earlier Protectorate administration, these forces were adumbrated as follows: "In the face of modern conditions (education, effects of mines, etc.) it appears the native institutions of the chiefdoms are no longer secure . . . Native institutions are likely to be more heavily attacked in the near future. Increasing

[20] H. Ross, *Annual Report of the Southern Province for the Year 1921* (Freetown, 1922), pp. 7, 11.

ease of travel and the attraction of mines means the influx of strangers into the chiefdoms, strangers who know what is done elsewhere, who criticize and despise a weak native government, or one which tends to be reactionary or oppressive."[21]

These changes in rural society provided the context for a fundamental transformation of the earlier Protectorate administration. It was now apparent that the earlier system, in Fenton's words, was geared too much to "the first responsibility of local administration"—namely, the preservation of law and order.[22] This meant, according to Fenton, that the traditional authorities were "preserved in form but are not sufficiently active and growing . . . It seems we cannot be absolved from trying to put life into the tribal authorities."[23]

D. THE NATIVE ADMINISTRATION SYSTEM: BEGINNINGS OF LOCAL ADMINISTRATION MODERNIZATION

Commissioner Fenton's reference to the need to put life into the traditional constituents of Protectorate administration was essentially a call to fit them to perform a wider set of functions, more expressly geared to facilitating colonial change, than those prescribed in the Protectorate Ordinance of 1896. This need to reorganize traditional authorities was partially recognized in the 1920's, as evidenced by the enactment of the Public Health (Protectorate) Ordinance, No. 26 of 1926, which provided that when need arose a Chiefdom could be declared a "Health Area" and the Chief designated "Health Authority" empowered to perform a small range of health, sanitation, and medical services. There were other measures of this sort concerned with road making, agriculture, and education, but all were *ad hoc* in nature, not systematically integrated into the over-all system of Protectorate administration.

21 J. S. Fenton, *Report on a Visit to Nigeria and on the Application of the Principles of Native Administration to the Protectorate of Sierra Leone* (Freetown, 1935), p. 11—cited hereafter as *Principles of Native Administration*.

22 *Ibid.*, p. 14. Cf. Lord Hailey, *Native Administration in the British African Territories* (London, 1951), IV, 1–12.

23 Fenton, *Principles of Native Administration*, pp. 11–12.

To remedy the limitations of these isolated attempts to improve Protectorate administration the Sierra Leone government turned for a model to the Native Administration (N.A.) or Native Authority system that had been developed in Nigeria at an earlier period.[24] Three essential principles of the N.A. system in Nigeria were applied to the rationalization of Protectorate administration in Sierra Leone in 1937: (1) the establishment of separate financial institutions, known as Chiefdom Treasuries, for each unit of administration; (2) the grant of tax authority to each Chiefdom unit of administration; and (3) authorization of Paramount Chiefs and other tribal authorities to enact by-laws and issue orders in pursuance of social services and development functions.

Although the traditional Chiefdom unit was adopted as the basis of the administrative structure within which the foregoing principles of executive local government operated, its composition and characteristics were expressly defined, unlike its amorphous status under the earlier Protectorate administration.[25] Under the Tribal Authorities Ordinance, No. 8 of 1937 the Chiefdom unit of administration was designated "Tribal Authority" and defined to mean "the Paramount Chief, the Chiefs, the councillors and men of note elected by the people according to native law and custom."[26] The Paramount Chief in particular was looked upon, for all practical purposes, as the sole Native Authority; he was held ultimately responsible by the colonial government for the performance of the statutory duties imposed upon the Native Administrations.

Apart from the maintenance of law and order which, of course, continued to be an important task of traditional authorities, the most significant aspect of their role under the new N.A. system

[24] Margery Perham, *Native Administration in Nigeria* (London, 1937). The term "Native Authority" is slightly different in connotation from "Native Administration" and is virtually limited to Northern Nigeria. Whereas the latter term denotes the whole unit of local colonial administration, the term "Native Authority" refers to the Emir's position in a "Native Administration" as the sole "Native Authority."

[25] For an outline of the traditional authority system, see J. S. Fenton, *Outline of Sierra Leone Native Law* (Freetown, 1933), and K. L. Little, *The Mende of Sierra Leone* (London, 1951).

[26] *Tribal Authorities Ordinance, No. 8 of 1937,* sec. 2.

was the operation of the Chiefdom Treasury. The Chiefdom Treasury was authorized to receive revenue of Native Administrations, keep account of revenue and expenditure, and maintain inventories of Native Administration property. The Governor-in-Council laid down the procedures followed by the Chiefdom Treasury and the tax it was authorized to levy, which was called a "Chiefdom tax" amounting to 4 shillings per adult male per annum. The tax was "assessed by and paid to a chief or headman" who was held responsible under criminal law for delivering the tax collected to the Chiefdom Treasury.[27] The tax provided the Treasury with about 50 per cent of its revenue; the remainder was derived from government grants, court fees and fines, and a rebate from the hut tax which continued alongside the new Chiefdom tax. Finally, the tax assessment and collection was to be done under the direction of the District Commissioner.

As the Native Administration system took shape, it became clear that the treasury function was the most adequately performed of all the tasks imposed on the Native Administrations, though abuses of tax authority were not uncommon. It was rather in the uses of the revenue available to Native Administrations that the colonial government had difficulty in making the N.A. system effective. From its inception in 1937 to its reformation after World War II, the politics of the N.A. system revolved around the use and misuse of Native Administration revenue.

27 *Chiefdom Tax Ordinance, No. 10 of 1937*, secs. 3, 5, 16.

CHAPTER 2 -

Politics and Functioning
of the Native Administration
System, 1937-1949

A. THE SETTING: INDIRECT RULE AND CHIEFS

Indirect rule is the method of local colonial administration through the agency of Chiefs who exercise executive authority. It was applied in one form or other throughout British colonial Africa and was, from the standpoint of the metropolitan power's budget, a form of colonialism-on-the-cheap.[1] In the 1920's, for instance, the average British colony in Africa used one administrator to every three used in a French colony. In 1926 Nigeria had one British administrator for every 100,000 persons in the Northern Province and one for every 70,000 in the Southern Province; in French West Africa (total population around 12,000,000 in 1922, compared to 18,000,000 in Nigeria in 1926) only the territory of Upper Volta (population 2,300,000 in 1926) even approximated the ratio of British administrator to population in Nigeria, the ratio being one French administrator for every 48,745 persons.[2]

Sierra Leone was a typical British colony in this respect. From 1896 to 1921 the British governed the Protectorate (population

[1] Lord Hailey, An African Survey (London, 1938), pp. 1449–1454.
[2] R. L. Buell, The Native Problem in Africa (New York, 1928), I, 983–984; Hailey, An African Survey, pp. 236–241.

24

around 1,200,000 in 1920's) with only five administrators (District Commissioners) and one circuit court judge. By 1921 and later the consequences of socio-economic change necessitated a closer administration of the Protectorate, which entailed the increase of the number of District Commissioners to ten and the addition of ten Assistant District Commissioners and three Provincial Commissioners.[3] Nevertheless, the ratio of British administrators to local population was still lower than that found in French colonies.

However, the administrative advantage claimed by indirect rule in regard to its comparatively low charge upon the metropolitan power's budget was somewhat offset by the rather large claims that Chiefs were permitted to make upon local sources of revenue. These claims were instituted at the foundation of the Sierra Leone Protectorate and were carried forward, in one form or other, under the N.A. system in the 1930's. Initially the British colonial authorities granted Chiefs a variety of financial incentives to participate in the administration of their subjects. These incentives included stipend payments pursuant to the Protectorate treaties, a 5 per cent rebate on collection of the hut tax, incidental gifts, entertainment allowances, and board and lodging fees when Chiefs traveled outside their Chiefdoms. By 1930 these payments represented 10 per cent of the expenditure on Protectorate administration. In addition, the fees and fines of Native Courts were permitted to accrue to Chiefs personally; by the 1930's these revenues were estimated at more than 20 per cent of the total hut tax collected per annum.[4] Carried forward under the N.A. system in 1937 in the form mainly of regular salaries for Chiefs,

---

[3] *Protectorate (Amendment) Ordinance No. 4 of 1920; Order in Council No. 11 of 1920,* Schedule B. A decade later the administrators in the Protectorate were augmented to thirty-one, who were responsible for twelve Districts grouped within two Provinces: viz., Northern Province—Bombali District (24 Chiefdoms), Kambia District (11 Chiefdoms), Karene District (19 Chiefdoms), Koinadugu District (35 Chiefdoms), Port Loko District (12 Chiefdoms); Southern Province—Bonthe District (16 Chiefdoms), Kailahun District (17 Chiefdoms), Kenema District (13 Chiefdoms), Kono District (16 Chiefdoms), Moyamba District (17 Chiefdoms), Pujehun District (20 Chiefdoms). See *Protectorate (Administrative Divisions) Order in Council, No. 21 of 1930,* Schedule B; N. A. Young, *Administrative Sub-Divisions of the Colony and of the Protectorate* (Freetown, 1930), pp. 3–4.

[4] *Sierra Leone Financial Report for the Year 1930* (Freetown, 1931), p. 24.

these expenses largely undermined the capacity of Native Administrations to undertake modern social services for the local populace.

B. CHIEFS' STATUS UNDER THE NATIVE ADMINISTRATION SYSTEM

The financial incentives provided for Chiefs under the earlier Protectorate administration were an important factor in determining their status under the N.A. system in 1937. It was apparent to the colonial authorities that some form of financial incentive was required for obtaining Chiefs' participation in the N.A. system, and it was decided to grant them regular salaries which would represent a commutation of their earlier sources of income. The former sources of income of Chiefs, on the other hand, were turned over to the Native Administrations, and, combined with the four shilling Chiefdom tax and the hut tax (together making an aggregate local tax of nine shillings per adult male per annum) they constituted the major part of Native Administration revenue.[5]

The Chiefs, however, were initially cool to this arrangement, and some opposed it outright, preferring not to enter the N.A. system at all. It was simply more advantageous financially for some Chiefs to remain under the earlier Chiefdom unit of Protectorate administration. As Lord Hailey put it: "The income of some of the Chiefs holding 'unreformed' [pre-1937] Chiefdoms [was] sufficient to add to their reluctance to come under the 're-formed' [Native Administration] system, for it is clear that they would lose materially by doing so . . ."[6]

To overcome Chiefs' reluctance to accept the N.A. system, the colonial government arrived at a curious compromise: Chiefs were permitted to exercise voluntary choice on whether to enter the N.A. system, and if they decided affirmatively, the share of

[5] *Notes on Native Administrations—Instructions to Native Administration Clerks,* C.S.O. Circular No. P/87/37 of 15th December, 1937 (mimeographed; Freetown, 1937), pp. 4 ff.

[6] Lord Hailey, *Native Administration to the British African Territories* (London, 1951), III, 305.

Native Administration revenue available for Chiefs' salary would be very much in their favor.

The need for such a compromise reflected a major dilemma for colonial administration—namely, how to rationalize local administration in the face of basic socio-economic change while preserving the authority of Chiefs as the premier legitimizing force. The government took as axiomatic the need to maintain Chiefs' authority, for without it indirect rule would be rather meaningless as a theory of colonial administration and precarious in practice. This compromise, then, was a makeshift arrangement, inherently contradictory, endeavoring to fit administration through Chiefs to new tasks without causing any significant diminution of chiefly authority.[7]

Accordingly, Senior District Commissioner Fenton, who formulated the N.A. system for Sierra Leone, proposed a model budget for the Native Administrations which, as shown in Table 1, al-

TABLE 1

Projected Budget of Native Administration, 1935

Revenue heads		Expenditure heads	
Tax	£ 635	Paramount Chiefs	£ 300
Court fees	30	Sub-chiefs	37
Government grant	299	Headmen	37
		Speaker	40
		Clerk	36
		Messengers	54
		Court sitting fees	35
		Others	425
Total	£ 964	Total	£ 964

Source: J. S. Fenton, *Report on a Visit to Nigeria and on the Application of the Principles of Native Administration to the Protectorate of Sierra Leone* (Freetown, 1935), p. 16.

lotted as much as 56 per cent of revenue for administrative expenditures, under which Chiefs' salaries claimed by far the largest

[7] For the way this problem evolved in the Gold Coast, see Amon Nikoi, "Indirect Rule and Government in the Gold Coast, 1844-1954" (unpublished Ph.D. dissertation, Harvard University, 1956). See also L. Gray Cowan, *Local Government in West Africa* (New York, 1958).

share. The social services to be provided by Native Administrations were supposed to be carried out with the revenue that remained. In clinging thus to the assumptions of indirect rule when formulating the financial policy of Native Administrations, the colonial government, so to speak, was seeking to have its cake and eat it too. The government, therefore, not surprisingly convinced itself that despite the extraordinary share given to Chiefs' salaries under the model budget proposed by Senior Commissioner Fenton, the Native Administrations would nonetheless be able to undertake basic social services. For instance, in commenting on a model budget similar to the one shown in Table 1, Fenton conceded that the share of revenue designated for Chiefs' emoluments (60 per cent in this case) "is high in proportion," but he added that "as much as can be given without crippling Native Administration activities should be allowed to existing chiefs to gain their goodwill, which is important."[8]

An evaluation of the functioning of the N.A. system in Sierra Leone will show how feeble indeed was Fenton's hope that the Native Administrations would not be crippled by the proportion of revenue claimed by Chiefs.

C. EVALUATION OF NATIVE ADMINISTRATION, 1937–1949

Although two model Native Administrations were established in 1936 the N.A. system was not given a statutory basis until 1937, in which year eighteen Administrations were instituted. The expansion of Native Administrations between 1937 and 1949 proceeded rather slowly, largely because Chiefs had the right to decide whether their Chiefdoms should be made Native Administrations. Nevertheless, a decade later there were 121 Native Administrations, representing 57 per cent of the total number of Chiefdoms in the Sierra Leone Protectorate, as seen in Table 2.

The financial records of Native Administrations constitute an adequate basis for evaluating their functioning, and the records used here cover the period 1937–49. The latter year is chosen as

[8] Fenton, *Principles of Native Administration*, p. 17.

TABLE 2

Establishment of Native Administrations, 1936–1947

Year of establishment	Number of Native Administrations[a]	Total	Year of establishment	Number of Native Administrations[a]	Total
1936	2	2	1942	24	97
1937	18	20	1943	1	98
1938	14	34	1944	9	107
1939	26	60	1945	6	113
1940	10	70	1946	7	120
1941	3	73	1947	1	121

Source: *Sierra Leone Protectorate Handbook, 1947* (Bo, 1947).
[a] There were 202 Chiefdoms in the Sierra Leone Protectorate in 1936 and 211 in 1947.

the terminal point because by then the colonial government was well on the way toward replacing Native Administrations with a more modern unit of local government called District Councils.

Table 3 shows the revenue and expenditure of Native Administrations for the period 1937–49, during which time the administrative expenditure head (the main subheads of which were personal emoluments of Paramount Chiefs, Section Chiefs, Headmen, Court Presidents, and Court Members) invariably claimed about 50 per cent or more of revenue. To some extent, the disproportionate share of revenue going to administrative expenditures stemmed from the small size of some Native Administrations. But this was by and large only a secondary contributor to the unproductive pattern of Native Administration expenditure, for the pattern was equally prevalent in the larger and wealthier Native Administrations found in Moyamba, Kailahun, and Kenema Districts, for example. Chiefs, even the educated ones, simply lacked the service-orientation toward local government which the adequate performance of social services by Native Administrations clearly required; and combined with the colonial government's approach to Chiefs, viewing them as an indispensable constituent of local administration, there was no other outcome for Native Administrations than that revealed in Table 3.

TABLE 3

Comparative Native Administration Estimates, 1937–1949

Year	No. of N.A.'s	Revenue (£)	Expenditure Heads (£)								Total expenditures (£)
			Admin.	Educ.	Agric.	Med. & Health	Forestry	Misc.	Works	Extra-ordinary	
1937	20	16,101	11,368	—	—	81	—	—	60	2,423	13,732
1938	34	29,887	21,124	—	—	227	—	—	271	7,071	28,693
1939	60	50,092	33,984	128	—	451	—	12	542	15,143	50,260
1940	70	57,448	39,979	—	78	484	—	60	635	17,135	58,371
1941	73	61,044	41,615	132	290	656	108	63	1,125	14,576	58,565
1942	97	75,578	53,491	467	1,606	751	781	18	1,848	14,591	73,453
1943	98	88,407	57,079	792	2,824	1,504	418	2,088	2,557	21,471	88,733
1944	107	104,483	62,312	1,505	2,961	2,925	700	2,553	3,828	27,661	104,455
1945	113	112,165	68,524	2,263	4,366	4,013	1,288	2,502	4,925	20,249	107,107
1946	118	117,385	73,547	3,270	4,071	5,647	1,992	3,377	6,645	30,595	128,329
1947	121	124,065	76,538	5,133	4,008	6,828	2,515	3,741	6,126	30,287	135,176
1948	128	134,302	83,870	6,565	4,380	8,160	2,786	4,046	6,194	26,844	142,845
1949	136	156,196	88,524	8,351	5,576	9,702	3,195	5,187	8,110	35,407	164,052

Source: *Sierra Leone Protectorate Chiefdom Estimates, 1949* (Freetown, 1949), p. 1.

A more detailed breakdown of the administrative expenditure head for all Native Administrations in 1949 is given in Table 4,

TABLE 4

Selected Expenditure Estimates, 1949

	Expenditure by province (£)			
Administration expenditure head	Southwestern province	Southeastern province	Northern province	Total
1. Salary of hereditary officials				
(a) Paramount Chiefs	9,668	6,725	6,677	23,070
(b) Sub-chiefs	2,587	1,904	1,827	6,318
(c) Speakers	2,489	1,544	1,175	5,208
(d) Village Heads	1,516	1,148	1,150	3,814
(e) Entertainment	1,089	732	1,122	2,943
Total hereditary officials	17,349	12,053	11,951	41,353
2. Personal emoluments of staff (clerks, messengers, etc.)[a]	18,552	10,350	11,560	40,462
3. Other charges (stationery, transport, etc.)	2,938	1,787	1,984	6,709
Total administration	38,839	24,190	25,495	88,524

Source: *Analysis of Chiefdom Estimates, 1949* (Bo, 1949), p. 5.

[a] Included under "personal emoluments" are sitting fees to members of Native Courts, and these payments amounted to £14,467 or 35 per cent of total personal emoluments. Since Chiefs and other hereditary officials are members of Native Courts, this sum should be taken as an additional part of their income.

and it is evident that, relative to the revenue available, Chiefs gained sizable emoluments under the N.A. system. The total administrative expenditure in 1949 was £88,524, representing 57 per cent of Native Administration revenue. Of this total some 92 per cent, or £81,815, was claimed by salaries or salary-related payments. Paramount Chiefs alone received £23,070, and, when combined with the emoluments of other chiefly personnel, the payment to hereditary rulers represented 51 per cent of the total salary outlay and 46 per cent of the total administrative expenditure. These proportions are even larger if the court fees accruing to Chiefs are calculated as part of the total payment to hereditary rulers.

31

The extent to which the pattern of Native Administration expenditure in Sierra Leone was a direct outcome of the position Chiefs held under indirect rule is further suggested by comparative data on other British colonies. Table 5 shows the expenditure

TABLE 5

Native Administration Expenditure in Three British Territories

Territory	Year	Admin.	Education & Health	Agric.	Works	Total expenditures (£)
			Expenditure heads by %			
Tanganyika	1935	68.1	10.6	6.4	5.3	n.a.[a]
Northern Nigeria	1936	57.0	11.5	6.3	23.2	973,468
Western Nigeria	1938	60.0	11.8	n.a.	28.0	677,034

Source: Hailey, *An African Survey*, pp. 427–428, 440.
[a] Total revenue of Tanganyika Native Administration was £186,468.

of 77 Native Administrations in Tanganyika in 1935, 492 in Northern Nigeria in 1936, and 114 in Western Nigeria in 1938, and the unproductive charge of Chiefs' salaries on revenue was no different from that in Sierra Leone. In the important case of the Kano Native Administration in Northern Nigeria, which was the largest and wealthiest polity of its kind, the administrative expenditure head claimed nearly 40 per cent of total expenditure in 1936–37, and the salary of the Emir alone represented 13 per cent of total expenditure.[9]

D. CONCLUSION

British colonial authorities in Sierra Leone and elsewhere in Africa were unable to rectify the unproductive features of the N.A. system. This was virtually impossible within the assumptions of indirect rule. As T. O. Beidelman has remarked in a study of indirect rule in a Tanganyikan Chiefdom: "Indirect Rule [through Native Administrations] was workable only through a serious

[9] Margery Perham, *Native Administration in Nigeria* (London, 1937), p. 118.

discrepancy between promulgated public policy and actual political action, a discrepancy which in the long run contributed to many of the difficulties of colonial administration and social change in Africa."[10] Thus, it was ultimately necessary to replace the Native Administrations with a new unit of local government whose conception and inspiration were free, or relatively free, of the assumptions of indirect rule. Indirect rule, after all, was a method of administration more suited for *controlling* backward populations undergoing colonial change than it was for *facilitating* the depth and scale of such change. In the nature of the case, this latter function of local administration required units of government representative of the new changing forces, which the Chiefs who manned Native Administrations were basically not.

What, then, can be said about the contribution of Native Administrations to the over-all process of political change and modernization in Sierra Leone? For one thing, it would seem that the N.A. system played an important role in modernizing the social and political relationships between Chiefs and the rural masses. In particular, the inept functioning of Native Administrations (which included a large measure of corruption, to be discussed in later chapters) created points of friction between Chiefs and the masses which weakened the latter's age-old allegiance to the former. Second, the N.A. system enabled Chiefs to modernize a fair part of their traditional sources of authority and power. These several aspects of the N.A. system will be discussed in later chapters.

[10] T. O. Beidelman, "Warfare in Court: Intertribal Tensions in a Local Government Court in Colonial Tanganyika" (unpublished MS, 1964), p. 3.

Part II -

Social Change and Colonial Modernization

CHAPTER 3

The Framework of Social
Change in Sierra Leone

For the analysis of African social change, it is of little value to view colonialism merely as a dominating social and political system. It was certainly a dominating system, but also something more than this: it was a revolutionary system of social change in the context of pre-literate or pre-industrial societies.

As far as I am aware, Karl Marx was one of the first social scientists to emphasize systematically the revolutionary character of modern colonial systems. As Marx saw it, the dynamic character of Western capitalist societies was such that their expansion to non-Western societies inevitably resulted in the reconstruction of the latter along modern lines. Marx considered this process of colonial modernization as a historic contribution to the development of non-Western societies. He conceived development primarily, though not exclusively, as change in the forces of production, technical and human. In this sense Marx accorded a progressive role to the colonial systems in non-Western societies.

As Marx put it in his essays on British rule in India which he wrote for the *New York Daily Tribune* in 1853:

... We must not forget that these idyllic village communities, inoffensive though they may appear, had always been the solid foundation of Oriental despotism, that they restrained the human mind within the smallest possible compass, making it the unresisting tool of superstition, enslaving it beneath traditional rules . . . England has to fulfill a double mission in India: one destructive, the other regenerating—the annihilation of old Asiatic society, and the laying of the material foundations of Western society in Asia. The political unity

37

of India, more consolidated, and extending farther than it ever did under the Great Moguls, was the first condition of its regeneration. This unity . . . will now be strengthened and perpetuated by the electric telegraph. The free press, introduced for the first time in Asiatic society, and managed by the common offspring of Hindoo and European, is a new and powerful agent of reconstruction . . . From the Indian natives, reluctantly and sparingly educated at Calcutta, under English superintendence, a fresh class is springing up, endowed with the requirements for government and imbued with European sciences. Steam has brought India into regular and rapid communication with Europe, has connected its chief ports with those of the whole south-eastern ocean, and has revindicated it from the isolated position which was the prime law of its stagnation . . . England, it is true, in causing a social revolution in Hindostan, was actuated only by the vilest interests, and was stupid in her manner of enforcing them. But that is not the question. The question is, can mankind fulfill its destiny without a fundamental revolution in the social state of Asia? If not, whatever may have been the crimes of England, she was the unconscious tool of history in bringing about that revolution.[1]

In West Africa no less than in India, the colonial system generated the conditions of basic social change. Through Western education in government and mission schools, the establishment of Western type political and administrative institutions, and the rise of commercial and some industrial economic activity, African social systems were shaken at their foundation and prepared, to one degree or other, for replacement by modern social systems. In the meantime the two social systems—traditional and modern —coexisted. They interacted with each other in a process that would ultimately give the new system a structure that reflected the African reality but was unquestionably modern.[2]

A. EDUCATION AND SOCIAL CHANGE

Education was a fundamental element in African social change, and possessed certain features not associated with other factors of social change. For one thing, education could normally be attained by Africans without conjuring up fear among Euro-

[1] Karl Marx and Frederick Engels, *On Colonialism* (Moscow, n.d.), pp. 23–81.
[2] Cf. J. H. Boeke, *Economics and Economic Policy of Dual Societies* (New York, 1953); J. S. Furnivall, *Colonial Policy and Practice* (Cambridge, 1948).

peans that its attainment would necessarily jeopardize their colonial prerogatives. Furthermore, Africans could gain education with much less effort than that involved in the attainment of other factors of social change such as large-scale commerce, industry, and capital. Under the right conditions, all an African required to secure education was a limited contact with the cash or money economy so as to obtain the money needed for school fees and related expenditures. A final feature of the unique role of education was that, once attained, education invariably altered the African's way of life and social position. The fact that the son of one peasant farmer secured missionary education and another did not meant that one had access to new occupational functions such as a clerk in a European firm or in colonial administration. The other remained perforce in his village attending his father's farm. Thus, as a factor of social change, education necessarily contributed to the rise of a new system of social stratification. Throughout this study our concern with social change will be oriented in terms of the new social stratification it produced.[3]

The educational basis of social change in Sierra Leone was laid at an early date as compared to other West African colonies. The first mission schools were instituted in Sierra Leone when the philanthropic settlement of the Colony occurred in 1787. The provision of mission education at this period was rather small. In 1792 there were only 300 pupils enrolled in mission schools. Education remained restricted to the Colony until the 1840's, at which time mission schools were established in the southern areas of the Sierra Leone hinterland. By the second decade of the nineteenth century the colonial government, having declared the coastal settlement a Crown Colony in 1808, entered the educational field on a small scale. By the mid-nineteenth century the combined educational efforts of government and missions resulted

[3] In this approach I follow the anthropologist and sociologist. "The anthropologist viewing change with structural principles in mind is mainly interested in alterations in the network of social relationships. He observes individuals, either of their own free will or by compulsion, disengaging themselves from social ties and entering into new ones, and he sees one set of groups disappearing and another emerging." H. Ian Hogbin, *Social Change* (London, 1958), p. 54. Hogbin's full discussion encompasses pp. 21–56. Cf. Morris Ginsberg, "Social Change," *British Journal of Sociology* (September 1958), p. 205.

in some forty-two schools (all primary) which enrolled some 6,000 pupils.[4]

Although this educational development was admittedly small, it nevertheless stimulated the rise of new social groups within the African community. As early as 1854 the educational activity among the Creoles had produced one African lawyer; in 1872 another African was admitted to the British Bar, as were seven others between 1878 and 1890. In the early decades of the twentieth century this development of a new elite was even more striking, as will be seen later.

The changes resulting from education were for a long time almost totally limited to the Colony. The hinterland of Sierra Leone was declared a Protectorate under British authority in 1896, and a decade or so passed before its educational development produced basic social change. The colonial government was a crucial element in this development. In 1914 the government spent 2 per cent of its total expenditure on education in the Colony and Protectorate; in 1922 the figure stood at 2.7 per cent and at 6.5 per cent in 1936. In 1921 the total number of schools was 173, of which 70 were in the Protectorate enrolling 1,200 pupils, as against 8,320 pupils in the Colony schools. Fifteen years later there were nearly 100 schools in the Protectorate and the number of pupils enrolled in schools throughout Sierra Leone was 32,347. In the postwar period these figures saw a marked increase throughout the territory.[5]

B. COMMERCE, GOVERNMENT, AND SOCIAL CHANGE

Sierra Leone was a good example of African initiative in the field of commerce and trade. Early in the life of the Colony, many Creoles turned actively to trade for a livelihood. In addition to the hawking of British-produced goods among the indigenous peoples of the hinterland, Creole traders collected the agricultural products of the hinterland (e.g., palm oil, palm kernel, rubber, kola

[4] Doyle L. Sumner, "Education in Sierra Leone" (unpublished MS), p. 4.
[5] See Martin Kilson, "Sierra Leone," in Helen Kitchen, ed., *Educated Africans* (New York, 1962).

nuts) for export to world markets. Creole trading in the hinterland also stimulated the systematic cultivation of cash crops by the indigenous tribes. This process was vividly described by Governor Rowe in a dispatch to the Colonial Office in 1879: "The genius of the Sierra Leone people is commercial; from babyhood the Aku girl is a trader, and as she grows up she carries her small wares wherever she can go with safety. The farther she goes from the European trading depots the better is her market . . . These people do more than collect the native produce, they stimulate its cultivation. Many bushels of palm kernels are collected by the native women that they may buy the handkerchief and the looking glass brought to their village by the Sierra Leone [Creole] adventurers. Had she never visited them these kernels would have been left to rot on the ground. Tons of colah are exported from Sierra Leone which would have never been gathered from the trees had not this pushing huckster found her way inland . . . The relations of the Sierra Leone Government with its aboriginal neighbours directly affect the security of these travelling traders, and their presence in a country or their being driven away from it directly influences the sale there of British manufactures and the export of African produce."[6]

The scale of such commercial activity during this period was, of course, rather small. Palm kernels were the largest cash earner, bringing in £157,457 on the world market in 1891. Annual rubber exports ranged from £79,195 to £43,729 in the period 1896–99. Within ten years of the founding of the Protectorate the total value of agricultural exports stood at £700,000, as against £450,000 in 1896. Palm kernels remained the major earner among agricultural cash crops; between 1901 and 1926 the output of palm kernels and palm oil increased threefold (from 21,135 tons to 67,865), and their export value increased fourteen times (from £175,565 to £1,205,812).[7] The post-Protectorate period also experienced some industrial development of the money economy,

---

[6] *Despatch No. 35 of October 13, 1879, to Sir Michael Hicks Beech,* cited in N. A. Cox-George, *Finance and Development in West Africa: The Sierra Leone Experience* (London, 1961), p. 149.

[7] *Trade Report for the Year 1926* (Freetown, 1927), p. 17.

especially the production of minerals in the early 1930's. By 1936 the value of mineral exports exceeded that of cash crops for the first time; and this situation has continued to the present. In 1957 diamond and iron exports represented 72 per cent (£10,975,000) of the value of all Sierra Leone's exports.[8]

Governmental administrative and economic functions grew apace with private commercial and industrial expansion. Colonial governments were particularly active in the development of railroads, roads, port facilities, telecommunications, and other facets of the economic infrastructure, because private firms in the colonies were not anxious to undertake them.[9] Most colonial governments, in fact, saw their role in development largely in terms of facilitating the activities of private entrepreneurs. In Sierra Leone, for instance, the Governor expressed the official view on this matter in 1933 as follows: "It is the duty of every African [colonial] Government, not to provide work for the workless, but so to govern that private enterprise is encouraged to do so; that trade is allowed to grow without hindrance; that business houses are given every facility and encouraged to start new productive works, and that the inhabitants are helped to cultivate and utilize the soil."[10]

The role of the Sierra Leone government in economic development may be gauged from a consideration of the government's pattern of expenditure. In 1898 the total expenditure stood at £121,112, and it increased to £853,320 by 1925.[11] The bulk of this expenditure during the early period of colonial government went to directly economic undertakings, as can be seen from the data in Table 6 for the years 1913–18. By the 1920's a major part of Sierra Leone's economic infrastructure had been established

---

[8] *Sierra Leone Protectorate Handbook, 1952* (Bo, 1952), p. 52; J. T. Jack, *Economic Survey of Sierra Leone* (Freetown, 1958), pp. 27–32.

[9] *Private Enterprise in British Tropical Africa*, Cmd. 2016 (London, 1924), pp. 18–21.

[10] Quoted in Cox-George, *Finance and Development in West Africa*, p. 296. Cf. *Legislative Council Debates, No. 1 of Session 1933–34* (Freetown, 1934), pp. 6–7.

[11] *Sierra Leone Report for 1898*, Cmd. 9498 (London, 1899), p. 6; *Sierra Leone Blue Book, 1926* (Freetown, 1927), p. 54.

TABLE 6

Sierra Leone Government Expenditure, 1913–1918
(Per cent of total)

Expenditure heads	1913	1914	1915	1916	1917	1918
Administrative	16.7	15.5	19.5	20.4	20.4	19.2
Economic	52.9	50.9	47.3	39.4	37.6	38.7
Defense	6.8	4.9	4.1	10.9	8.9	9.8
Social	9.6	9.1	13.0	14.1	13.8	14.0
Transfer (debts)	9.8	14.9	13.3	13.6	16.2	15.2
Unclassified	3.8	4.3	2.6	1.3	2.7	2.9

Source: Cox-George, *Finance and Development in West Africa*, p. 208.

through government expenditure, and thereafter the economic expenditure head claimed a smaller proportion of total expenditure. Thus by World War II the economic expenditure head claimed 24.2 per cent of total expenditure, and only in the last year of the war did it approximate the prewar level. It stood at 37.3 per cent of total expenditure in 1945.

The social expenditure head expanded significantly during the 1930's; it represented 18.7 per cent of total expenditure in 1939, as against 9.1 per cent in 1914, and was 20.7 per cent of expenditure in 1945.[12] This increase was related to earlier changes in the economy, for as new economic institutions such as the port facilities, railways, and telecommunications emerged, there was need for more educated manpower to manage them. Education was accordingly an important element in the increase of the social expenditure head during the 1930's. The Sierra Leone government had a keen appreciation of the significance of education to over-all development. For instance, in a note appended to the estimates of 1919 the Governor remarked that: "Progress is impossible while . . . intelligence remains undeveloped. It is for this

[12] These and the preceding expenditure figures are taken from Cox-George, *Finance and Development in West Africa*, p. 259.

reason that I am anxious to see more attention paid to education
... in the Protectorate ..."[13]

Another reason for the increase in the social expenditure head
was the whole range of new problems in the fields of health,
medicine, and social welfare that accompanied the increase of
town-dwellers. The Sierra Leone government, like most colonial
governments, recognized the need to attend to these problems lest
their neglect should impair over-all colonial efficiency. Thus, in
defense of his estimate proposal to increase medical and health
expenditures in 1939, Sir Douglas Jardine, the Governor, informed
the Secretary of State for the Colonies that "during my visits to
the Protectorate I have been gravely perturbed by the lack of
medical and health facilities, and the increases under Heads XI
and XIA (Medical and Health Heads) provide for the first steps
to meet claimant needs in this direction. In this connexion I
would refer you to my despatch No. 792 of the 30th November,
in which I have dealt at length with the necessity for the provision of more ample funds under this and certain other Heads
of the Estimates if what I consider Imperial obligations to this
Dependency are to be met."[14]

The significance of the contribution of colonial government to
the social and economic development of African colonies cannot
be overemphasized. The colonial bureaucracy was in a unique
position to control the revenue required for such development,
and it was in keeping with their conception of modernization
that they should pursue it. There is little doubt that had the
colonial bureaucracy in Sierra Leone and elsewhere in Africa not

[13] Quoted in *ibid.*, pp. 208–209. The British government fully shared this viewpoint. Replying to a proposal of the Sierra Leone government in 1927 to allocate
£35,500 for an agricultural school and teachers' training college in the Protectorate, the Secretary of State for the Colonies remarked: "I desire to assure you
that I entirely agree with the attitude taken [on the significance of education] . . .
by the Government . . . during the debate in the Council and I am strongly in
favour of the adoption of these proposals. I attach the greatest importance to the
progress of the College of Agriculture and Teachers' College and I shall be deeply
interested in following the progress of the scheme." *Despatches in Connexion with
the Estimates for 1927, Sessional Paper No. 3 of 1927* (Freetown, 1927), p. 5.

[14] *Despatches in Connexion with the Estimates for 1939, Sessional Paper No. 4
of 1939* (Freetown, 1939), pp. 1–2.

shouldered this development, the degree of social change would be much less than it was.

C. SOCIAL CHANGE AND NEW SOCIAL GROUPS

Although we will later deal at length with the rise of new African social groups, we should note here the general features of such groups as they emerged during the late nineteenth century and the first several decades of the twentieth century. The available data are limited to the Colony area, but they give us an idea of how colonial socio-economic change led to a new form of African social stratification.

Data for 1888 show that of a total African population of 75,000 in the Colony, some 12,700 were occupied as merchants, traders, and hawkers; and 12,317 were classified as farm laborers. Since the Colony was an area of rather dense population, other occupations emerged to serve the specialized needs and demands attendant upon urbanization. In addition to the thousands occupied in trading and cash-crop agriculture, there were 2,611 persons occupied as mechanics, butchers, bakers; 1,964 fishermen and seamen; and some 3,767 domestics. There were, finally, some 679 persons occupied in such government services as transport, postal service, and general administration.[15]

By the second decade of the twentieth century the number of Africans employed in modern enterprises had increased. An official population count in the Colony in 1921 showed that of a total African population of 85,163, some 40,750 persons were occupied in the money economy. Represented among these Africans were 17,755 traders and hawkers, 12,963 cash-crop farmers and farm laborers, 5,203 mechanics and craftsmen, 1,255 clerks and merchants, and 1,159 government employees. A decade later the number of Africans occupied in the money economy in the Colony was 60,954 among a total population of 96,422, or 64 per cent of

[15] *Sierra Leone Report on the Blue Book for 1888*, Cmd. 5897 (London, 1889), p. 9.

the Colony's population.[16] A rough estimate of the occupational grouping of those gainfully employed at this time is provided in Table 7.

TABLE 7

Occupations of the Colony Population, 1931

Occupations	% of employed population (60,954 employed)
Agriculture	13.1
Fishing	2.1
Commerce	21.1
Professions	0.8
Government	1.7
Skilled trades	7.0
Laborers and servants	7.2
Miscellaneous	2.5
Unemployed	34.5

Source: *Annual Report on the Social and Economic Progress of the People of Sierra Leone, 1933* (London, 1934), p. 14.

One special feature of the new African social groups for many decades was the disproportionate number of Creoles among them. Given their earlier educational and economic experiences in the colonial society, the Creoles advanced more quickly into the modern occupations. They were particularly predominant in the professions, in the well-paid government jobs, and in the more lucrative merchant and business undertakings. As the Protectorate became increasingly involved in the modern money economy, the favored position of the Creoles was slowly but surely called into question. But it was not until the emergence of representative government and party politics in the post-World War II period that the Protectorate population was able to countervail against the Creole advantage.

[16] *Report of Census for the Year 1931* (Freetown, n.d.), pp. 36–38, 52, and *passim*.

D. THE ROLE OF EUROPEAN OLIGARCHY IN SOCIAL CHANGE

The role of the European colonial community or oligarchy in African social change was of such significance that it deserves special consideration. A crucial feature of the European influence upon colonial social change was the European monopoly of political power and authority. Their authoritarian political status enabled the expatriate groups more or less to impose whatever pattern they wanted upon African social change. As a result, the political consequences of social change were rendered much more predictable than would have been the case if this change were free from authoritarian political direction.

To some extent much of colonial social change was akin to the reorganization of society which occurred in Communist Russia. The colonial state in Africa, like the authoritarian state created by the Russian Communist Party, sought to regulate social change and to direct its political consequences into channels acceptable to the ruling oligarchy. The colonial system, however, had certain unique features not found in the Soviet pattern.

For one thing, the dominant groups in colonial Africa differed racially and culturally from the majority of the population. Politically, this meant that the alien colonial groups could hardly ever claim for themselves a natural legitimacy stemming from common racial and cultural characteristics. Sociologically, the colonial oligarchy's alien status and superior technological culture clearly marked it off from the majority of the population. Colonial groups were even distinct from that small segment of the indigenous majority who secured some of the attributes of modern power, influence, and wealth. However advanced this small indigenous segment might become, it remained subordinate to the overwhelming monopoly of power and wealth claimed by the colonial oligarchy.

This in turn had its own political consequence. The new indigenous social groups eventually recognized that to approximate the position of the colonial oligarchy presupposed the ultimate destruction of colonial rule. Short of this there was, as Georges

47

Balandier puts it, an "upper limit" beyond which the colonial oligarchy hesitated to let Africans advance.[17] It was the circumstances surrounding the maintenance of this "upper limit" that gave the colonial system much of its dynamic character—especially its political dynamic. An important part of the problem of political change in colonial Africa concerned the conditions required to preserve or regulate the European predominance over the ingredients of modern social change such as education, capital, technology, bureaucratic skills, and the like.

Another aspect of the European role in colonial social change was paradoxically its contribution to the fluidity or openness of modern African social stratification. Since the dominant European position prevented any given segment of the African population from being secure in whatever degree of modern social change it achieved, there was a tendency for any advanced African segment to attend to the needs of all Africans involved in the modern social system. Thus, the most advanced African groups such as businessmen, professionals, and intellectuals exerted pressure upon the colonial system not merely in their own interests but also on behalf of the wage-laboring and farming elements as well. The result of this was to keep access to the ingredients of modern social change comparatively open to a variety of African elements, with no single African group being able to monopolize "modernization."

This situation is not, however, a permanent feature of the process of modern African social stratification. It may be radically altered in the post-colonial period; for once political power is transferred from Europeans to Africans, there is a good chance that the African elite will monopolize this power and thereby dominate a major part of the ingredients of social change. A keen observer of Nigerian politics noted this tendency rather soon after the transfer of political power to Africans: ". . . Consumption by the wealthy in Nigeria is conspicuous. Large cars, fine clothes, big houses, the possession of refrigerators and radiograms all point to a man's success in life. In some ways this is expected of him, and

---

[17] Georges Balandier, "Social Changes and Social Problems in Negro Africa," in Calvin W. Stillman, ed., *Africa and the Modern World* (Chicago, 1955), pp. 60–69.

the class structure in Nigeria still appears open enough to allow anyone to attain these dizzy heights of opulence. Nevertheless the strata are hardening. Education, for instance, is already showing signs of division into that available for the privileged few on the one hand, and the less fortunate many on the other. Private schools are numerous and often get the best of both worlds, subsidized by the Government and at the same time charging fees high enough to restrict attendance to the children of the rich."[18]

Apart from political power, the European role in colonial social change rested upon its socio-economic predominance. It is thus necessary to obtain some idea of the scale of this predominance if we are to appreciate fully the European influence on social change.

Recent data for Sierra Leone presented in Tables 8 and 9 give us some notion of the European economic position. Of the total assessable income in 1957–58 of £7,392,971, some 43 per cent was attributed to exclusively European-owned enterprises operating in Sierra Leone (i.e., the category designated "Companies assessed in U.K."). Furthermore, 12 per cent of the assessable income was claimed by primarily European-owned enterprises (i.e., the category designated "Companies assessed in S.L."), though some of these were Lebanese-owned firms and a few were African-owned. For comparative purposes, it is notable that Nigerian data for 1955–56 show that of a total taxable profit of £12,155,000, about 57 per cent, or £7,017,000, was claimed by forty exclusively European-owned companies which represented only 15 per cent of the total number of companies in Nigeria.[19]

Another facet of the European economic predominance may be seen from the Sierra Leone data in Tables 8 and 9. A number of Europeans were included among the 935 parties with an aggregate income of £1,274,779 subject to assessment under the category of "Non-company trades and professions" in 1957–58, though a sizable proportion was Lebanese and the remainder African. Even among the 796 assessments under the category

[18] K. W. J. Post, "Nigeria Two Years after Independence," *The World Today* (December 1962), p. 524.
[19] *Federation of Nigeria Digest of Statistics*, Vol. 6, No. 3 (Lagos, 1957), p. 19.

TABLE 8

Categories of Taxpayers Assessed, 1948–1958

Year of assessment	Companies assessed in U.K.	Companies assessed in S.L.	Non-company trades and professions	Government employees	Pensioners	Non-government employees	Total assessments
1957–58	22	32	935	796	21	920	2,726
1956–57	22	42	993	773	32	959	2,821
1955–56	29	40	1,011	806	39	770	2,695
1954–55	30	48	981	796	40	728	2,624
1953–54	35	44	968	823	44	798	2,712
1952–53	37	49	892	822	42	689	2,531
1951–52	35	48	999	748	50	741	2,621
1950–51	39	48	1,085	736	158	655	2,721
1949–50	33	39	1,007	646	82	716	2,523
1948–49	28	33	1,001	649	104	694	2,509

Source: *Report on the Income Tax Department 1958* (Freetown, 1959), Table II (a), p. 4.

TABLE 9

Assessable Income of Taxpaying Groups, 1948–1958
(in £)

Year of assessment	Assessable income	Companies assessed in U.K.	Companies assessed in S.L.	Non-company trades and professions	Government employees	Pensioners	Non-government employees	Total assessable income
1957–58	7,392,971	3,168,514	888,027	1,274,779	958,639	24,194	1,078,818	7,392,971
1956–57	7,150,457	2,850,361	1,220,592	1,253,536	889,736	28,920	897,312	7,150,457
1955–56	6,927,027	2,210,641	1,507,935	1,198,886	1,255,951	31,789	721,825	6,927,027
1954–55	7,761,949	3,877,094	1,162,980	1,163,622	895,956	36,053	626,244	7,761,949
1953–54	6,447,886	3,646,259	154,856	1,119,774	803,138	35,054	688,805	6,447,886
1952–53	6,089,670	3,288,295	354,593	1,132,817	688,459	33,992	591,514	6,089,670
1951–52	5,464,008	2,807,299	356,541	1,135,091	603,715	30,853	530,509	5,464,008
1950–51	4,893,517	2,509,340	196,786	1,132,992	571,904	50,539	431,956	4,893,517
1949–50	4,437,206	2,418,626	289,449	811,246	459,042	36,622	422,221	4,437,206
1948–49	2,491,937	436,427	415,923	774,228	420,074	13,952	431,333	2,491,937

Source: *Report on the Income Tax Department 1958* (Freetown, 1959), Table II (b), p. 5.

designated "Government employees," whose assessable income was £958,639 in 1957–58, a significant proportion was European. Senior civil servants are the main group of government employees assessable for taxation, and during this period Europeans constituted 58 per cent of all senior civil servants.

Thus in terms of capital or business ownership and of salaried income, Europeans possessed an immense predominance over African groups. This predominance, moreover, persists during the early post-colonial period and has considerable importance in the new African states.

CHAPTER 4 -

Transformation of the Traditional Elite

A. NEW SOURCES OF CHIEFS' WEALTH

A much neglected feature of the study of colonial change in Africa has been the transformation of the traditional elite. As a group they claimed a disproportionate share in modern social change, owing largely to their role in local colonial administration. Their position enabled them to retain traditional authority while simultaneously pursuing wealth and power in the modern sector of colonial society. Among the sources of new wealth available to Chiefs were (1) direct money payments by governments, (2) tax extortion, (3) salary payments by Native Administrations, and (4) the commercialization of Chiefs' customary economic rights.

1. Direct Payments and Tax Extortion

Direct money payments to Chiefs began with the foundation of the Protectorate in 1896 and continued in various forms until the 1930's. The most important payment was the 5 per cent rebate from collection of the hut tax. The rebate on tax collection was common throughout sub-Saharan Africa, and in French territories it continued alongside regularized salary payments well into the post-World War II period.[1] Other direct payments to Chiefs in Sierra Leone included treaty stipends, annual gifts, and

[1] V. Thompson and R. Adloff, *The Emerging States of French Equatorial Africa* (Stanford, 1960), pp. 74–75.

53

entertainment allowances.[2] Though these payments were never large in absolute terms, they were significant relative to the incomes available to other groups in rural areas.

As the Chiefs strengthened their position in the Native Administrations after the late 1930's, additional incomes became available through illicit use of tax authority. Though it is difficult to provide precise figures on the sums accruing to Chiefs through tax corruption, there is some evidence on this issue. For instance, in the report of inquiry into the tax riots in 1955–56 it was revealed that Chiefs had been accustomed to providing for themselves modern houses, automobiles, and sundry other modern conveniences through tax corruption.[3] One Paramount Chief, who was a member of the Sierra Leone Legislature, had levied an unauthorized tax upon his subjects in order to finance a modern house costing £5,000; at the same time he owned three other modern houses also believed to have been financed by illicit taxes. Another Paramount Chief owned a four-storey concrete house which cost somewhere between £10,000 and £15,000.[4] The man in question, Paramount Chief Bai Farima Tass II, who was in the Legislative Council, claimed before the commission of inquiry that this house cost only £4,000; but this was flatly rejected by the commissioner: "Having seen the house I do not believe it cost only £4,000 if all the labour and materials were paid for at current rates. It must have cost much more than that sum . . . If the sum of £4,000 mentioned by him is correct, then it only reinforces my opinion that forced labour was used to keep the cost down to a minimum."[5] Another instance revealed by the inquiry

---

[2] *Sierra Leone Financial Report for the Year 1930* (Freetown, 1931), p. 24.

[3] Sir Herbert Cox, *Sierra Leone Report of Commission of Inquiry into Disturbances in the Provinces, November 1955–March 1956* (London, 1956), esp. pp. 151–160. Such behavior was widespread in West and East Africa. Lloyd noted in 1956 that among the Yoruba "some of the more popular *obas* have made a town levy to contribute towards the cost of their car." P. C. Lloyd, "The Changing Role of the Yoruba Traditional Rulers," in *Proceedings of the Third Annual Conference of the West African Institute of Social and Economic Research* (Ibadan, 1956), p. 61.

[4] Interview with District Commissioner, Kambia District, April 1960.

[5] This and the following examples are taken from *Reports of the Commissioners of Enquiry into the Conduct of Certain Chiefs* (Freetown, 1957), pp. 51, 67.

was that of Paramount Chief Bai Bairoh II, who forced his subjects to contribute £300 in unauthorized levies to purchase an automobile for his personal use.

2. Native Administration Salaries

Another source of modern wealth available to Chiefs in Sierra Leone was the regularized salary payment from Native Administration revenues. Table 10 shows that within a decade of

TABLE 10
Average Salaries of Paramount Chiefs by District, 1947

Districts	Salary (£)	Districts	Salary (£)
Bo	180	Kenema	212
Bombali	164	Koinadugu	104
Bonthe	197	Kono	176
Kailahun	197	Moyamba	226
Kambia	147	Pujehun	180
Karene	101	Tonkolili	109

Source: *Annual Report on the Sierra Leone Protectorate, 1947*, p. 8.

the establishment of Native Administrations, the average salary of Paramount Chiefs ranged from £101 in Karene District to £226 in Moyamba District. Although by the immediate postwar period illegal or quasi-legal sources of income may have contributed more to Chiefs' total income than their salaries, during the 1950's the latter increased significantly and became an important component of total income. Table 11 shows that between 1949

TABLE 11
Salary Payments to Paramount Chiefs, 1949–1956

Year	Salary payments (£)	Year	Salary payments (£)
1949	23,070	1953	49,448
1950	29,942	1954	53,770
1951	34,456	1955	61,114
1952	42,681	1956	63,664

Source: *Report on the Administration of the Provinces, 1956* (Freetown, 1959), p. 22.

and 1956 the total salary payments to Chiefs more than doubled and these payments were supplemented by a central government grant that totaled £141,998 during 1957–60.[6] As regards the more recent salaries of some Chiefs, their range may be gauged from the salaries of Paramount Chiefs in Tonkolili District as shown in Table 12.

TABLE 12

Salaries of Paramount Chiefs in Selected Chiefdoms,
Tonkolili District, 1960

Chiefdom	Salary (£)	Chiefdom	Salary (£)
Yoni	579	Kholifa-Mabang	360
Bonkolenken	600	Sambaia	700
Kholifa	822		

Source: *Tonkolili Chiefdom Estimates, 1960* (District Commissioner's Office, Tonkolili).

It may be noted by way of comparison that even larger salaries were claimed by traditional rulers elsewhere in Africa. Some of the highest chiefly salaries anywhere in Africa were found in Nigeria. The Emir of Kano Native Authority, for example, received a £7,700 salary in 1960; the Emir of Kazaure Native Authority received £1,320; the Emir of Argungu Native Authority received £1,430; and many Yoruba *obas* claimed salaries of £2,000 in 1956.[7] In East Africa traditional rulers received somewhat smaller salaries on the average, but relative to the incomes available to most of the population these salaries were comparable to those of West African traditional rulers. For instance, in 1953 the Sukuma Chiefs in Tanganyika received salaries ranging from £100 to £500; the Bunyoro County Chiefs in Uganda received

[6] *Sierra Leone Government Estimates of Expenditure and Revenue, 1959–1960* (Freetown, 1959), p. 43.

[7] *Native Administration Estimates, 1959–1960, Kano Province* (Kaduna, 1960), pp. 60, 117; *Native Administration Estimates, 1959–1960, Sokoto Province* (Kaduna, 1960), p. 6; Lloyd, "The Changing Role of the Yoruba Traditional Rulers," pp. 60–61.

salaries from £400 to £500; and Ganda County Chiefs in Uganda received salaries from £270 to £600.[8]

3. Commercialization of Traditional Economic Relations

It is seldom recognized that much of colonial socio-economic change was mediated by traditional relationships. Such traditional economic relations as Chiefs' customary rights to tribute and labor were carried forward as social and economic modernization proceeded. During the early period of colonial rule in Africa, such customary rights were not merely left undisturbed by colonial government but were often embodied in colonial laws. The Sierra Leone Protectorate Native Law Ordinance of 1905, for instance, sonctioned Chiefs' rights to customary tribute through the medium of sub-Chiefs and Headmen and upheld as mandatory Chiefs' rights to free labor: "Every Paramount Chief in his capacity as Chief . . . shall continue to have the same powers with respect to obtaining labor that they have heretofore possessed, that is to say, the farms of such Chiefs . . . shall be worked by the labourers of such Chiefs and by all the people respectively recognizing each such Chief . . ., and such people respectively shall continue to supply labour sufficient to enable the farms of their Chief to be properly worked."[9]

The maintenance of these customary rights under colonial modernization necessarily gave Chiefs an initial advantage over other segments of the population. Under the money or exchange economy Chiefs' customary rights to tribute and labor were readily convertible from a status of wealth in kind to modern forms of wealth—money and capital. Thus, having accommodated to colonial rule, it was of no surprise that traditional rulers were among the first groups in local African society to participate in the market economy through cash-crop production and marketing. Three years after the promulgation of the Protectorate and a year after the Hut Tax War, the Colonial Secretary informed the

[8] A. I. Richards, *East African Chiefs* (London, 1960), pp. 64–65, 92–93, 244; John Beattie, *Bunyoro: An African Kingdom* (New York, 1961), p. 43.

[9] *Protectorate Native Law Ordinance, No. 16 of 1905*, sec. 15, pp. 17–20.

British government in London that Sierra Leonean Chiefs were accommodating to indirect rule and were especially "taking to trade and beginning to understand that there are other chattels besides a multiplicity of slaves and wives which conduce to material wealth and prosperity . . ."[10]

When the Native Administrations were established in 1937, Chiefs theoretically surrendered customary rights to tribute in return for regular salaries. (The British used this policy throughout Africa when establishing systematic local government through Chiefs.) In reality, however, these rights continued and were more or less acquiesced in by the colonial government, save on occasions when their use resulted in peasant rebellion. Only in 1956, under pressure of widespread peasant disturbances, did the Sierra Leone government finally put an end to exaction of customary tribute by Chiefs.[11]

As regards customary rights to labor, the Forced Labour Ordinance of 1932 modified the application of these rights as laid down in the Native Law Ordinance of 1905 but did not terminate them. It provided that peasants need render free labor to Chiefs for no more than thirty days per year and no more than six days in any week, whereas the earlier requirements were much more onerous. Under Native Administrations, however, the Chiefs' exercise of customary rights to labor became very oppressive and was a major factor underlying the peasant tax riots in 1955–56. These riots, in fact, led the Sierra Leone government to outlaw customary labor claims once and for all.[12]

Chiefs employed several methods in converting their customary rights into modern economic gain. First, they marketed the sizable stores of agricultural products secured as tribute from peasants; second, they expanded their own cash-crop output with the aid of free labor; third, they utilized traditional authority to establish and protect markets for themselves; and fourth, they

---

[10] *Sierra Leone Report for 1899*, Cmd. 354 (London, 1900), p. 45.

[11] *Statement of the Sierra Leone Government on the Report of the Commission of Inquiry into Disturbances in the Protectorate* (Freetown, 1956), p. 12.

[12] Cox, *Sierra Leone Report of Commission of Inquiry into Disturbances in the Provinces*, p. 162; *Statement of the Sierra Leone Government on the Report of the Commission of Inquiry into Disturbances in the Protectorate*, p. 13.

manipulated their role in the traditional land-tenure system to expand their own cash-crop holdings and especially to claim rents or royalties from expatriate mining firms in return for mining concessions backed by the colonial government. Unfortunately, there is not sufficient evidence to document fully the scale of the Chiefs' penetration of the money economy by these methods. Undoubtedly, however, this penetration was considerable. The reports of the inquiry into the 1955–56 peasant disturbances show one Paramount Chief, for example, who claimed £375 per annum from the sale of surplus rice. Another claimed £400 from the sale of similar products; one established a mineral water factory and transport firm in addition to the sale of surplus products; and another Chief, whose total Chiefdom income was nearly £4,000, gained £1,666 per annum from rent paid by an expatriate iron-mining concern.[13] When set against the income of thirty shillings per head or £4.10s. per adult male claimed by the average farmer, these chiefly emoluments certainly placed Chiefs in a very high income bracket.[14] Some Chiefs' incomes equaled and even surpassed those of the more modernized African income groups such as merchants, businessmen, lawyers, and doctors. Furthermore, despite the traditional setting or environment in which Chiefs performed their ruling functions, their style of life had much in common with that of the urbanized modern groups. As will be seen later, this situation was significant in the political ties between Chiefs and the modernized elite.

B. POLITICAL CONSEQUENCES OF CHIEFS' ROLE

The colonial transformation of traditional rulers had a considerable impact upon their relations with the peasantry. The Chiefs, exposed to both colonial administration and the market economy, became a mediating agency through which much of modernity—especially its socio-political orientations—reached

[13] *Reports of the Commissioners of Enquiry into the Conduct of Certain Chiefs,* pp. 38–39, 51, 68; Cox, *Sierra Leone Report of Commission of Inquiry into Disturbances in the Provinces,* pp. 153, 160, 161 n. 2.

[14] J. T. Jack, *Economic Survey of Sierra Leone,* p. 6.

the masses in rural society. The particular use Chiefs made of this function, especially the furtherance of their own modernization, influenced the changing political relationships between them and the peasantry.

1. Political Awakening of the Peasant

Perhaps the most important consequence of Chiefs' abuse of local tax administration was the emergence of a characteristically modern group conflict in local African society. This conflict was characterized by a form of rural "radicalism," which in some instances constituted a virtual peasant revolt against traditional rulers and authority.

In Sierra Leone this rural radicalism was evident in the 1930's, and it was particularly strong in the immediate postwar years (1946–51) and has sometimes flared up since then. On one occasion (October 1950) it took the form of a violent riot which involved some 5,000 peasants and hinterland town-dwellers in Kailahun District. Commenting on this riot in his annual report to the Governor, the Chief Commissioner observed that "the extent and violence of the rioting, which spread from Kailahun to outlying towns and villages . . . with casualties and considerable damage to property, made it necessary to summon police help from Freetown."[15] In late 1955 and early 1956 a recurrence of rural radicalism approximated a peasant revolt properly so-called; the commission of inquiry described it as a "mass disobedience to authority." The disturbances, known commonly as tax riots, involved "many tens of thousands" of peasants and hinterland town-dwellers and entailed widespread property destruction (especially Chiefs' property—e.g., cattle, surplus crops, modern homes), with damages estimated at £750,000.[16]

Rural radicalism has occurred elsewhere in Africa, and it is such a potential source of instability in post-colonial African states that it warrants much more attention from social scientists than it has received. All we can do here, however, is to note its

[15] H. Childs, *Report on the Sierra Leone Protectorate for the Years 1949 and 1950* (Freetown, 1952), p. 5—cited hereafter as *Protectorate Report* by year.
[16] Cox, *Sierra Leone Report of Commission of Inquiry into Disturbances in the Provinces*, esp. pp. 13–17.

extent and character. In remarking upon the impact of social change on the relationship of Yoruba *obas* in Western Nigeria to their people, Peter Lloyd observed that "great strains have been produced which have resulted in local conflicts . . . The excitement, occasionally leading to rioting, which breaks out over chieftaincy disputes or tax collection, is a similar manifestation of strain."[17] Other instances are worth mentioning here. The peasant disturbances in Chad in 1957–58 have been described as "symptomatic of a revolt, widespread in northern and eastern Tchad, on the part of the peasantry against the exactions of their customary chiefs."[18] Of the riots in Uganda in 1945 and 1949, J. E. Goldthorpe remarked that "chiefs and wealthy Africans were the main objects of mass disapproval"; and peasant rioters in Tiv areas of Northern Nigeria in October, 1960, destroyed much property.[19]

As regards the political meaning of this rural radicalism, it is perhaps best described, following Max Gluckman's distinction between revolution and rebellion, as peasant *rebellion*.[20] The previously mentioned peasant riots seldom entailed demands for the destruction of the existing system of traditional authority (which Gluckman would call a revolution) but instead were aimed at ameliorating aspects of its use (what Gluckman would call a rebellion). Such a distinction assists us in grasping the rather peculiar ambivalence of many Africans (literate and illiterate, rural and urban-dwelling) toward traditional rulers. Lucy Mair has underlined this ambivalence in the case of West Africa as follows: ". . . In the eyes of the same persons the Chiefs may be symbols of reaction, symbols of group unity, and symbols of pride in national history. That is why there has been no move to eliminate them from the political system altogether."[21]

---

[17] Lloyd, "The Changing Role of the Yoruba Traditional Rulers," p. 57.

[18] Thompson and Adloff, *The Emerging States of French Equatorial Africa*, pp. 76–78, 455.

[19] J. E. Goldthorpe, "Social Class and Education in East Africa," in *Transactions of the Third World Congress of Sociology* (London, 1955), pp. 115–122; David Williams, "The Tiv Are in Turmoil," *Daily Times* (Lagos), October 20, 1960, p. 5.

[20] Cf. Max Gluckman, *Custom and Conflict in Africa* (London, 1955).

[21] L. P. Mair, "African Chiefs Today: The Lugard Memorial Lecture for 1958," *Africa* (July 1958), pp. 200–201.

Sociologically, this ambivalence toward traditional authority is related to the fragmented process of African social change. This means, among other things, that there is a tendency for some facets of a social and cultural system to change in a modern direction while other facets remain intact or simply lag. Values (and attitudes toward traditional rulers fall within the realm of values) would appear to be one facet of culture least likely to change rapidly or in the first instance, as compared to such things as the mode of economy, dress, food, and the like. This is so because values more than other aspects of culture are, as it were, highly integrated into the total culture. They become fixed at the level of thought and in individual personalities and tend to take on a momentum of their own, separate from the peculiar historical circumstances within which they originated.

Politically, the ambivalence toward traditional authority has significant implications for the mode of change. It is likely to be one of the crucial factors in local African society that make for a stable, non-revolutionary pattern of political development. Peter Lloyd has observed this process among the Yoruba and formulated his view of it as follows: "The hostility against many *obas* is against their persons and not their office; in fact, many crises peter out because no means can be found for punishing the individual without degrading the throne."[22]

For this process to succeed as a key stabilizing element in postcolonial African states, however, presupposes that traditional rulers (and other elite groups linked to them) will not use their position as an excuse for reaction and corruption. In Northern Nigeria, for instance, an ambivalent respect toward traditional authority on the part of both educated and uneducated commoners has prevailed and has unquestionably facilitated a non-revolutionary political change. But the situation whereby the traditional elite uses its power to recruit its own educated kin into higher educational institutions and government posts, to the relative neglect of commoner or pagan children (even though the latter's "performances at the local N.A. elementary school

[22] Lloyd, "The Changing Role of the Yoruba Traditional Rulers," p. 64.

have regularly surpassed those of the Hausa boys") is likely to prove a source of serious conflict and instability.[23]

Apart from the foregoing, there are additional consequences of the role of traditional rulers in colonial change. In Sierra Leone, Chiefs' involvement in cash-crop production and marketing created a competitive relationship between chiefs and the peasantry that had no precedent in tradition. The relationship was essentially modern or Western in nature. It stemmed from the money economy and related institutions established by colonial rule. It depended upon colonial legal and political support. Since there was no basis in the indigenous scheme of things for legitimizing this economic role of Chiefs, the peasantry could not be expected to relate to it in traditional terms.

As it happened, the peasantry viewed the Chiefs' role in the cash economy in modern competitive terms. It was seen as an unfair competitive advantage. As early as 1903 a Sierra Leone government report to the Colonial Office recognized this situation: ". . . The Chiefs cannot understand . . . that their young men prefer leaving their villages for work on the railway and in Freetown; but, considering that they got a good wage for their labour, from 9d. to 1s. a day, *they naturally prefer it to unpaid labour in their villages under their chiefs.*"[24] Similarly, a correspondence to the *Sierra Leone Weekly News* in 1930 related the economic relationships between Chiefs and peasants in the following terms: ". . . The Protectorate Youths are forced to come to the Colony proper because of the almost inhuman oppression that seems to be going on. The natives are forced to make the Chiefs' Farms, to do all Public Buildings for the Chiefs, all Government Buildings, and the monies for all work done are paid to the Chiefs; and

---

23 Smith, *The Economy of Hausa Communities of Zaria*, p. 92.

24 *Sierra Leone Report for 1903*, Cmd. 2238 (London, 1904), p. 28. (italics added.) The new mobility in rural society was widespread in colonial Africa. Professor Wrigley noted it in Uganda at an early period: ". . . In the 1890's, it had been noted that the independence of the peasantry had been much enhanced by the opportunity to gain an income otherwise than by the service of the chiefs . . . Though habits of deference died hard, the Ganda masses were incomparably freer under the new dispensation than under the old . . ." C. C. Wrigley, "Buganda: An Outline Economic History," *Economic History Review* (August 1957), p. 77.

if they refuse to turn up or are late, they are fined heavily; and they have to provide their food whilst doing these public works. Over and above that, they are fined heavily at Court even beyond their means, and if they can manage a little time to make a small farm, the Chief's portion is also demanded. If you produce a good quantity of rice in your farm, the Chief is sure to know it, and some charge is brought against you to take all that rice away . . . Further, if you show any attitude of resistance or unwillingness to conform to the Chiefs' dictates, you are either recommended for imprisonment or for deportation."[25]

Although the average peasant's attitude toward the Chiefs' advantage in the market economy was essentially economic in origin, it eventually became part of a wider outlook which would prove a basis for political action. A District Commissioner's Report for the year 1921, for instance, already mentioned that the "collection of tribute is the most fertile source of abuse and complaint."[26] The transmutation of specific economic grievances into a broader social and political consciousness, however, had to await the penetration of local African society by the middle-class nationalism of the post-World War II period.

2. Modernization of Chiefs' Authority and Power

The participation of Chiefs in the colonial economic system has made it exceedingly difficult to categorize them simply as a "traditional elite." In reality they are both traditional and modern authorities. This situation has both weakened and strengthened their authority and power, depending upon the particular combination of modern circumstances confronted by Chiefs at any given point in time.

As regards their authority, Chiefs had superficially the best of both worlds: they freely invoked either traditional or modern justifications as circumstances required. In reality, however, this double standard was not easy to uphold unless the peasant masses remained unqualifiedly attached to traditional authority. The fact

[25] *Sierra Leone Weekly News*, November 22, 1930, p. 8.
[26] H. Ross, *Annual Report on the Southern Province for the Year 1921* (Freetown, 1922), pp. 7–9.

of the matter was that the same forces of change that made Chiefs what may be called a traditio-modern elite equally influenced the peasantry and undercut or questioned allegiance to traditional authority. As we have shown, some peasants considered the Chiefs' role in the modern economy an unfair competitive advantage and refused, often in violent ways, to accept it.

As regards their power—i.e., the physical means enabling Chiefs to command or influence people—there is little doubt that traditional rulers have become essentially modern. Most if not all of their traditional sources of power (e.g., slavery, war making, economic preemption) were either destroyed or regulated by the colonial state. What remained of these (e.g., customary rights of tribute, labor, land rights) was so closely articulated to the colonial processes of social and economic change that they can scarcely be called "traditional."

The political implications of this situation are, I think, crucial for understanding the role of traditional rulers in African political change. The traditional rulers may be expected to support that political arrangement which will enable them (1) to maximize modern sources of their power and (2) simultaneously maintain as much as possible of traditional authority. Under colonial rule this political arrangement prevailed in its purest form: *ergo*, the accommodation by Chiefs to the colonial system. Similarly, in the period of nationalist political change one can expect to find the traditional rulers shifting, especially as the central political power shifts, slowly but definitely away from accommodation to colonial rule toward a shrewd selection of political alliances among competing nationalist groups. Again, this shift will be governed by the Chiefs' calculation of which nationalist group will best enable them to maximize modern sources of power and simultaneously retain much of their traditional authority.

This pattern of Chiefs' politics was widespread in African political change, though in Northern Rhodesia one observer, J. Clyde Mitchell, saw a rather different process at work. Professor Mitchell maintains that "to some extent the chiefs . . ., as paid officials of the Administration, have been caught up in the struggle for a superior standard of living and for a 'civilized way of life,' but fundamentally their interests are vested in the tribal system and they must forever remain opposed to the aspirations of Congress [i.e., the nationalist African National Congress] and the urban middle class it represents."[27] I would myself question Mitchell's argument, for it assumes a static situation in the traditional or tribal sector of colonial society, which is surely not the case in Northern Rhodesia.[28] Modern changes have been extensive in this territory, and recent evidence on the political behavior of Chiefs suggests that their use of politics to adjust to the new changes is not essentially different from the proposition I offer.[29]

Apart from the manner in which the Chiefs' authority and power were modernized, a number of other circumstances enabled Chiefs to pursue the political strategy I attribute to them. For one thing, the new elite nationalist leaders were frequently the direct kin of traditional rulers. They were thus disposed to assist Chiefs in making the transition from traditional to modern society while at the same time upholding the traditional authority of Chiefs. The fact that the kin of Chiefs have become political leaders in emergent African societies is itself linked to the greater opportunities Chiefs had to take advantage of social change. Their favored status under colonial administration and the wealth they derived from it enabled traditional rulers to provide their kin with the best education available. In the Sierra Leone Protectorate and elsewhere in Africa the educated kin of Chiefs were among the first African professionals and the first senior African members of the colonial civil service. From these preferred positions they readily moved into nationalist political leadership.

Another factor that enabled traditional rulers to pursue the political strategy sketched here is that, though traditional values were shaken by social change, their hold on the rural masses did not dwindle completely. Despite the important occasions of peas-

[27] J. Clyde Mitchell, "The African Middle Classes in British Central Africa," in INCIDI, *Développement d'une classe moyenne dans les pays tropicaux et subtropicaux* (Brussels, 1956), p. 231—hereafter cited as *Développement d'une classe moyenne*.

[28] See Hortense Powdermaker, *Coppertown* (New York, 1962).

[29] Cf. Robert I. Rotberg, "What Future for Barotseland?" *Africa Report* (July 1963), pp. 21–23.

ant rebellion against certain uses of traditional authority in the context of modernization, the masses displayed the ambivalence toward Chiefs and traditional authority that we have already noted. Thus there is still a real sense in which Chiefs continue as the sole legitimate representatives of traditional values (especially as they relate to personal or group allegiances to authority) in the eyes of most people. In the context of modern political change this was a fact of considerable significance. The nationalistic new elite, in its attempt to secure mass political support beyond the urban centers of its own origin, normally accommodated its political organization, methods, and policies to the strategic position held by Chiefs in local society. As seen later in this study, such was particularly the case for the Sierra Leone People's Party, the dominant party in the rise of postwar nationalism in Sierra Leone.

CHAPTER 5

Emergence of the New Elite

A. NATURE OF THE NEW ELITE

Usually the more advanced elements among the new African "social categories" arising under colonialism and afterward have been regarded as essentially a "new elite."[1] It is felt that in composition and structure the new elite group is still too heterogeneous, too mixed-up with respect to old (African) and new (Western) ingredients to warrant a more precise sociological designation. Persons enter this elite through a variety of channels and arrive without any clear-cut idea of what their relationship is with each other or with the bulk of the African population. Thus it is argued that the characteristics of "social class" as understood in the Western world are still largely absent from the structure of the new African elite. More specifically, it is felt that since this elite has not gained a solid and independent foothold in economic ownership and function, it does not warrant designation as a "class."[2]

I am myself inclined toward this approach to the issue, and throughout this study the term "new elite" is employed largely in this way. I would, however, be more prepared than some observers to differentiate the new elite group into several components and to consider its upper level as possessing the characteristics of a "social class."[3]

[1] Georges Balandier, "Conséquences sociales du progrès technique dans les pays sous-développés," *La Sociologie Contemporaine*, III (1954–55), 45.
[2] St. Clair Drake, "Social Change and Social Problems in Contemporary Africa," in W. Goldschmidt, ed., *The United States and Africa* (New York, 1963), p. 254.
[3] S. F. Nadel, *A Black Byzantium* (London, 1942), pp. 127–128.

In terms of the political, economic, occupational, and educational factors considered by S. F. Nadel and others to be crucial in determining social class, the upper level of the new African elite is distinct from the lower strata of the elite as well as from the bulk of the African population. By virtue of their occupation, wealth, and prestige senior civil servants, wealthy merchants or traders, wealthy planters, bankers, contractors, some manufacturers, African managers in European firms, the political elite, and members of the liberal professions constitute a veritable upper class. Those engaged in such occupations are not merely functionally distinct from the lower level of the new elite (e.g., junior civil servants, clerks, tailors, carpenters, seamstresses, masons, medium traders); they are equally distinguished by their affluence and style of life and by their significantly higher level of education. They are also differentiated from the lower level of the new elite insofar as they have normally dominated the development of modern nationalist politics.

Another reason for viewing the upper level of the new African elite as a social class is that it is a politically conscious group which enters politics to advance its over-all position in society and ultimately to become a ruling or governing class. In this respect, the upper level of the new elite is like the early bourgeoisie in Western Europe who employed politics to become a ruling class or a politically effective group within the ruling community. In the context of colonial modernization, the African middle class's attempt to become a ruling class means that it must (1) replace the expatriate ruling oligarchy as the "standard-setting group," to use Nadel's expression, in the modern sector of society and (2) appropriate for itself the prestige of the traditional elite as the most legitimate authority in the eyes of the black masses who still reside largely in traditional society.[4]

The first of these requirements of ruling-class status was met by the upper level of the new elite through the political nationalism that they created and organized. To meet the second require-

[4] S. F. Nadel, "The Concept of Social Elites," *International Social Science Bulletin*, Vol. III, No. 3 (1956), 415 ff.

ment, they often "return" to traditional society in order to assume the symbols, titles, and other badges of prestige and rank which still carry weight with the common man.

During the early 1950's, for instance, Philip Garigue observed this process evolving among the Yoruba new elite in Western Nigeria. He noted the consolidation of power of the new elite through "transfers from the ranks of the successful 'new' political leaders into the 'traditional' authority structure; certain of the former, who would not otherwise have any claim to such appointments, are being given titles as chiefs."[5] Similarly, Morton-Williams has remarked on this process in Western Nigeria, noting that although "the successful big-business man and cash-crop farmer among the Yoruba commands respect . . ., to achieve the certain standing of members of an elite they need to identify with an established elite which enables them to assume its insignia, its badges of prestige. Economic activity alone cannot . . . qualify one for membership of a Yoruba *elite*. Cocoa farmers, bankers, traders may be in the *elite* not because their success gives them wealth, but because they are able to make their wealth politically effective."[6]

In Northern Nigeria this same process is evident, but with certain unique features of its own. For one thing, many of the persons who possess upper-level new-elite attributes are an integral part of the traditional elite. In this respect the process of legitimizing the new elite in Northern Nigeria is like that in Sierra Leone, though in the latter country the professional and business elements in the new elite that evolved in the Protectorate normally claim immediate kinship with traditional rulers but do not hold traditional office themselves. As regards the commoner new-elite elements in Northern Nigeria, M. G. Smith describes their process of legitimation as follows: "Wealth carries great prestige, but little political weight in traditional terms . . . What then can these unfortunate merchants with surplus income do? One answer

[5] Philip Garigue, "Changing Political Leadership in West Africa," *Africa* (July 1954), p. 224.

[6] P. Morton-Williams, "A Discussion of the Theory of Elites in a West African (Yoruba) Context," *Proceedings of the Fourth Annual Conference of the West African Institute of Social and Economic Research* (Ibadan, 1956), p. 30.

is to go to Mecca, preferably by the most expensive means—the aeroplane. In 1950 the airway services were extended in the direction of Mecca to accommodate the growing number of successful Hausa merchants." Having secured the title *Alhaji* through an expensive pilgrimage to Mecca, the Hausa businessman derives an economic benefit, according to Smith. ". . . By the style of his pilgrimage, commercial confidence in him is increased, and is usually expressed by an increasing volume of trade, with the consequence that he may soon become even wealthier than before. At this stage the merchant . . . often starts making loans on a more substantial scale than before, for which the salaried Native Authority officials, who habitually live beyond their means, provide an open market whose risks are covered by a high and irreligious rate of interest (25 per cent per month)."[7]

Thus in view of one way in which the African middle class rose to a ruling position it is not altogether correct to say that this group's success has "displaced the upper strata in traditional societies."[8] Although there has certainly been a good measure of elite displacement under colonialism and since, traditional forces have qualified the process of displacement at several crucial points. First, traditional rulers have been able to modernize themselves to the point of assuming many new-elite attributes. Second, a not inconsiderable proportion of the professional and business elements among the new elite are the offspring of traditional rulers. Third, the new-elite persons of commoner origin have sought the symbols and badges of prestige, status, and rank controlled by the traditional elite. This process has been particularly evident in West African states and in East Africa, especially Uganda.[9]

Accordingly, what will finally emerge in the new African societies as a legitimate ruling class will more than likely be a peculiarly African amalgam of the traditional elite and the upper level of the new elite. Marriages and the school system will probably

[7] M. G. Smith, *The Economy of Hausa Communities of Zaria* (London, 1955), pp. 100–101.

[8] G. Almond and J. S. Coleman, eds., *The Politics of Developing Areas* (Princeton, N.J., 1960), p. 283.

[9] David Apter, *The Political Kingdom in Uganda* (Princeton, N.J., 1962).

bring them together. Even more important perhaps will be the sharing of political power.[10]

In both English-speaking and French-speaking African states of today, political cooperation between the old and new elite groups is normal. The attainment of political independence by many African states was dependent upon the social and political ties between these elites during the decolonization period. This was so in Sierra Leone, as we will see in detail later, and in other areas such as Western Nigeria, Northern Nigeria, Senegal, Mauritania, and the Ivory Coast. For the latter country, one observer has described this process as follows: ". . . Through planting most of the educated elite kept deep roots in the countryside. Rivalry between traditional and modern elites was cushioned since chiefs who earned money through planting sought the best possible education for their children. The distance between traditional commoners and chiefs was also reduced, within the planter class, as both came to accept money as a sign of high status. Even the distinction between traditional and official chief faded among the planters, and a man like Félix Houphouet-Boigny, of but minor traditional status, but a *chef de canton* and Ponty-trained, came to be accepted as a spokesman of chiefs . . . Official chiefs were related to the new planter class and therefore . . . to the RDA [Rassemblement Démocratique Africain]."[11]

[10] In this connection I would disagree with the recent argument of Professor Lipset that since "traditional legitimacy is absent . . . in much of contemporary Asia and Africa . . ., [legitimacy of the new polities and their elites] can be developed only through reliance on legal and/or charismatic authority." Lipset's proposition neglects the actual experience of African traditional authority under colonial modernization. As I have shown in the earlier chapters of this study, it was the unique feature of colonial change in Africa that traditional authority was employed, however inefficiently, as an agency of modernization in local society. As a result the Chiefs were able to modernize the material bases of their power while simultaneously transferring an effective part of traditional legitimacy to the modern social and political institutions. Thus members of the new elite of commoner origin found it desirable to embrace the holders of traditional authority as a means of legitimizing their power. No doubt charismatic forms of legitimacy are of some consequence, but Lipset, influenced by Apter's work on the Gold Coast, gives too much consideration to them. Seymour M. Lipset, *The First New Nation: The United States in Historical and Comparative Perspective* (New York, 1963), pp. 17–18. Cf. David Apter, *The Gold Coast in Transition* (Princeton, N.J., 1955).

[11] Ruth Schachter Morgenthau, *Political Parties in French-speaking West Africa* (Oxford, 1964), p. 172.

African states have differed in the way newly secured political power has been divided among the old and new elites. In some states (e.g., Senegal and the Ivory Coast) the old elite has simply sought to maintain and extend its influence and power in the modern sector of local society, leaving positions in the central political system to the new elite. In other areas (e.g., Sierra Leone, Mauritania, Northern Nigeria, Western Nigeria) the old elite has secured political standing and office at the center of the political system. For instance, by early 1962 there were eight eminent Yoruba *obas* who sat as Ministers without Portfolio in the Western Nigeria government, and the Governor-General of Western Nigeria was none other than the Oni of Ife, the most eminent traditional ruler in the Region. Traditional rulers in Western Nigeria also have a separate legislative chamber, and a number sit as directors on the boards of government statutory corporations.

Seating traditional figures at the head of modern institutions is akin to certain practices which developed when a powerful bourgeoisie emerged in eighteenth- and nineteenth-century Britain and which Walter Bagehot characterized as "the *theatrical show* of society."[12] For Bagehot this referred to the process whereby the power exercised by the emergent bourgeoisie was partially hidden from the masses through manipulation of traditional institutions and symbols associated with the nobility and monarchy. Politically, this "theatrical show of society" was, in Bagehot's view, a shrewd strategy which partly freed the new elite from popular and conservative restraint. By the same token, the use of traditional rulers in African politics and the assumption by the new elite of chiefly badges of traditional prestige have a similar effect: they suggest to the masses that "real power" rests in some way with traditional institutions and rulers.

There is a final characteristic of the upper level of the new African elite that justifies our designating it a "social class"—

12 Walter Bagehot, *The English Constitution* (London, 1867), pp. 51–56. See also pp. 9, 85–86, 325 ff. It is noteworthy that Marx and Engels also recognized the traditional elements in the attempt of the British bourgeoisie to legitimize its status; but what Bagehot called "the theatrical show of society" Engels termed "an ornamental caste of drones . . ." (F. Engels, "Socialism, Utopian and Scientific," in Karl Marx and Frederick Engels, *Selected Works* [Moscow, 1962], II, 112).

namely, its consciousness of itself. According to Nadel, another component of social class besides the occupational, educational, and economic ones is what he called "consciousness of class."[13] "The essence of class (as of any group)," as Nadel put it, "lies in the consciousness of group membership; and consciousness of class is the consciousness of [a] 'common scale of values.' " A more elaborate statement of this view has been offered by A. L. Epstein and J. Clyde Mitchell: "The concept of social class implies some degree of consciousness of kind, some feeling of common cause with others in the same position vis-à-vis those either below or above one in the prestige scale, and this degree of common cause must be sufficiently well developed to be able to manifest itself in corporate action in certain stress situations. Social classes, therefore, when they come into being operate particularly within a framework of political relationships within the community."[14]

In Sierra Leone, Ghana, Nigeria, Senegal, the Ivory Coast, and elsewhere, a measure of group consciousness or corporateness has prevailed among the well-educated and well-to-do members of the new elite. One institution that both produced and reflected this group consciousness was the press, especially the African-owned press. The first African newspaper in Sierra Leone, the *New Era,* was founded as a weekly in 1855 by one William Drape, a Creole.[15] By 1900 Sierra Leone's educated population had been exposed to thirty-four newspapers at one time or other. Most of these were African-owned and operated, among them the *West African Herald* (1868–72), the *West African Reporter* (1874–84), the *Sierra Leone Weekly News* (1885–1915), the *Artisan* (1884–88), and the *Sierra Leone Times* (1891–1912). In Ghana, nineteen different newspapers appeared by 1900, all but two of them African-owned, and twenty-five newspapers were published between 1931 and 1956. Nigeria lagged somewhat behind these territories, but by 1900 some seven newspapers had appeared, and

13 Nadel, *A Black Byzantium,* pp. 127–128.

14 J. Clyde Mitchell and A. L. Epstein, "Occupational Prestige and Social Status among Urban Africans in Northern Rhodesia," *Africa* (January 1959), pp. 35–36.

15 C. H. Fyfe, "The Sierra Leone Press in the Nineteenth Century," *Sierra Leone Studies* (June 1957), p. 228.

a larger number appeared from the mid-1920's onward.[16] In French West Africa, newspaper development lagged behind that in British West Africa. An Ivory Coast paper founded in 1910 and called *L'Indépendant* was a rarity in its day. What one observer has called "the true press" did begin to evolve in French West Africa during the 1930's, however, and burgeoned in the postwar era. Expatriates played a more important part in the development of African newspapers in French West Africa than they did in British territories.[17]

In British West Africa the development of the press reflected increasing self-consciousness among the new African elite. As one authority has observed, the English-speaking African press of the late nineteenth and early twentieth century was "published by the best educated and wealthiest—often the 'professional'—classes, and read mostly by their own kind. In these conditions the public opinion which it created was compact, and effective . . ."[18] Furthermore, this press was an explicit expression of the political consciousness of the emergent elite. The African editors and owners of the press were directly active in the early political organizations of this group. For instance, the African owner of the *Gold Coast Leader* at the early part of this century, J. P. H. Brown, was a leader of the Aborigines Rights Protection Society; the same was true for the editor of the *Gold Coast Methodist Times*, Rev. Attoh Ahuma.[19] Similarly, the African editor-owner of the *Sierra Leone Weekly News*, the best newspaper in prewar West Africa, was a leader of the Sierra Leone branch of the National Congress of British West Africa, and his newspaper served as the party's organ.

[16] K. A. B. Jones-Quartey, "The Institutions of Public Opinion in a Rapidly Changing Africa," in *Conference on Representative Government and National Progress* (mimeographed; Ibadan, University College, 1959), pp. 2–3; Jones-Quartey, "The Ghana Press," in *Report on the Press in West Africa* (Dakar, 1960), pp. 32–35; Increase Coker, "The Nigerian Press: 1929–1959," *ibid.*, pp. 74 ff.

[17] J. de Benoist, "The Position of the Press in French-speaking West Africa," *ibid.*, pp. 1–31.

[18] Jones-Quartey, "The Institutions of Public Opinion in a Rapidly Changing Africa," p. 4.

[19] David Kimble, *A Political History of Ghana, 1850–1928* (Oxford, 1963), pp. 371–380.

Another aspect of the press as an expression of group consciousness among the emergent elite was the attention it gave to the social life of this inner circle. Notices of marriages and of gatherings of all sorts were regularly carried by both African and European-owned newspapers. This in turn reflected the compactness of the elite within the urban environment. A social distance was beginning to open up between the new elite and other Africans. Although this social distance has yet to become as distinct as it is in Western societies, it is nonetheless apparent and has contributed to the self-consciousness of the new leading groups.

Whatever the future shape and contours of the evolving social stratification system in African societies may become, the new elite will certainly be a major constituent of it. The contemporary attributes of this elite cannot be understood outside the historical context within which it evolved; we will therefore consider the salient features of its evolution in Sierra Leone in the remainder of this chapter.

B. BACKGROUND OF THE NEW ELITE

To a large extent, European decisions on where to locate schools, plantations, agricultural extension services, railways, and other modern enterprises in African colonies determined which tribal, regional, and religious groups would rise to the top of African society. In Sierra Leone, the fact that the initial settlement of the Colony at the end of the eighteenth century was intended as a haven for freed slaves goes a long way to explain the large Creole representation in the new elite. When the Anglican Church Missionary Society established Fourah Bay College in Freetown in 1827 (affiliated to Durham University for degree purposes in 1876), Creoles naturally gained a favored position in this institution of higher learning. The Register of the College reveals that "up to the 1920's all Sierra Leone students came from the Colony, and only in the 1940's, with the extension of teacher-training courses, were substantial numbers of students from the Protectorate admitted." On a tribal reckoning, of the ninety-one students at the College between 1870 and 1889, all but two were

76

Creole; and of the 134 students who received degrees between 1878 and 1949, Creoles were overwhelmingly in the majority.[20]

As modern education penetrated the Protectorate it was the Mende who received the lion's share. The fact that the Mende were largely pagan, as against the Islamized tribes in the north, caused Western missionaries to concentrate the bulk of their activity among them. Government-sponsored education likewise favored the pagan and later the Christianized Mende areas over the Islamized north. The first government school in the Protectorate was opened at Bo in 1906, and though admission was opened to all tribal groups, the Mende were preferred. In 1915, for instance, a classification of pupils at Bo School by district showed that of the 113 pupils, fifty-three were from the Railway District (Mende), sixteen from the Northern Sherbro District (Mende and Sherbro), twenty-five from Karene District (Temne), seventeen from Ronietta District (Mende), and two from Koinadugu District (Kuranko).[21] Nearly a generation later, Mende pupils still constituted the largest single bloc at Bo School, with 37 per cent of the student body, followed by the Temne with 28 per cent. In 1938, the year in which Bo School was elevated to a secondary school, 80 per cent of all schools in the Protectorate were situated in areas where the Mende predominated. These areas, mainly in the south and southeast, had 5 per cent of school-age children in school by 1938, compared to 1 per cent for the northern areas.[22]

These educational advantages gave the Mende a much wider representation in modern occupations than that of any other tribe; they were also, of course, more highly ranked in these occupations. In the African police force, for instance, the Mende predominated among the higher ranks during the 1930's, and 78 per cent of the Mende police were literate, as against 46 per cent of

[20] P. E. H. Hair, "An Analysis of the Register of Fourah Bay College, 1827–1950," *Sierra Leone Studies* (December 1956), pp. 157, 158.

[21] *Annual Report on the Protectorate Education for the Year 1915* (Freetown, 1917), p. 5.

[22] *Annual Report of the Education Department for the Year 1938* (Freetown, 1940).

the Temne.[23] Mende also claimed the higher posts in other areas of government employment, in private employment with European firms, and were invariably the first Africans in the Protectorate to enter the liberal professions.

Just as the Mende as a whole were favored by the colonial educational establishment, so were certain groups within the tribe given special consideration in this regard. This was particularly so for the Chiefs whose offspring gained special access to Bo School. The Government Notice announcing the founding of the school in 1906 declared its doors open solely "for the sons and nominees of Chiefs." This policy was later applied to other government-sponsored schools in the Protectorate, as in the case of the government school at Bumpe, Kenema District, opened in 1915. At the opening ceremony for the Bumpe School, the District Commissioner explained the basis for selection of pupils in the following terms: "It should not be open to all and sundry, but only to selected pupils chosen from a strata slightly, but not much, beneath those eligible for Bo School. The upper and leading classes must be educated before the lower or working classes."[24]

Not only was the traditional system of rank used as the yardstick for selection at the Bo and Bumpe schools, but many features of traditional social organization were incorporated in the school's regimen. Pupils at Bo, for instance, lived in compounds similar to those in their tribal villages, ate tribal foods, and had their relations with one another ordered along tribal lines.[25] In the Government Notice announcing the opening of Bo School, it was observed that the aim was "to enable the boys to acquire a good education without loss of their *natural* attachment to their respective tribes. Tribal patriotism is to be strengthened; Mende pupils, for instance, are to be taught in such a way that they will prefer Mendiland to any other country; so with Timinis, and all the other various tribes represented in the school."[26]

Besides its concern to prevent Western education from alienating pupils from their tribal moorings, the government's adherence

[23] *Annual Report of the Police Force for the Year 1933* (Freetown, 1934), p. 9.
[24] *Annual Report of the Railway District, 1915* (Freetown, 1917), p. 8.
[25] *Sierra Leone Report for 1909*, Cmd. 4964 (London, 1910), p. 33.
[26] Quoted in T. J. Alldridge, *A Transformed Colony* (London, 1910), p. 139.

to a traditional organization in the regimen of Bo School aimed at producing literate personnel for Chiefdom administration and related activities. This goal was partly attained, as evidenced by the fact that of the 166 boys who had graduated from Bo School by 1922, some 32.5 per cent entered Chiefdom administration. By 1934, however, this figure had declined to 15 per cent, though 22 per cent had entered the central government service and were not infrequently placed in posts related to local administration.[27]

The political significance of both the Mende advantage in the educational system of the Protectorate and the traditional regimen within which Western education was dispensed will become apparent later in this study. Suffice it to say here that the colonial government's aim of securing a continuity of ruling elites in the Protectorate was largely achieved, for the political success of the dominant party in postwar Sierra Leone was characterized by an apt alliance of Chiefs and their educated offspring.

C. PROFESSIONAL AND BUSINESS COMPONENTS OF THE NEW ELITE

1. The Liberal Professions

Law and medicine were the first liberal professions in which Sierra Leone Africans received full formal training. A Sierra Leonean lawyer secured admission to the English Bar in 1854, and by 1890 twelve of his compatriots had done likewise.[28] With the establishment of Fourah Bay College as an affiliated institution of Durham University in 1876, a major opportunity for the schooling of professionals opened up. The register of the College shows that before 1900 some nineteen African students studied law, and between 1900 and 1949 at least twenty-five graduates of the College became lawyers.[29] Close to one hundred African law-

---

[27] Sierra Leone Report for 1922, No. 1165 (London, 1923), p. 24; Legislative Council Debates, No. 1 of Session 1924–1925 (Freetown, n.d.), p. 53; Annual Report of the Education Department for the Year 1934 (Freetown, 1935), p. 19.

[28] J. D. Hargreaves, A Life of Sir Samuel Lewis (London, 1958), pp. 14–15, 107–111.

[29] Hair, "An Analysis of the Register of Fourah Bay College, 1827–1950," p. 159.

yers were to be found in 1960 in Sierra Leone, and a much larger number were studying law in Britain.[30]

African doctors, clergymen, teachers, and senior civil servants have also been known in Sierra Leone for a considerable time. The first Sierra Leonean qualified in medicine in 1858 after training at St. Andrews University, Scotland. From 1858 to 1901 some twenty-five Sierra Leoneans (all Creoles) qualified as doctors; and from 1906 to 1956 some sixty-three qualified, all but five of whom were Creoles.[31] About fifty Sierra Leonean doctors were practicing in 1960, and about one hundred students were training overseas in medicine.

Fourah Bay College was a prominent place for the education of clergymen. Its register shows that between 1871 and 1900 some fifty-five clergymen graduated from the College, and ninety-three graduated between 1900 and 1940. For the period from the founding of the College in 1827 to 1950, clerics were by far the major professional group trained at Fourah Bay: 250 clerical graduates received degrees during this period, of whom 200 were Anglican and fifty belonged to other denominations.[32] Many of these clergymen, however, practiced outside Sierra Leone, in Nigeria, Ghana, Gambia, and Liberia.

Schoolteachers are by far the largest single group among the liberal professions in Sierra Leone; they numbered 680 in 1938, 1,173 in 1952, and 2,521 in 1959–60.[33] However, teachers have not been as well educated as lawyers, doctors, or clergymen. For this reason only a small portion of them can truly claim membership in the upper level of the new elite. Prestigious Fourah Bay College graduated only twenty-five schoolteachers before 1900, and between 1900 and 1939 only ninety-five were trained there.[34] The

[30] Interview with Registrar of the Sierra Leone Law Courts, August 1960.

[31] M. C. F. Easmon, "Sierra Leone Doctors," *Sierra Leone Studies* (June 1956), pp. 81–96.

[32] Hair, "An Analysis of the Register of Fourah Bay College, 1827–1950," p. 159.

[33] *Annual Report of the Education Department for the Year 1938*, p. 34; *Annual Report of the Education Department for the Year 1952* (Freetown, 1953), p. 48; *Education Statistics, 1959* (Freetown, 1959), pp. 5–7.

[34] Hair, "An Analysis of the Register of Fourah Bay College, 1827–1950," p. 159.

caliber of their education left much to be desired, and it was not until after World War II that the matter received serious attention. A half-dozen teacher-training institutions were in operation in Sierra Leone by 1960, and though progress is being made in the quality of training, teachers still remain on the whole the most poorly trained element among the liberal professions.

On the basis of income, education, and prestige higher civil servants certainly rank among the upper level of the new elite. There were twenty Africans in the senior civil service during the mid-1920's and about fifty in the immediate postwar period.[35] Soon after, the pressure of African nationalist policies resulted in a significant augmentation of African senior civil servants. The number of Africans in pensionable senior posts more than tripled between 1953 and 1959. There were 381 African senior pensionable servants in 1959, and they held 56 per cent of all pensionable posts.[36] On the eve of independence, nearly 600 Africans had reached the senior service category. Next to teachers, they now constitute the largest group among the professions, and they claim larger incomes than teachers, ranking next to doctors and lawyers in this respect.

There were 9,651 junior civil servants immediately prior to independence.[37] Generally the education and income of this group are markedly inferior to those of senior servants, as is their standard of living. However, a small portion of junior servants are fairly well educated, claim middle incomes, and aspire to a style of life quite different from that of the farming community or the urban wage-laborers in railways, docks, manufacturing and other enterprises. These junior servants are more properly ranked as part of the lower level of the new elite.

2. Wealth of Professionals

Although adequate figures are impossible to come by, it appears that lawyers, doctors, and senior civil servants have

---

[35] See *Colony of Sierra Leone Staff List: Part I, Senior Service* (Freetown, 1948).
[36] *Government Statement on Africanisation, Sessional Paper No. 4 of 1959* (Freetown, 1959), p. 1.
[37] *Sierra Leone Government Staff List 1960* (Freetown, 1960).

been the most affluent groups among the professional component of the Sierra Leonean middle class. Sir Samuel Lewis, the prominent Creole barrister of the late nineteenth century, was in an income bracket that enabled him to purchase "an extensive estate" in 1882 on which he built "a substantial three-storied house from which to enjoy the 'pleasure of rural life.'" Sir Samuel also invested £800 in commercial crops and in cattle breeding.[38] Available data for the 1920's provide a fair sample of the incomes enjoyed by professional elements. African medical doctors in government service (of whom there were eight in 1925) claimed incomes that ranged from £500 to £650 per annum, excluding rent allowances that ranged from £30 to £80 per annum. Somewhat lower incomes were received by other African senior servants: African Assistant Colonial Secretary—£420; African Assistant Treasurer—£460; African Surveyor—£250; African Assistant Government Printer—£164; and African Engine Driver—£150.[39]

In the postwar period all professionals experienced a significant increase in wealth, as may be seen from the incomes claimed by those in government service. Lawyers employed as police magistrates received incomes that ranged from £984 to £1,720 in 1960, and puisne judges received £2,650. Lawyers in private practice also claimed high incomes, which ranged from £1,000 to £8,000 upward. The African medical doctors in government service received incomes ranging from £958 to £2,400 in 1960.[40] Furthermore, most doctors in government service pursued private practice as well. In 1949–50 the private incomes of doctors in government service ranged from £146 to £1,500.[41] Finally, at the lower rung of the incomes claimed by professional elements were schoolteachers. In 1949 teachers in government or government-assisted schools (which meant most teachers) claimed incomes that ranged from £42 per annum for primary teachers with lowest qualification (i.e., Standard VI or Junior Cambridge)

[38] Hargreaves, A Life of Sir Samuel Lewis, p. 28.
[39] Sierra Leone Blue Book, 1925 (Freetown, 1926), pp. 126–127.
[40] Sierra Leone Government Staff List, 1960, pp. 20–22.
[41] Report on Medical Salaries and Private Practice, Sessional Paper No. 3 of 1954 (Freetown, 1954), p. 5.

to £500 for secondary schoolteachers with highest qualification (i.e., university degree or education diploma).[42] By the mid-1950's this income range had expanded to £840 for the best qualified teachers, with most teachers falling in the £60 to £168 range.[43]

3. Business Groups

Since the business community in Sierra Leone and other African countries consists largely of traders or merchants of some sort, it is not easy to classify businessmen in relation to other segments of the middle class. One thing is certain: the many thousands who are described in colonial reports as "petty traders" or "hawkers" could hardly be included. Professor Sol Tax has rightly characterized the economic activity of these elements as "penny capitalism"; most of them claim little more income than the daily pay of unskilled workers and are no better educated. On the other hand, we would certainly include middle-sized and large-scale traders or merchants as members of the new elite, as well as many of those who own service firms which do tailoring, printing, butchering, and the like. Entrepreneurs properly so-called would also be included in the new elite; these include African bankers, cement manufacturers, contractors, large transport owners, and large-scale cash-crop planters.

As regards the early development of business groups in Sierra Leone, data relating to the second half of the nineteenth century show that some African merchants obtained sizable wealth. For instance, of 300 African merchants who petitioned the colonial government in 1875, about a dozen were importers of commodities valued at £75,000 per annum. About forty other merchants who signed the petition were described as occupying "a position in society somewhat less substantial," and the remainder claimed annual incomes around £100.[44]

The relative good fortune of a few African businessmen should

---

[42] *Revision of Teachers' Salaries, Sessional Paper No. 9 of 1948* (Freetown, 1948), pp. 1–6.

[43] *Revised Conditions of Service and Revised Salary Scales for Teachers in Government and Assisted Schools* (Freetown, 1952), pp. 4–9.

[44] Hargreaves, *A Life of Sir Samuel Lewis*, pp. 23–24. Cf. *Sierra Leone Report on the Blue Book for 1888* (London, 1889), p. 9.

not be overestimated, however. Of the sixty companies registered in Sierra Leone during the period 1937–56, only about a quarter were exclusively African-owned, and nine others had part African ownership. Excluding a firm whose share capital was £250,000 and which was merely incorporated in Sierra Leone but operated in the Gambia, the average share capital of African-owned companies was £12,393.[45] By contrast, the average share capital of expatriate companies was £45,500 for Syrian-Lebanese companies, £52,000 for Indian, and £40,085 for European companies. Moreover, the firms doing the largest amount of business in Sierra Leone were registered in Britain. In 1953 the capital of nine foreign-registered companies doing business in Sierra Leone ranged between £100,000 and £500,000, three between £500,000 and £1,000,000, and six over £1,000,000.

The position of African ownership of business in Sierra Leone up to the 1960's was not much different from that elsewhere in West Africa. Of the 2,000 companies registered in Nigeria between 1912 and 1959, Africans owned only about 37 per cent of them. In 1959 the median share capital of 647 of these African-owned companies was only £2,000; some twenty had over £50,000, and only one had over £1,000,000.[46] The situation was even more one-sided in French West Africa. In 1935 Africans owned only forty-four of the business establishments in Dakar, Senegal, as against 455 owned by Lebanese and 102 by Europeans.[47] More recently, it is reported that the African group in Senegal "to which the name 'commercial bourgeoisie' has been given, is still too small to have much influence; almost all African traders are small shopkeepers and make no appreciable impact on the affairs of the community as a whole . . . The middle-man trade is practically monopolized by the Lebanese colony . . ."[48]

---

[45] N. A. Cox-George, *African Participation in Commerce* (Freetown, 1958), pp. 14–15.

[46] J. D. Nyhart, "Notes on Entrepreneurship in Africa" (unpublished MS; Harvard Center for International Affairs, 1961).

[47] Jean Paillard, "La Fin des Français en Afrique noire," *Les Oeuvres Françaises* (Paris, 1935), p. 59.

[48] P. Mercier, "Evolution of Senegalese Elites," *International Social Science Bulletin*, Vol. III, No. 3 (1956), 443 n. 5. Cf. Assane Seck, "La Formation d'une classe moyenne en Afrique occidentale française," in *Développement d'une classe moyenne* (Brussels, 1956), pp. 161–162.

Another index of the smallness of African participation in business is the share of imports and exports handled by African-owned enterprises. In 1952 African firms claimed only 2.9 per cent of Sierra Leone imports by value (£234,468). Indian concerns claimed 10.5 per cent (£860,526), Syrian-Lebanese 16.2 per cent (£1,328,876), and European firms 70.4 per cent (£5,770,598). Similarly, data for selected exports in 1955 show that African firms claimed only 1.4 per cent (£111,871) of these exports. Even with 32 per cent of that year's exports by value under the control of the Produce Marketing Board, an agency of the Sierra Leone government, European firms handled 55 per cent of exports.[49]

It is thus evident that the business component of the African middle class in Sierra Leone and elsewhere in West Africa is neither particularly large nor wealthy. Significantly enough, its wealth is not much greater on average than that of some professional groups within the new elite such as doctors and lawyers. Note, for instance, the following report of the wealth and general affluence of a Ghanaian medical doctor: "A doctor, who estimates his income for 1953 at about £6,000, has a house which can scarcely be distinguished from a British country mansion, a description of which can be found on the last page of almost any copy of the London *Times*. It has 20 rooms (to house 8 people), running water, 4 flush lavatories and 3 bathrooms. It is built of concrete and stone. The furnishings of the house follow the European pattern, although on a more modest scale . . . The family possess 3 cars, a radiogramme, gramophone, sewing machine and typewriter. Savings are kept in the form of investments, cash in the bank, and ownership of 4 lorries."[50]

Cognizant of the weak position of the business element in the African elite, the new African regimes have endeavored to ameliorate this situation, though not without difficulty. The political elite tends to shape policy so as to favor Africans in commerce, but few privileged Africans choose a business career. A survey

[49] Cox-George, *African Participation in Commerce*, p. 8.
[50] W. B. Birmingham, "Standards of Living in the Gold Coast," in *Proceedings of the Third Annual Conference of the West African Institute of Social and Economic Research* (Ibadan, 1956), pp. 28–29.

of 139 arts students and 104 science students at the University College of Ghana revealed that only 9 per cent of the former and 4 per cent of the latter chose "business" as the vocation they would like to be in twenty years after receiving their college degree. A small percentage of students did name "agriculture" as their future vocation, and the reporter of the survey underlined that agriculture "is almost without exception conceived as a business venture," but an overwhelming majority chose the professions as their long-run occupational aim. A similar survey of adults and schoolchildren in Dakar showed that between 65 per cent and 80 per cent of the adults who were questioned preferred that their children pursue the professions; and more than 80 per cent of the children questioned wanted to enter professions, "with commerce far behind." It is interesting that in his explanation of this preference for professional occupations, the author of the survey, Professor Mercier, felt that "material security (e.g., that enjoyed by civil servants) seems to be desired more often than actual wealth."[51] This is no doubt an important factor underlying the preference for professions, but what the colonial legacy offers in an objective sense affects the individual's idea of what he can get. Africans simply recognize that, given the overwhelming expatriate predominance in business and commerce, they have little hope of access to large-scale wealth in these fields. Hence the strong preference for the professions which are relatively open to Africans and which do not require the capital, managerial skills, and influence that big business undertakings do. If through their own efforts or with outside help the new elite can create more favorable opportunities for Africans, business careers may come to attract the ambitious.

D. ESTIMATED SIZE OF THE NEW ELITE

If literacy in English were used as the index of new-elite status, then from 5 per cent to 15 per cent of Sierra Leone's population would fall into this category. Every literate person, however, could hardly be considered a member of the new elite in

[51] Mercier, "Evolution of Senegalese Elites," pp. 448–449.

Sierra Leone or in any other African country; hence the rather limited value of gross literacy statistics. Any meaningful index of new-elite status must surely take account of such factors as the *degree* of education, wealth, and general social standing vis-à-vis other educated persons, occupational standing, and the like. By my reckoning, hardly 2 per cent of Sierra Leone's population can be included in the new-elite category.

As regards the numbers involved, the income-tax assessments for 1959–60 report some 2,000 or so Sierra Leoneans whose incomes of between £500 and upwards of £10,000 warrant categorizing them as members of the new elite. If we added to this figure, on a generous reckoning, the large number of teachers with incomes between £70 and £500 (perhaps some 2,000 or so teachers fall in this category) and most of the 9,651 junior civil servants who receive similar incomes, we would have some approximation of the size of the combined middle and upper group.

E. SOME SPECIAL CHARACTERISTICS OF THE UPPER LEVEL

1. Asymmetrical Structure

One important characteristic of the professionals, businessmen, and civil servants who largely constitute the upper level of the new elite is the asymmetrical structure of the group. By this I mean that persons falling within the upper category are usually alone among their kin in holding a high social status. Their immediate kin—brother, sister, mother, father—are poor peasants or wage-laborers. In short, such persons attain modern elite status without carrying their whole family unit with them.

Thus in Sierra Leone one can find a senior member of the civil service who has a semi-literate sister residing in slum dwellings, while he himself was educated in law at a British university, earns a salary of £2,650 per annum, and lives in a modern concrete house that is valued at £10,000–£20,000 and is located in the affluent residential section of Freetown. Obviously this sociological asymmetry, widespread throughout West Africa, is a function of the slow rate of social change and can be expected to move toward greater symmetry as more intensive and extensive social change occurs. Meanwhile it constitutes an important force in the social and political relations of the new elite.

For one thing, it tends to restrict the new elite from becoming a close-knit social class separate from other segments of the population. The members of the upper level are impelled, by force of traditional obligations, to assist their poorer kin, and usually in ways that mitigate a great widening of the social distance between the upper and middle categories and the poorer sections. Wealthy Africans, for instance, often build annexes to their modern homes in which they house their poorer kin; or they incorporate their poorer kin directly into their household, not infrequently as servants.

This pattern is widespread among the upper level throughout West Africa, but especially among political leaders of all sorts. The establishment of a framework of representative government during the period of decolonization gave a certain measure of political influence to the poorer orders, and members of the new elite who enter politics have felt obliged to recognize this influence by consenting to the social-security claims of their poorer kin. Neglect of such claims would be interpreted by the more tradition-bound masses as disrespect of indigenous values and would be intensely unpopular. Even when the framework of representative government is discarded for the authoritarian single-party regime, as it has been in most of West Africa, the political leadership has not felt politically capable of disregarding social-security obligations to poorer kin. Thus there may be a sense in which the asymmetrical structure of the new elite operates as a mechanism through which the poorer masses may keep their new rulers responsive to their needs.

If the asymmetrical structure of the new elite has limited its political power, it has also restricted its economic development. Family interests not infrequently take precedence over class or occupational interests, resulting in a slow pace of the development of entrepreneurship. In particular, the accumulation of capital by professionals and businessmen has been retarded by the manifold claims of the poorer kin on the richer. As K. D. S. Baldwin put it in a report on entrepreneurship in Western Nigeria:

"Very few Africans have been able to accumulate enough capital to start enterprises of their own. Even if they can, they are often deterred by the obligations of the indigenous family system which requires 'rich' members of the family to respond to calls for assistance made on them by other poorer and, very often, distant, relatives. Admirable though this may be as a social security scheme, it is a serious detriment to autochthonous development since it drains away the rich man's resources and removes the incentive of providing benefit to himself or his children."[52]

This situation, combined with the concentration of large-scale capital and managerial skill in expatriate hands, has caused the new elite to turn to government resources for both entrepreneurial and professional development. But these resources are themselves limited, in the nature of the case, resulting therefore in the use of corrupt methods to secure them. Such corruption by the political elite is widespread in West African states and is a potential source of political instability in these states. It is unlikely to be brought into reasonable bounds as long as this elite, and its allies, are obligated to respect the social-security claims of the African family system.

2. Nationalism and Elite Development

The main phase of the development of the new elite in Sierra Leone coincided with the rise of anti-colonial nationalism. World War I marked a watershed for both of these developments. The old middle class of the late nineteenth and early twentieth century, whose style of life may be described in Werner Sombart's terms as "bourgeois, old style," emphasizing thrift and hard work as the conditions for getting ahead in modern society, gave way at this time to a different type of middle-class outlook which focused upon the resources of the colonial government as the more effective means of advancement. This change in middle-class outlook was partly related to the fact that increasing num-

---

[52] Quoted in Bernard Blankenheimer, "Economic Policy in Emergent Africa," *SAIS Review* (Winter 1959), p. 14. Cf. Elizabeth Colson, "Native Cultural and Social Patterns in Contemporary Africa," in C. Grove Haines, ed., *Africa Today* (Baltimore, 1955), pp. 72–84.

bers of professional Africans found government service the most suitable outlet for their skills. In 1925, for instance, 57 per cent of the medical doctors in Sierra Leone were so employed. This, in turn, whetted the appetite of the new elite for more government jobs, as well as for direct government assistance in training and preparation for government posts.

Stripped to its essentials, the anti-colonial nationalism that emerged after World War I was merely the ideological projection of the expanding appetite of middle-class Africans for new jobs and related perquisites which only the government could provide. Inevitably, this nationalism confronted the sizable expatriate personnel, who claimed the most desirable posts in the colonial establishment, as the main barrier to its goal. This barrier, it was soon discovered, could be overcome only with the demise of the colonial regime itself. Hence the anti-colonial orientation of African nationalism.

The National Congress of British West Africa, founded in Accra, the Gold Coast, in March 1920, with branches in Sierra Leone, the Gambia, and Nigeria, was the major organizational expression of the new middle-class nationalism after World War I.[53] The aims of the NCBWA covered the whole gamut of essentially middle-class needs, among which were greater African representation in central colonial government, expansion of the franchise, and "the establishment of a British West African University to give British Africans technical and scientific training, and especially the training necessary for the holding of positions in the Colonial Service."[54] Only a small portion of these aims was even partly achieved during the 1920's and 1930's. At the end of World War II, however, the colonial authorities moved toward greater African representation in central government, which widened the possibilities for greater use of government resources for the development of the African elite.

This development, as the elite saw it, was basically a matter of the replacement of expatriate personnel at all levels of the colonial

[53] *Sierra Leone Weekly News,* January 4, 1919, p. 11.
[54] Quoted in *Journal of the African Society* (July 1920), p. 331. See David Kimble, *A Political History of the Gold Coast, 1850–1928* (Oxford, 1963), pp. 374–403.

establishment. In Sierra Leone this policy of "Africanization" commenced in the late 1940's and by the end of the 1950's had no small achievement to its credit. Table 13 shows how the num-

TABLE 13

Africanization of Senior Civil Service Posts
in Sierra Leone in the 1950's

Year	Expatriates[a]	African	Total	African % of total
1953	315	166	481	24
1958	296	332	628	53
1959	297	381	678	56

Source: *Government Statement on Africanization, Sessional Paper No. 4 of 1959* (Freetown, 1959), p. 1.

[a] Figures in this column refer only to pensionable senior servants and do not include the expatriate senior servants hired by contract. If the 179 contract (temporary) expatriate officers were added to the 1959 figure, then the readjusted African proportion of the total would be 48 per cent.

ber of Africans in senior civil service posts augmented during the 1950's; it is to be underlined that professional Africans were the main beneficiary of this increase. By 1956 some 80 per cent of the medical doctors were in government service, compared to 57 per cent twenty-one years earlier, and in 1960 nearly 40 per cent of the lawyers were so employed. Furthermore, a majority of the doctors and lawyers pursued private practice along with government employment. Africanization also applied to the training of professionals. Whereas the colonial government in Sierra Leone had sent fewer than one hundred students overseas for higher education in the period 1943–49, the Sierra Leone People's Party (SLPP) government, elected to office in 1951, had sent over three hundred students for higher education overseas by 1959.[55] The SLPP government also assumed full financial responsibility for Fourah Bay College (now the University College of Sierra

[55] *Sierra Leone Government White Paper on Educational Development, Sessional Paper No. 4 of 1958* (Freetown, 1958), pp. 4–5, 6–14.

Leone) during this period; today most students at the College receive government scholarships.[56]

The SLPP government has also extended wide assistance to the business community among the African elite. In the mid-1950's the government announced that "it is Government's policy to encourage private enterprise . . .," and by the end of the 1950's a number of measures had been instituted to this end.[57] Manufacturing machinery was purchased and sold to African capitalists at less than original cost; African produce firms were given special consideration by the Sierra Leone Government Produce Marketing Board when purchasing cash-crops for export; the Development of Industries Board was established to provide loans and easy credit to African businessmen; a variety of assistance, including credit, was extended to the large cash-crop planters organized into cooperatives; and, finally, government pressure was brought to bear upon expatriate firms to expand their African managerial personnel and to upgrade it without let or hindrance.[58]

With the establishment of the independent state of Sierra Leone in April 1961, the new elite, now with a governing class, obtained incomparable opportunities for further development. But it is no longer quite so easy for the new elite to justify claims upon government resources precisely in the same nationalistic mode that prevailed before independence. The range of self-serving policies that the new elite could have accepted by the African majority in the pre-independence period as being in the public interest is much more limited in the post-independence era. Yet there will always be a lot of room for maneuver by the elite in this regard.

For instance, it is certainly arguable that the use of government resources to expand professional categories like that of medical doctors is as much in the public or national interest as it is in that of the new elite. Throughout West African states medical

[56] For details see Martin Kilson, "Sierra Leone," in Helen Kitchen, ed., *The Educated African* (New York, 1963).

[57] *House of Representative Debates, First Session 1957–1958* (Freetown, 1958), pp. 81–82.

[58] *Ibid.; Sierra Leone Estimates of Expenditure and Revenue, 1959–60* (Freetown, 1959), p. 99.

doctors shun many crucial areas of medicine because, as a report of the Nigerian government has noted, they "offer very little or no scope for remunerative practice."[59] In 1958 such important medical fields in Nigeria as pathology, dermatology, malariology, nutrition, anaesthetics, among others, had only a few or no practitioners. This situation necessarily affects the efficiency of any developing state in tropical Africa and cannot be left wanting; and to the extent that it is attended to, the result is as much in the public as in the new elite's interest.

Yet every instance of government assistance to the professional and business categories of the elite can hardly be rationalized invariably in this way. Much of this assistance is purely and simply self-serving, with little or no gain for the public interest. Even so, it must be recognized that what we call public interest is a meaningless notion separate from specific group or class interest; the evaluation of the claims of both upon government resources must, therefore, take into consideration the relative nature of the relationship between them. As V. O. Key has put it: "Private groups have a remarkable facility in the rationalization of private gain with the public interest . . . The principal driving forces in politics are class interests and group interests; they make themselves felt regardless of the kind of government or social organization that exists. [Yet] . . . the promotion of the public good cannot be accomplished apart from class or special interest. The public good is, after all, a relative matter."[60]

F. CONCLUSION

The role of the elite in the new African states will be decisive in many spheres. Its monopoly of professional, technical, and bureaucratic skills ensures this; no other combination of African groups outside the elite constitutes a threat in this regard, though the crucial position of expatriate interests represents a

[59] *Matters Rising from the Final Report of the Parliamentary Committee on the Nigerianisation of the Federal Public Service, Sessional Paper No. 2 of 1960* (Lagos, 1960), pp. 25–26.

[60] V. O. Key, Jr., *Politics, Parties and Pressure Groups* (New York, 1956), pp. 174–176.

limiting factor. The historical pattern of the elite's evolution, the nature of its nationalism, and the sociological setting of its relationship to the wider populace are significant for understanding the elite's post-colonial behavior. The role of corruption, for instance, so widespread in all West African states, is closely linked to these aspects of the elite's development. So, too, is the widespread tendency toward authoritarianism. The elite's heavy dependence upon government resources, and hence the political process, for its expansion, combined with the desire of groups outside the elite for access to these same limited resources, is unlikely to be conducive to the maintenance of the rather fragile institutions of representative government (including the mass franchise) inherited from the decolonization period of the 1950's.

Part III -

Colonial Constitutional Change

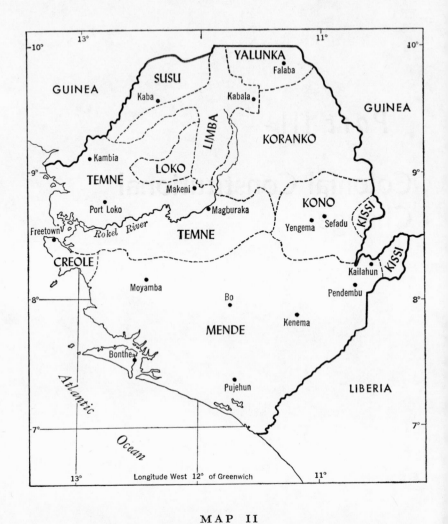

MAP II

PRINCIPAL TOWNS, LINES OF TRANSPORT,
AND ADMINISTRATIVE DISTRICTS

CHAPTER 6

The Political Context of

Constitutional Change, 1863-1931

A. BEGINNINGS OF CONSTITUTIONALISM, 1863–1900[1]

1. Representation of the Creole Elite

Established as a Crown Colony in 1808, the Sierra Leone peninsula and the areas directly to the south of it were governed by a Governor-in-Council who combined both executive and legislative authority. This system prevailed until 1863 when the executive and legislative functions were divided between an Executive Council and a Legislative Council. Though the new Councils marked a step away from the earlier form of colonial autocracy, they were not intended as a move toward self-government. For as Christopher Fyfe has put it, "the new constitution was devised to govern an expanding Colony more efficiently, not to let its citizens govern themselves."[2] But the seed of a form of representative government was embedded in the new constitutional arrangement; the growing need for efficiency in colonial administration—a need which was to assert itself even more

[1] Throughout this and the following chapters, my view of constitutional change or the constitution-making process is based upon Carl Friedrich's conception of constitution making "as the process by which governmental action is effectively restrained . . ." As Friedrich suggests, this conception takes account of the organization or structure of government, of who participates in it, and of the purposes any particular organ of government serves. Moreover, though to restrain governmental action gives the appearance of a negative approach to power, in actuality it is not infrequently a mere prelude to an even greater use of power once a new constitutional structure has been secured. Cf. Friedrich, *Constitutional Government and Democracy* (Boston, 1941), pp. 119–130.

[2] C. H. Fyfe, *A History of Sierra Leone* (Oxford, 1962), pp. 107 ff.

sharply during the twentieth century—entailed a search for constitutional methods of accommodating the rising group of articulate Africans.

At this time, and until the first decade of the twentieth century, Creole merchants were by far the most politically articulate segment of the African community. They were also of direct value to the early efforts of the colonial regime to penetrate the Sierra Leone hinterland. This value was not lost on the colonial government and was given official recognition within six months of the promulgation of the Legislative and Executive Council in 1863. In December 1863 two African merchants (Charles Heddle, a planter, and John Ezzidio, a merchant) were appointed nominated members of the Legislative Council, and they sat in the Council as acknowledged spokesmen of Creole merchant interests. In fact, the appointment of Ezzidio was made in consultation with the Sierra Leone Mercantile Association, an organization of Creole merchants founded in the early 1850's.[3]

Between 1863 and 1903 the African members of the Legislative Council were largely merchants (nine out of twelve). The first professional African to attain full nominated membership of the Legislative Council was a lawyer, Sir Samuel Lewis, who was appointed in 1882. Sir Samuel, the first black man to be knighted by the British Crown, served in the Legislative Council until his death in 1903, during which period he was joined by two additional lawyers and a physician. In 1910 another lawyer was appointed temporary member of the Legislative Council, and in 1911 a lawyer gained full nominated membership.[4] It was not, however, until after World War I, when a new constitutional structure was established in 1924, that the professional group gained ascendancy in African representation in the Legislative Council. It was also at this time that Chiefs were first appointed to the Council.

[3] *Sierra Leone Blue Book, 1863* (Freetown, 1864). I have consulted a handwritten copy in the Government Archives. Cf. C. H. Fyfe, "The Life and Times of John Ezzidio," *Sierra Leone Studies* (June 1955), pp. 219–223; Fyfe, *A History of Sierra Leone*, p. 318.

[4] The foregoing data are from J. L. John, "Memorandum on the Evolution of the Legislative Council of Sierra Leone," in *Legislative Council Debates, Session 1924–1925* (Freetown, n.d.), pp. 243–244.

2. The Political Heritage and Colonial Constitutionalism

In British Africa it was not a matter of chance that the colonial authorities employed constitutional procedure in the accommodation of articulate African interests. It was rather the result of the British democratic political heritage which was accepted by the colonial establishment as a moderating force upon its efforts to govern backward societies. Whereas in German, Portuguese, and Belgian African territories coercive measures of one form or another were more often than not applied to articulate African political demands, in British Africa (and to a lesser extent in French Africa) these demands were normally met within a constitutional framework—that is, a framework in which a set of rules or procedures were established whereby articulate African interests could affect (restrain) government action.

Evidence of the prevalence of a democratic heritage in British West African colonies was apparent at the very start of constitutional development. For example, in 1868 a Circular Despatch of the Secretary for the Colonies established the limits within which a variant of constitutionalism would apply to articulate non-official interests represented in the colonial Legislative Council. The Circular Despatch advised that the nominated member of the Legislative Council "will naturally understand that holding his seat by nomination of the Crown, he has been selected for it in the expectation and in the confidence that he will co-operate with the Crown in its general policy, and not oppose the Crown on any important question without strong and substantial reasons; but of the validity of these reasons he will be himself the judge . . . It will be his duty to exercise a vigilant supervision over the measures introduced by the Government lest in any case local official interests, which are no doubt strongly represented in the Legislature, should prevail to the prejudice of public interests."[5] Several years later, in 1870, the Secretary of State for the Colonies, in a dispatch to the Governor of Sierra Leone, further stipulated the conditions that would guarantee a measure of democratic

[5] Quoted in Martin Wight, *The Development of the Legislative Council, 1606–1945* (London, 1946), p. 112.

intent, if not full-fledged democratic procedure, in the colony's lawmaking body. "A Governor," the dispatch observed, "should choose [as African nominated members] not only those who are most likely to support Government, but those who will be taken to represent and will really inform you of the wishes of the intelligent portion of the community."[6]

Limited though these institutional extensions of the British democratic heritage to colonial government were, they nevertheless infused the small Sierra Leonean elite with a belief in the values of parliamentary constitutionalism. Sir Samuel Lewis, the acknowledged spokesman of the unofficial nominated members, was, according to his able biographer, "especially vigilant for any sign of neglect of the rights and privileges of the Legislative Council. Members of Council, he held, had the right to the fullest information about all matters they were asked to discuss, especially if money was to be voted; members of the public, in turn, should be kept informed about the work of the Council. The Governor should not enforce the passage of measures by the votes of the official majority without giving proper consideration to the views of the unofficials, and to any petitions they might present."[7] For Sir Samuel the right of unofficial nominated members to discuss fully all matters was, moreover, sacrosanct. Unofficial members, he believed, should refuse on principle "only to say 'yes' to every clause of a Bill, and register by their votes the will of the Secretary of State."[8]

Yet Sir Samuel fully recognized that a colonial government, whatever its adherence to a democratic heritage might be, represented a set of autocratic, oligarchic interests. However one, as a colonial subject, might feel about these interests, they had a certain legitimacy in the context of their civilizing and modernizing functions. Sir Samuel Lewis thus admitted a certain community of interest between colonial government and the small articulate

[6] Quoted in A. T. Porter, "The Social Background of Political Decision-makers in Sierra Leone," *Sierra Leone Studies* (June 1960), p. 6.

[7] J. D. Hargreaves, "Sir Samuel Lewis and the Legislative Council," *Sierra Leone Studies* (December 1953), pp. 42–43.

[8] *Legislative Council Debates, 11 June 1898;* cited in J. D. Hargreaves, *A Life of Sir Samuel Lewis* (London, 1958), p. 35.

African element; and this community of interest in turn necessitated some limitation upon the constitutional rights of African members of the legislature. One such limitation, as Sir Samuel saw it, was that unofficial members were bound to support colonial policy whenever they reasonably could, rather than mount unnecessary opposition for its own sake. As Sir Samuel put it: "Unlike the Unofficial Members in some of Her Majesty's Colonies, those in Sierra Leone do not study to oppose any and every measure proposed by the Government, but rather to give it frank support whenever they can honestly do so."[9]

Here, thus, was a process of political acculturation of educated Africans to the constitutional norms of the colonial oligarchy. This acculturation, in turn, minimized the apprehension of the colonial oligarchy over granting political concessions to articulate African interests. As long as articulate African groups were, or appeared to be, committed to the constitutional procedures of colonial government, the extension of these procedures to them was a means both of legitimizing the colonial system and increasing its efficiency in the face of expanding functions. In a sense, then, colonial constitutional change is essentially a matter of creating procedures by which the African elite may be acculturated to the political norms and rules of the metropolitan power. This accomplished, the skills and aspirations of the African elite are more readily available to the colonial government.

B. BEGINNINGS OF MODERN MIDDLE-CLASS POLITICAL
EVOLUTION, 1909–1924

The year 1909 marked the true commencement of modern-style politics in Sierra Leone. In that year the urban elite founded the first of several Ratepayers' Associations whose main function was to contest elections to the Freetown Municipal Council, a body that had included elected African members since its foundation in 1895. In addition to these electoral associations other political groups were formed during this period, and most of them

9 *Legislative Council Debates, 23rd May 1892;* cited in Hargreaves, "Sir Samuel Lewis and the Legislative Council," p. 42.

expressed an incipient nationalist orientation. The Civil Servants' Association (1907–9), the Aborigines Protection Society (1919), the Sierra Leone Bar Association (1919), the African Progress Union (1919), the Sierra Leone branch of the National Congress of British West Africa (1920), and the Young People's Progressive Union (1929), for example, fall into this category.

These groups exercised varying degrees of political influence in the colonial system, depending partly upon the extent to which they were founded as explicitly political organs. Even the primarily occupational groups, such as the Civil Servants' Association and the Bar Association, were of some political significance, inasmuch as the pursuit of professional interests was often inseparable from politics. For instance, the Civil Servants' Association's aim of "Africanization" of the civil service inevitably entailed political pressure upon the colonial regime. Furthermore, the leaders and members of the occupational groups frequently belonged to the explicitly political groups. Thus Mr. L. E. V. M'Carthy, a lawyer, was simultaneously Joint Secretary of the Bar Association and Secretary of the Sierra Leone Committee of the British West African Conference, the preparatory body for the founding of the National Congress of British West Africa, Sierra Leone branch (hereinafter referred to as SLNC), in 1920. Similarly, Mr. (later Sir) E. S. Beoku-Betts was leader of the Sierra Leone Bar Association, Secretary of the Public Welfare Association, and Vice President of the SLNC.[10]

This overlap of the leaders of the political and occupational organizations virtually made them a single, unified political force. It also provided a more efficient utilization of the limited educated, intellectual, and financial resources available to the emergent African elite. Both types of organization endeavored, in one way or other, to modify the imbalance in social and political power between Africans and the imported oligarchy of government officials, technicians, private entrepreneurs, and missionaries. The essentially occupational Civil Servants' Association, for instance, endeavored to act as "a medium whereby representations

[10] *Sierra Leone Weekly News* of February 15, 1919, pp. 8–9; of October 4, 1930, p. 4; and of October 18, 1930, p. 9.

can be made to Government on all matters affecting the interests of the African Staff . . ., to make collective representations constitutionally to the Head of the Executive and . . . the Secretary of State for the Colonies when necessary . . ., [and] to ensure that mutual improvement and support of its members are maintained."[11] The explicitly political SLNC, on the other hand, sought not merely the modification of relationships between blacks and whites but the eventual transformation of the colonial system into a "national" system: ". . . Among the objects of the Congress shall be the promotion of the common interests of the British West African Dependencies . . .; to promote and effect 'Unity of Purpose and of Action' among the people; . . . to promote commercial and industrial intercourse of the people . . .; to aid in the development of the political institutions of British West Africa under the Union Jack, so as eventually to take her place beside the sister nations of the Empire, and in time, to ensure within her borders the government of the people, by the people, for the people; to ensure equal opportunity for all; to preserve the lands of the people for the people; and to save them from exploitation in any shape or form."[12]

While political organizations were springing up among the African urban middle class, a similar development began in the hinterland towns of the Protectorate. By the 1920's an educated elite had emerged in the Protectorate, and, like its counterpart in the Colony, it was cognizant of the need to influence colonial government. Unlike the Colony middle class, however, the small educated group in the Protectorate had close ties to the traditional social structure, particularly to its ruling elite. Those Chiefs who had been educated and given new sources of affluence and power were obviously already capable of participating in modern institutions. It was regarded as desirable for traditional rulers to be equipped for leading positions in the emergent social and political systems. The colonial government encouraged this atti-

[11] *Ibid.*, November 26, 1927, p. 9; D. N. K. Browne, "The African Civil Servants' Association," *The Civil Servant* (Freetown, December 1948), pp. 2 ff.
[12] *Constitution of the National Congress of British West Africa*, secs. 18, 19. Text found in *Sierra Leone Weekly News*, October 4, 1930, p. 5.

tude in hopes that Chiefs who were acceptable to educated Africans would have a moderating influence and forestall precipitous demands. From the 1920's onwards, this policy shaped every facet of political development in the Sierra Leone Protectorate.

Another form of government influence upon the early politics of the hinterland was the policy of administering the Sierra Leone territory through two distinct political systems of Colony and Protectorate. This led the articulate Africans of the hinterland to define their needs and interests in terms of the territorial, administrative limits of the Protectorate. Thus the Protectorate's first organized political group, the Committee of Educated Aborigines (CEA), formulated its declaration of aims, drawn up initially as an Address of Welcome to the Governor, Sir Alexander Ransford Slater, in 1922, in terms of the Colony-Protectorate division: "Since the foundation of the settlement of Sierra Leone up to date, no other Governor has been so marvellously acute to detect this 'anomaly of a somewhat glaring character' [i.e., absence of Protectorate representation in the central legislature] . . . Educated aborigines were aware of it ages ago but, as they could not have voiced the question before now, they reluctantly adopted the 'wait-and-see policy' innate in them, and waited till the hour strikes. The only reason one could accurately ascribe to that lamentable political blunder you have observed in the Sierra Leone Legislature, and we would also add, in the Sierra Leone Branch of the National Congress of British West Africa is simply the wilful neglect of the thorough education of Protectorate aborigines, on the same standard as the Africans in the Colony."

If the colonial government had succeeded in compartmentalizing Sierra Leone, however, this did not prevent educated Africans on both sides of the administrative division from seeking nearly identical objectives. Thus, the CEA's desire to overcome what it called the "wilful neglect" by colonial government of Protectorate needs was little different from what the SLNC sought for Colony interests. In its own address of welcome to Sir Alexander Ransford Slater, the newly appointed Governor, in May, 1922, the SLNC proclaimed that "our first and foremost reform is popular representation and the Elective Franchise, a valuable preparation towards political manhood . . . We are . . . hoping that Your Excellency will make an early pronouncement with reference to this burning question of the day."[13]

The combined demands of the articulate Protectorate and Colony groups set the stage for the first major constitutional reorganization of the Sierra Leone government since 1863. The appointment of Sir Alexander Ransford Slater as Governor in 1922, was, in fact, partly related to the need of colonial government to arrange a new mode of constitutional accommodation of the political forces that emerged in the post-World War I era. An additional factor which caused the colonial government to move toward a new stage in constitutional change was the incipient, and often riotous, growth of political activity among the inarticulate masses. This latter development, as seen by colonial authorities, added a qualitatively new dimension to the problems of colonial government and could not be left to its own machinations.

C. EARLY POLITICAL EVOLUTION AMONG THE MASSES, 1919–1931

1. Urban Wage-Laborers

Tenuously situated in the modern sector of colonial society, the urban wage-laborers experienced a pattern of political change that differed in certain basic ways from that of the new elites. Yet the efforts of wage-laborers to evolve modes of political expression relevant to their own needs were no less significant for the over-all development of African politics in colonial society.

The first trade union in Sierra Leone, the Carpenters' Defensive Union, was formed in 1895, though it was not until after World War I that trade unionism approached the status of a coherent movement of wage-earners.[14] The founding of the Sierra Leone Railway Skilled Workmen Mutual Aid Union (later called the

---

[13] The SLNC Address to Governor Slater appeared in the *Sierra Leone Weekly News* of May 20, 1922, pp. 8–9. The CEA address to the Governor ran on the same pages in the issue of September 9.

[14] *Sierra Leone Blue Book, 1926* (Freetown, 1927), pp. 370b–370c; I. T. Wallace-Johnson, *Trade Unionism in Colonial and Dependent Territories*, Part I (London, 1946), pp. 3 ff.

Railway Workers' Union) in September 1920 marked the beginning of such a movement. It emerged in the midst of two railway workers' strikes in July and October 1919, which were called because of the colonial government's delay in granting railway workers a promised War Bonus.[15] The subsequent development of the Railway Workers' Union was also associated with a series of strikes in 1926, 1931, and 1955, each of which played an important role in the political education of the railway workers in particular and the urban masses in general.

Strikes, in fact, were the one major means of political education for the wage-laborers, because the political organizations and activities of the new elite were normally beyond their ken. The Railway Workers' Union strike of 1926 was an especially good instance of this. The violence accompanying the strike brought the wage-laborers, and the urban masses generally, into direct encounter with the coercive power of the colonial government, thereby providing for the workers an important lesson in the role of force in the maintenance of colonial authority.[16] The Sierra Leone Battalion, the Police Force, and special police volunteers (who were educated Africans) were deployed against the strikers and the riotous crowds. The use of educated Africans as special constables (some 160 were involved) was a particularly salutary lesson for the urban masses; it represented direct evidence of the extent to which some Africans had, as it were, a stake in the system.[17]

The strike also revealed, however, that other segments of the educated African community were capable of recognizing a certain community of interest with the urban masses, or more specifically the skilled wage-laborers, however momentary it might be. In the earlier Railway Workers' Union strike in 1919 there was no evidence at all of this orientation among the educated classes. Indeed, they were unanimously opposed to the strikers and to

[15] An account of the strike is given in the *Sierra Leone Weekly News* of July 26, 1919, pp. 8–9; and news of the founding of the union appears in the issue of October 9, 1920, p. 5.

[16] *Sierra Leone Weekly News*, January 13–February 27, 1926; *Legislative Council Debates, No. I of Session 1926–1927*, pp. 4–5.

[17] *Legislative Council Debates, No. I of Session 1926–1927* (Freetown, n.d.), p. 84.

the riotous crowds who filled the streets of Freetown in their support, pillaging and burning in their wake. The leading newspaper of the educated classes derided the strike, describing its participants as "ruffians," and a Committee of Citizens was formed by the Freetown Municipal Council (composed of educated Africans and colonial officials) to assist the government in collecting funds to meet damages to property that resulted from the strike.[18] In contrast, a segment of the educated classes openly embraced the 1926 strike, hoping to extend their leadership to the wage-laborers. The SLNC in particular organized a measure of favorable public opinion toward the strike and collected a benefit fund of £1,000 for the strikers, whose stoppage lasted for nearly two months (January 13 to February 26).[19] This, however, was only a limited attempt by a segment of the elite to embrace the wage-laborers; it was not followed up by an organized effort to include them in the SLNC. Though the government actually feared this would happen, it did not in fact occur until after World War II.[20]

Finally, there was a rather persistent tendency for the strikes of skilled workers to act as a stimulus to riotous behavior by the unskilled, urban poor. Such behavior was associated with the railway workers' strikes in 1919 and 1926, resulting in the pillaging and burning of expatriate stores, warehouses, and homes—especially those of Lebanese merchants. As one observer recorded the riots accompanying the 1919 strike: "The community of Freetown woke this morning and found the City all in confusion and wild consternation. Organised bands of ruffians and irresponsible men were reported to have concentrated at different centres where they made forcible entry into several premises occupied by Syrians, broke open their stores and took away whatever they could lay hands on. A large quantity of cotton goods, rice, palm oil and cash were looted."[21] Lebanese businessmen estimated their prop-

---

[18] *Sierra Leone Weekly News,* October 18, 1919, p. 5.

[19] *Ibid.,* February 13, 1926, p. 2.

[20] *Legislative Council Debates, No. I of Session 1926–1927,* pp. 4–5.

[21] *Sierra Leone Weekly News,* July 19, 1919, p. 12. For detailed accounts of the 1919 riots, see *Sierra Leone Royal Gazette,* October 16, 1920; *Sierra Leone Weekly News,* October 30, 1920. On the treatment of expatriate merchants, see R. B. Winder, "The Lebanese in West Africa," *Comparative Studies in Society and History* (April 1962), p. 300.

erty damage in this riot at £250,000, some £45,000 of which was eventually compensated for by the Sierra Leone government from a special levy imposed on the Freetown community.

2. Urban Poor

Although the urban poor were particularly prone to seize upon strikes as occasion for anomic political expression, they did in fact evolve a rather more sustained form of at least quasi-political evolution. At their own level of peripheral contact with the modern sector of colonial society, the urban poor improvised a variety of voluntary or mutual-aid associations which were not without political relevance. They provided their members with a set of norms and procedures capable of mediating their members' interaction with the urban environment; eventually they, in Professor Wallerstein's words, "made men civil, responsive to the controls of the new social order."[22]

The rise of voluntary associations among the urban poor occurred just about at the same time as trade unions were formed among skilled and semi-skilled workers. In 1865 the Jubilee Society, a benefit body, was founded "for relief of members during sickness, death, loss in fire."[23] Beginning in 1900 such groups flourished in the urban environ of Freetown, Sherbro, and Bonthe. By 1925 there were twenty-three voluntary associations of various sorts; they claimed 13,415 members, which meant that they embraced a not inconsiderable portion of the adult urban population of this period (44,000 total population for Freetown in 1921).

The organizational pattern of these groups was, in the nature of the case, quite heterogenous. At times they were tribal in character; sometimes occupational; occasionally both tribal and occupational; and still others were mainly religious or religious and tribal. Thus the West End Limba and Limited Creole Society (founded in 1916, with 650 members in 1925) was restricted to

[22] Immanuel Wallerstein, "The Political Role of Voluntary Associations in Middle Africa," in *Urbanization in African Social Change: Proceedings of the Inaugural Seminar held in the Centre of African Studies, University of Edinburgh* (Edinburgh, 1963), p. 153.

[23] *Sierra Leone Blue Book, 1926*, pp. 370b–370c. The following data on early voluntary associations in Sierra Leone are from this document.

the tribe designated in its title; whereas the Mixed Kru Tribal Association (founded in 1900, with 75 members in 1925) was organized by Kru but open to all "irrespective of tribe." The Kru Tribe Seamen's Union Friendly Society (founded in 1916, with 650 members in 1925) was limited tribally to Kru and occupationally to seamen. The Ekewam Keyarati Mandingo Muslim Society (founded in 1918, with 97 members in 1925) was limited to Muslims irrespective of tribe. The Seamen's Defensive Union Friendly Society (founded in 1916, with 76 members in 1925) was restricted to seamen irrespective of tribe, and the John Bull Line Co. Society (founded in 1915, with 72 members in 1925) was limited to seamen employed by a given shipping line.

The aims and purposes of these associations equally reflected their mixed character. Although they could all be classified under the general category of "mutual aid," the specific type of aid rendered was as varied as the different organizational composition of the associations. Thus the previously mentioned Jubilee Society concerned itself with "relief of members during sickness, death, loss in fire . . . ," while the Ikhwanul Ahawamil Islamiya provided "loan of money for members," and the Mixed Kru Tribal Association rendered "assistance to adult Krus and their Children . . . and for building a place of religious worship and education for them."

A final feature of these associations was their syncretism: within the same association there co-existed traditional and modern elements. This reflected the effort of the depressed urban folk to fit themselves, on their own terms, for the strain and stress of urban social change, while simultaneously holding on to some of the old ways. Given this syncretistic character, these associations were highly attractive to the poorer urban masses; they contained patterns of behavior and modes of communication recognizable to them. As one observer has noted with regard to the Martha Davies Confidential Benevolent Association (founded in 1910), through the use of a musical form known as "shouts," which were rooted in traditional religious expression, the Association had a greater mass appeal than those religious bodies purely Western in format: "There are hundreds of those shouts in circulation not only in Freetown, but elsewhere in Sierra Leone, and in other parts of West Africa. The shouts touch the deepest religious feelings of the average Sierra Leonean more than any other form of Christian Hymn-singing . . . They are easily memorized and easily translated into the vernaculars of the country, and the illiterate can understand them . . ."[24]

Politically, the voluntary associations among the poor urban folk did not make clear-cut demands upon the colonial regime. In this they differed markedly from the Railway Workers' Union and other associations of the skilled and literate elements; these combined the friendly society functions with explicitly political ones. Instead, the voluntary associations among the poor, as already intimated, gained much of their political consciousness and experience mainly through anomic acts such as riots, looting, and arson. The perpetration of such acts by the poorer laborers often coincided with strikes by skilled workers. Strikes vividly denoted to the poorer urban elements a weakening of the colonial regime's control over them and were thus construed as an opportune occasion for riot. (This, incidentally, was the main reason why all colonial regimes feared strikes as an instrument of African politics.)[25] Yet this mode of political evolution among the poorer urban groups was undoubtedly unsatisfactory. It lacked the long-run effectiveness of an articulate political agency like a trade union, political party, or pressure group. The urban masses had to await a closer linkage between their voluntary associations and the nationalist parties before they could bring their full political weight to bear.

3. The Peasantry

Rural life necessarily provided much less experience of the flow of new ideas, things, and people that are natural to the urban situation and often give the urban masses an advantage in politics. This does not mean that the peasantry was immune to political change. As with the poorer urban elements, riots and related

[24] I. M. Ndanema, "The Martha Davies Confidential Benevolent Association," *Sierra Leone Bulletin of Religion* (December 1961), p. 66.
[25] Cf. *Legislative Council Debates, No. I of Session 1926–1927*, p. 5.

anomic acts were often their first form of political expression. Throughout the post-World War I period innumerable riots and disturbances occurred in the Sierra Leone hinterland: in Moyamba in 1923–24, in Kambia in 1930, in Pujehun in 1931, in Kenema in 1934, and elsewhere.[26] Similar disturbances were evident in other African territories: in the Ivory Coast in 1915 and 1934, in Kenya in 1921–22, in the Gold Coast throughout the 1920's and 1930's, in southern Nigeria in 1929 and 1931, in French Soudan in the mid-1930's, and on the copperbelt and surrounding areas of Northern Rhodesia in 1935.[27]

In general, the peasant disturbances in Sierra Leone were not very explicit in their political expression, though certain incidents might be interpreted otherwise—especially the Idara Rebellion in Kambia in 1930–31. But whereas the urban disturbances invariably reflected an anti-colonial political reaction, characterized by widespread pillaging of expatriate property, this type of reaction was not associated directly with peasant disturbances. Instead, peasant violence and vandalism were aimed at the property, person, and authority of Chiefs. This was so, of course, because Chiefs were the main agency through which colonial change touched and affected the rural masses. This meant in turn that the stress and strain consequent upon colonial change were readily identified with Chiefs.

An equally important feature of anomic acts by the peasantry was that they were often well organized—much more so than comparable acts by urban masses. This organization was effected normally through traditional agencies or institutions, most of which were free of interference from Chiefs—a freedom which

[26] *Legislative Council Debates, No. II of Session 1931–1932* (Freetown, 1932), pp. 4, 33; *Legislative Council Debates, No. I of Session 1934–1935* (Freetown, 1935), pp. 20, 111.

[27] *Despatch by the Secretary of State Regarding Report of Commission of Enquiry into the Disturbances at Aba,* Cmd. 3784 (London, 1931); *Report of the Commission of Enquiry Appointed to Inquire into the Disturbances in the Calabar and Owerri Provinces, December 1930, Sessional Paper No. 28 of 1930* (Lagos, 1930); *Papers Relating to Native Disturbances in Kenya,* Cmd. 1691 (London, 1922); *Report of the Commission Appointed to Enquiry into the Disturbances in the Copperbelt, Northern Rhodesia . . . November, 1935* (Lusaka, 1935).

itself was related to the impact of colonial change on rural African society. In Sierra Leone, the Poro Society (a secret society that originated among the Mende) was one such institution which, according to an informed Mende scholar, "can act independently of the chiefs. They may admittedly be members of the inner circle, but it does not follow that they govern or influence the concerted action of the Poro."[28]

The Poro Society was decisive in the conduct of the Hut Tax War in 1898, though at this period Chiefs were the main manipulators of Poro.[29] During the disturbances in the 1920's and 1930's there is reason to believe that Poro also played a major role, though precise information is not available.[30] There is, however, evidence on Poro's role in the peasant tax riots in 1955–56, and we may usefully refer to it at this point. "The reports from administrative and police officers on the disturbances contain references to the singing of Porro songs; we have ourselves heard such songs at the termination of our public sessions, and indeed the strength of the Society has been openly displayed as have their dresses, signs and tokens. There have been references in the course of the evidence to the Porro Society . . ., and one or two witnesses have been 'persuaded' by their brothers that they were going too far in giving information regarding Porro . . . We are quite satisfied that Porro played an important part in facilitating the disturbances and may well partly account for the extreme secrecy which shrouded the prevailing discontent. Porro almost certainly caused the pattern of complaint made to us which was remarkably consistent despite differing circumstances in the various chiefdoms. The influence of the Porro Society is secret, profound and universal. The aloofness in some few cases of the chiefs from the Society has enabled them to be undermined, for it is a

[28] Max Gorvie, *Old and New in Sierra Leone* (London, *ca.* 1939), p. 31. For examples of this in Ghana during the 1920's and 1930's, see Martin Kilson, "Sociological Aspects of African Politics," *Ghana Journal of Sociology* (February 1966), pp. 5–6.

[29] Sir David Chalmers, *Report by Her Majesty's Commissioner and Correspondence on the Subject of the Insurrection in the Sierra Leone Protectorate 1898*, Part II, Cmd. 9391 (London, 1899), pp. 35, 382–383—cited hereafter as *Report on the Insurrection of 1898*.

[30] Gorvie, *Old and New in Sierra Leone*, pp. 38–39.

cult which almost at will can become a primitive government of its own."[31]

4. The Idara Rebellion: A Peasant Insurrection

In addition to secret societies, indigenous religious symbols and institutions were also utilized by the rural populace for political expression. The Idara Rebellion in northwestern Sierra Leone in 1931 was a fascinating instance of this.

The leader of the rebellion, one Idara (or Haidara) Contorfilli, was a Muslim missionary (presumably literate in Arabic but illiterate in English) who entered Sierra Leone from French Guinea in early 1930 and began mission work at Kambia, Northern Province. His message was initially religious; he sought to reform African religious practices along the lines of his own conception of proper behavior. Idara adumbrated his beliefs in an awkwardly composed letter to the Provincial Commissioner, dated February 2, 1931: "I have the honour . . . to particularly inform you Sir, that I am a man who is sent to all the muslims of the universe ordained by God, to prophecy about the prophecy of Mohamed. In subsequent to this there are one or two very important cases I should like to put for your understanding that is, about the burning of every kind of Native swear, and further to give all unmarried women to husbands however the case may be. It must be observed that native swear is very harmful and dangerous to human beings; in fact it is the law of the Koran to strictly prohibit swearing. My name is Haidara I can change the sun into moon and play wonders of the world. My song is Alla, Alla, and I am bound to turn every body into muslim."[32]

Neither Idara's teaching nor his eccentric claim of vast super-

[31] Sir Herbert Cox, Sierra Leone Report of Commission of Inquiry into Disturbances in the Provinces, November 1955–March 1956 (London, 1956), pp. 11–12; Commenting on the role of Poro in the Hut Tax War in 1898, one official remarked that "the rising is not to be attributed directly to 'Poro' laws and customs, although the 'Poro' organisation appears to have been made use of for the purpose of arranging the details of the raid." E. D. Fairtlough, "Memorandum on Disturbances," in Chalmers, Report on the Insurrection of 1898, Part I, Cmd. 9388 (London, 1899), p. 146.

[32] The text of the Idara letters quoted in this section is given in B. M. Jusu, "The Haidara Rebellion of 1931," Sierra Leone Studies (December 1954), pp. 147–149.

natural powers was initially disturbing to the government. In a report to the Legislative Council on another letter sent by Idara to the Acting Colonial Secretary, T. N. Goddard, the government observed that "this communication though foolishly expressed, contained nothing subversive of British rule or tending towards defiance of the Government; it was written solely from the point of view of professors of the Moslem faith."[33] Indeed, Idara himself initially made a special effort to ensure the government of his political rectitude: "I really thank the English people for telling the natives to build Masidis for praying. I am praying for you to have more power in the world. I pray for you Fridays and Saturdays."

All was not as it seemed at first sight, however. Idara directed his teachings to the poorer peasants and posed as guardian of their interests. His style was aggressive and oblivious of the established social relations. When the latter stood in his way, he challenged them head on. In a letter to the District Commissioner in Kambia, dated February 2, 1931, Idara gave signs of violent intentions: ". . . The people that know how to follow Annabi's road and totally refuse to do so are going to be killed. I have asked you now to look and listen for the way the world is praying and also pulling boys to teach them Arabic. Those that call themselves Mohammedan and never help the poor people but take the money from again instead. If this is not stopped the beginning of the killing will start from them and the ending also to them."[34]

The "populist" element in Idara's teaching gained him many followers who, according to a contemporary eyewitness, paid him homage that went "beyond mere hero-worship."[35] And Idara was a true hero, impeccably consistent in his self-appointed role as guardian of his followers' interests. These interests, as he first saw them, were basically religious in character. But circumstances soon lent them a political turn. By 1931 the impact of the world

---

[33] *Legislative Council Debates, Session 1930–1931* (Freetown, 1932), pp. 132–133. Mr. T. N. Goddard's report to the Legislative Council constitutes the most detailed account available of the Idara movement. Valuable material may also be found in the pages of the *Sierra Leone Weekly News,* January–March 1931.

[34] Text of letter in Jusu, "The Haidara Rebellion of 1931," p. 149.

[35] *Sierra Leone Weekly News,* February 21, 1931, p. 13.

depression was widely felt in local African society; peasants experienced great difficulty in satisfying their limited demand for imported goods and especially in paying the hut tax. Neither the Chiefs nor the colonial government appeared able or willing to ameliorate the situation. Consequently, many peasants sought their own solution; it was here that Idara's religious movement became an instrument of peasant political expression.[36] As Colonial Secretary T. N. Goddard observed: "The people must have complained to him of the hardness of the times due to the considerable fall in price of kernels and other staple products and their difficulty or inability to pay the tax . . . Some of the people readily believed and rejoiced that at last some one had come to rid them from the burden of taxation and acclaimed him an Angel of God."[37]

As a leader, Idara had a touch of the charismatic, as the colonial government soon recognized: "Illiterate and comparatively ignorant as he was, Idara had the power of inflaming the passions and seizing the imagination of an ignorant and excitable section of the community."[38] It is doubtful, however, that the government's characterization of him as "ignorant" was correct. Idara was most skillful at locating the sources of peasant grievances in colonial society and at articulating these grievances in a manner comprehensible to the most simple peasant. He was also courageous in his role as guardian of peasant interests, representing them to the colonial authority with firm conviction. In this respect, Idara Contorfilli compared favorably with another religious leader of rebellious peasants, who, when faced with a situation similar to Idara's, proved a less courageous man—namely, Martin Luther.[39] For Idara did not shirk an open encounter, to the death, with the established authorities. In an open letter to his followers in Kambia, dated February 10, 1931, Idara declared that such an encounter was now unavoidable: "In the name of God Only.

[36] *Legislative Council Debates, Session 1930–1931*, pp. 133–134.

[37] T. N. Goddard, "Idara, the Muslim 'Prophet' and the Unrest in the Kambia District," *Sierra Leone Weekly News*, February 21, 1931, p. 9.

[38] *Legislative Council Debates, Session 1930–1931*, p. 142.

[39] Cf. Frederick Engels, *The Peasant War in Germany* (Moscow, 1956), pp. 62 ff.

Peace be unto all . . . I send you all greetings after that my former name was Idara my present name is Mohammed Madihu; this is a letter to all the inhabitants of Kambia; all who are not for me should be on the left hand of Kambia . . . I am telling you or giving this parable that if 'a cow does not rely on his horns he will not dig the ground with it.' God sends his messengers without guns or sword staffs or daggers. But he gives them something which is more than a gun or sword but I have the name of God with me, you should look at what is in the air, so you should not fear the European be he French or English as the four corners of the earth are guarded by the prophet Mohammed all creatures are made by God. Bai Inga [Paramount Chief of Mange Chiefdom, Kambia] and the Government have all fallen. I have also curse everybody who is under the Government. I am also telling you not to pay your House Tax to any Paramount Chief. You have been hearing about me. Birds, Ants, Beasts and all living creatures knows about me."[40]

Idara's grandiose declaration of war against the colonial order was backed by machetes and guns which he distributed to his followers. So challenged, the colonial government proceeded to subdue the rebellious Idara, whose declaration of war it described as "the rapid mental expansion of the megalomaniac."[41] A platoon of the Royal African Frontier Force (thirty-four men) was dispatched against Idara's forces at Bubuya, Northern Province, on February 16, 1931. The encounter was brief: Idara's forces were decimated, and Idara was killed, as was the commanding officer of the government troops.[42]

Thus in the rise of the Idara movement the colonial government confronted an attempt by peasants at political expression on the basis of the raw materials known to them. It was soon apparent

[40] Text of letter in Jusu, "The Haidara Rebellion of 1931," p. 150. Though his declaration might suggest it, Idara was not a victim of the behavior Marx referred to when he remarked that "weakness [took] refuge in a belief in miracles, fancied the enemy overcome when he was only conjured away in imagination, and it lost all understanding of the present in a passive glorification of the future that was in store for it . . ." Karl Marx, "The Eighteenth Brumaire of Louis Bonaparte," in Karl Marx and Frederick Engels, *Selected Works* (Moscow, 1951), I, 229.

[41] *Legislative Council Debates, Session 1930–1931*, p. 133.

[42] *Ibid.*, pp. 136 ff.

that such expression by a backward peasantry undergoing colonial change was intolerable: it threatened the very security of colonial rule and development. The government thus had little alternative but to respond with military force to the Idara movement, as in fact all colonial governments have so responded to similar movements elsewhere in Africa. As the Acting Colonial Secretary noted in a report to the Legislative Council: "It [the use of military force] was instrumental, by leading to the immediate destruction of Idara, in nipping in the bud an attempt at subversion of the Government's power which might have had prolonged and costly consequences . . . Had his activities not been speedily terminated, he might have been the means of involving the country in considerable embarrassment and expense . . . The Government is tolerant enough of empty, though foolish, talk, and was tolerant towards Idara himself until it became clear that he was bullying the more ignorant people in the name of religion and openly preaching sedition and defiance of authority. But no Government worthy of the name would tolerate activities such as he adopted latterly, or would fail in its duty of taking strong measures against those who preach sedition, whether orally or by the written word."[43]

D. A NOTE ON THE "MASS FACTOR" IN AFRICAN POLITICAL CHANGE

Political change among rural and urban masses is one of the most neglected aspects of the study of modern African politics. Our picture of African political change will never be three-dimensional until our research and analysis encompass more than the politics of the new elite.

In seeking to understand what may be termed the "mass factor" in African political change, the main problem is to define empirically and conceptually the way in which institutional modernization among the masses relates to the over-all process of colonial political change. Empirically, the definition of the mass factor in political change is basically a historical problem. It is a problem

[43] *Ibid.*, p. 142.

rooted in the time lag between the initial colonial contact with a given part of an African society and the eventual establishment of effective colonial administration in depth and on a territory-wide basis.

In the case of Sierra Leone it is evident that the advantages gained by the groups that first experienced Western contact automatically rendered them an elite. Given the limited scale and resources of the early colonial regime, there was necessarily a delay in the spread of Western practices and standards to the wider population. From the middle of the nineteenth to the turn of the twentieth century a small elite of Creole merchants, traders, and professionals monopolized whatever political influence was available to Africans.[44] The hinterland peasants, barely linked to the coastal colonial settlement through trade in cash crops, were politically inert. The same was true of the small group of wage-laborers in the coastal towns who, though geographically a part of the colonial settlement, had only a fitful relationship to the modernizing forces. Moreover, when the colonial regime was extended to the hinterland in 1896, it was the traditional ruling elite —not the peasantry or the wage-laboring groups—who initially received the lion's share of the benefits generated by colonial institutions.

Conceptually, the problem of the mass factor in African political change is more difficult. The historical situation suggests that any reckoning of political influence based on such criteria as education, wealth, and economic function should relegate the mass factor to a minor political role, as against that of the elite. Yet the historical situation also suggests that this set of circumstances is tentative: a stage is reached where the differential in political influence between elite and masses decreases. The further expansion of the elite's political influence becomes increasingly dependent upon mass support, owing to the role of the metropolitan democratic heritage in the functioning of the British and French colonial systems. Under these systems, emergent African political pressures are likely to be accommodated within a proto-demo-

---

[44] Arthur Porter, *Creoledom: A Study of the Development of Freetown Society* (London, 1963), pp. 19–65.

cratic framework. Accordingly, the emergent elite groups must project their demands in the name of the masses, the *demos;* and at the mature stage of colonial transformation these demands should be representative of the masses.

There is another manner in which the mass factor may be envisaged as a crucial feature of African political change. By themselves the peasants and urban poor evolve their political expression along lines essentially incongruous with the proto-democratic central colonial government. They are simply un-tutored in the rational norms and procedures of central colonial government and politics. Moreover, the system employed to govern the masses in local colonial society both incorporates and strengthens the authoritarian features of the traditional society, and, needless to say, it is far removed in spirit from any Legislative Council (or Conseil Colonial in French West Africa), or limited franchise (allowed after World War I in most of West Africa). Thus to a large extent the political expression of the masses takes a violent, riotous form because there is no institutional arrangement to provide otherwise. This pattern of political expression, however, can hardly be tolerated in a modernizing colonial system. It must be transmuted into a more predictable factor in political change.

To this end, the African educated or middle-class elite comes forth as the arbiter between colonial government and the masses. It is suited for this task because of its acculturation to metropolitan standards. This means, among other things, that any political expression influenced, organized, or controlled by the African elite is comprehensible to colonial government and can thus be dealt with in terms of the government's rational, proto-democratic procedures. The elite is itself cognizant of this strategic function required of it in the process of political change; indeed, it often asserts its eligibility for this role before the colonial oligarchy recognizes it. This situation tends to generate conflict between the colonial authorities and the African elite. At the mature stage of colonial transformation, the African elite's movement for national independence is, in view of the foregoing, essentially a question of exacting maximum advantage from performance of its strategic mediating role. The main point to be made here, however, is that it is the pattern of the masses' political expression that creates the situations that call forth the African elite as the key arbiter of political change.

Why is the closed network of expatriate interest groups impelled to employ the African elite as an arbiter of mass political pressures? As we have noted, these pressures are normally violent; as such they render colonial security precarious. To this extent they are viewed more ominously by colonial government than political pressures from African elite groups. The Sierra Leone government, for instance, seldom found cause to suspect the elite of opposing the very basis of the colonial state. But the Colonial Secretary, we recall, was moved by the populist Idara Rebellion to speak of "taking strong measures against those who preach sedition."

A similar concern for security characterized the government's response to the Railway Workers' Union strike of 1926 and to the riots that accompanied it. The Governor, Sir A. R. Slater, in a confidential dispatch to the Colonial Office in 1926, underlined the "serious character of the strike in that it revealed a widespread defiance of discipline and revolt against authority."[45] In the postwar period, the colonial government responded similarly to the Railway Workers' Union strike and riots of February 1955 and to the peasant tax riots of December 1955–April 1956.

It was, in fact, only on those occasions when the political activity of the new elite groups appeared to sympathize with or embrace the violent forms of populist expression that the colonial government viewed this activity with a sense of grave concern. One such occasion was the railway strike of 1926. The government firmly reprimanded that segment of the elite which supported the strikers and, by implication, their riotous supporters. The Colonial Secretary to the Governor, Mr. H. C. Luke, proposed to the Executive Council that "as a mark of their displeasure with the unworthy behaviour, in this crisis, of the entire Creole com-

---

[45] *Despatch of Sir A. Ransford Slater, Governor, to Rt. Hon. L. S. Amery, Secretary of State for the Colonies, 20th April, 1926.* (Copy in Sierra Leone Government Archives.)

munity, His Majesty's Government should be asked to suspend, for an indefinite period, that part of the constitution which provides for an elected element in the Legislative Council."[46] The Governor, however, considered Luke's proposal too harsh and too dangerous. He feared particularly the impact of such measures among the skilled wage-laborers and some of the less advanced mass elements who appeared to be on the verge of turning to the educated elite for leadership. Instead, the Governor proposed to punish the elite only by decelerating the pace of integrating educated Africans into the decision-making bodies of colonial government. The Governor's statement of his case is worth quoting here *in extenso:*

In my opinion the harm that demagogues of the type of Dr. Bankole Bright and Mr. Beoku-Betts can, and undoubtedly do, cause is to some extent mitigated rather than accentuated, by the fact of their membership of the Council. Their sense of responsibility as legislators is, it is true, painfully low but it is occasionally discernible . . . In my judgement, to oust from the Legislative Council the members who were chosen of the people less than two years ago would, by making martyrs of them, increase their power for harm far more than continued tolerance of their presence can do . . . It would . . . in all probability antagonize the moderate section on whose tacit, if timid, support we can now depend . . . *It would tend to drive underground the disorderly and undisciplined elements always unhappily present in the Colony of Sierra Leone and thereby gravely enhance the danger arising from such elements* . . . I consider that the more dignified course for the Government to adopt is . . . to refuse to let that deplorable exhibition of political perversity deflect us . . . from our course of seeking patiently to educate public opinion by the means deliberately adopted in 1922. At the same time . . . the events of the last few months have supplied Government with abundant reasons for proceeding at a much slower pace with Africanisation of the Service and for tightening up control generally by legislative and other measures, while they obviously afford unanswerable arguments against any requests for further constitutional development in the present generation. Already one of the newspapers . . . is clamouring for a House of Assembly with unofficial control of the purse strings. Even if the community had behaved with consistently exemplary correctness during the last few years, such a claim would of course be preposterous. I have always made it abso-

[46] Quoted in *ibid.*

lutely clear that there can be no question for many years of conceding the smallest modicum of self-government—but the 'strike attitude' of so large a proportion of the educated community has furnished us with an additional and crushing reason for uncompromising rejection of such a demand.[47]

E. CONCLUSION

In view of the above analysis of how the mass elements may be conceived as active agents in African political change, there are grounds for reformulating the model most frequently used to study African political change. This model tends to relegate mass elements to a passive or merely supportive role in African political change, while those factors associated with the elite are considered decisive. As Thomas Hodgkin has pointed out in a review of Perham's book *The Colonial Reckoning,* this model is quite unsatisfactory: ". . . The whole conception of militant-intellectual-elite-operating-upon-passive-masses is naive, and remote from the facts as I have observed them . . . If we want to take [African political change] seriously we must pay attention . . . to the various activities and contributions of different sectors, strata, groupings, organizations, within a given African system."[48]

The salient features of my own reformulation of the elite-oriented model are as follows: The elite's role in African political change was mainly to mediate the variety of African pressures upon the colonial system. The masses, on the other hand, created or stimulated much—though by no means all—of the situations of political instability that brought the elite's mediating function into play and enabled it to be effective. In other words, the pattern of political evolution among the masses widened the range of receptivity within the colonial system for fundamental political change; this rendered the strategic position of the new elite serviceable to the colonial regime, in return for which basic constitutional concessions were granted.

[47] *Ibid.* (Italics added.)
[48] Thomas Hodgkin, "Reflections on the African Revolutions," *New Statesman* (August 3, 1962), p. 148.

The foregoing permits a broader and dialectically sharper grasp of African political change. Moreover, it places the apparatus of the colonial state nearer to the center of the analysis of political change than does the elite-oriented model. The institutions of local colonial administration are especially elevated to a central position in the analysis, for it is through these that the masses obtain their greatest contact with colonial modernization.[49]

[49] Cf. the excellent study by A. L. Epstein, *Politics in an Urban African Community* (Manchester, 1958).

CHAPTER 7 -

The Making of the
1924 Constitution

A. TOKEN DEMOCRACY

If the peasant and wage-laboring groups were crucial in stimulating greater receptivity for basic change in the structure of colonial government, it was the emergent elite which exerted the greatest influence upon the colonial constitution-making process. This was so largely because of the qualitative features that distinguished the new elite and the educated Chiefs from the masses. The necessary skills, knowledge, and connections were theirs.

Until 1924 the Legislative Council in Sierra Leone was composed of six official members, including the Governor, and four nominated unofficial members, three of whom were Africans and the other European. This arrangement was reconstituted by the *Sierra Leone (Legislative Council) Order in Council, 1924,* which provided for twelve official members and ten unofficial members. Of the ten unofficial members, two were to represent "commercial, banking and general European interests, one of these being appointed on recommendation of the [European] Chamber of Commerce."[1] The remaining eight unofficial members represented emergent African interests as follows: three elected Africans and two nominated Africans representing the Colony; three nominated Paramount Chiefs—two from the Mende tribe and one

[1] Governor's Address to Legislative Council, December 28, 1922; text in *Sierra Leone Weekly News,* December 30, 1922, p. 5.

124

from the Temne—each representing a Protectorate Province.[2] The Executive Council, the primary source of government policy, was not affected by the changes in the structure of the Legislative Council; it remained a purely European organ.

For the purpose of electing three unofficial members of the Legislative Council, the Colony was divided into three voting districts: Freetown District, Sherbro Judicial Urban District, and the Rural Areas District.[3] The franchise in these districts embraced only elite Africans. In addition to meeting a literacy qualification, an elector was required to be an "owner or occupier of any house, warehouse, counting house, shop, store or other building . . . in the electoral district of which the annual value is in the urban electoral district not less than ten pounds [and] in the rural electoral district not less than six pounds . . ., or is in receipt of a yearly salary in the urban electoral district of at least one hundred pounds a year and in the rural electoral district of sixty pounds a year."[4]

The urban wage-laborers could not possibly meet these qualifications; on the average, they barely received one shilling income per day, and the great majority lived in overcrowded, dilapidated slum-dwellings owned by wealthier Africans.[5] When the 1924 voting lists were drawn up, only 1,866 persons were eligible to vote, and of these 1,016 were registered in the two urban districts of the Colony and 339 in the Colony's rural district.[6] (The adult population of Freetown was roughly 25,000 at this time.)

Just as the Colony provisions of the 1924 Constitution made a place only for those few Africans who were rising to European standards, so did the provisions relating to the Protectorate benefit only the modern-style Chiefs and their educated kinsmen. The demands of the educated Africans who formed the CEA were partly met through the reconstitution of the Legislative Council

[2] Sierra Leone (Legislative Council) Order in Council, 16th January 1924, secs. 4–7.
[3] Ibid., sec. 7.
[4] Ibid., sec. 23.
[5] Cf. Report of the Slum Clearance Committee, Sessional Paper No. 9 of 1939 (Freetown, 1939), pp. 6–13.
[6] Legislative Council Debates, Session 1924–25 (Freetown, n.d.), p. 225.

as the Legislature of the Protectorate and Colony, in which Paramount Chiefs were eligible for membership if literate in English.[7] Chiefs were acceptable to the new elite in the Protectorate because they had attained a fair measure of modern education and wealth. By 1926, for instance, five of the 223 graduates of Bo Government School had become Paramount Chiefs; and of the 412 who had graduated by 1934 some thirteen became Paramount Chiefs and two sub-Chiefs.[8] The Protectorate new elite was also prone to alliance with Chiefs because of kinship ties. For instance, the founding Vice President of CEA, J. Karefa Smart, and its Assistant Secretary, W. C. M. Caulker, were sons of Paramount Chiefs.[9]

B. THE SPECIAL POSITION OF TRADITIONAL RULERS

The relationship between the new and old Protectorate elites was of such significance in the formulation of the 1924 Constitution that it should be elaborated more fully. Nearly two years before the enactment of the 1924 Constitution the leaders of the CEA, in their address of welcome to the Governor in September 1922, had already intimated a favorable attitude toward traditional ruling institutions. They observed, among other things, that "without the consent of the 200 Ruling Houses in the Protectorate, no Elective Franchise should be granted to a handful of Colonial [Colony] Africans on behalf of Protectorate Aborigines." Although the Address did not state explicitly that Paramount Chiefs should be chosen as Protectorate representatives in the Legislative Council, it certainly implied that their selection was not ruled out by the new elite. Moreover, when requesting that educated persons who were not Chiefs should be chosen as Protectorate representatives, the CEA had in mind primarily those who were related by blood and experience to traditional rulers.

[7] *Protectorate Order in Council, 16th January 1924,* secs. 6–7; *Sierra Leone (Legislative Council) Order in Council, 16th January 1924,* sec. 4.

[8] *Legislative Council Debates, No. I of Session 1925–26* (Freetown, n.d.), p. 59; *Annual Report of the Education Department for the Year 1934* (Freetown, 1935), p. 19.

[9] *Sierra Leone Weekly News,* May 21, 1922, p. 12.

In the same address of welcome to the Governor, the CEA observed: "Educated Aborigines are few and far between in the Protectorate, but in the Southern Province [Mende country] . . . competent candidates could even now be obtained to directly represent in the Legislature the still unrepresented 1,350,000 Aborigines in the Protectorate. To continually keep the Legislature supplied with qualified aboriginal members, the Sons and Nominees of Protectorate Chiefs at present attending the Bo School should be trained for it before finishing their course . . ."[10]

Thus, as regards which elite element in the Protectorate should sit in the new Legislature, the government had more or less the best of both worlds. Neither group threatened the position of the colonial oligarchy. The Protectorate educated elite, like the middle class in the Colony, was fairly well acculturated to metropolitan standards and as such understood and accepted the "rules of the game." The same was true for the educated Chiefs. The latter were also too dependent upon the colonial authority to constitute a threat; under the Protectorate (Amendment) Ordinance of 1918 the Governor was empowered "to depose any chief who in his opinion is unfit for the position, and to appoint a person to be chief in his place."[11]

When confronted with this sort of alternative among claimant elites, colonial authorities in British and French Africa pursued the same type of policy. Insofar as the more articulate demands for constitutional change emanated from the new elite, these authorities endeavored to qualify such demands by giving their support to the traditional elite.[12] Thus, the Sierra Leone government, with the consent of the Colonial Office, chose two educated Paramount Chiefs to represent the Protectorate in the new Legislative Council established under the 1924 constitution. The government's choice of Paramount Chiefs was also influenced by its view of what type of persons were eligible candidates for legis-

[10] *Ibid.*, September 9, 1922, p. 8.

[11] *Protectorate (Amendment) Ordinance, No. 12 of 1918*, sec. 80.

[12] For the Gold Coast, see David Kimble, *A Political History of Ghana, 1850–1928* (Oxford, 1963), pp. 441–442; for the Conseil Colonial in French Africa, see Kenneth Robinson, "Senegal," in W. J. M. Mackenzie and K. E. Robinson, eds., *Five Elections in Africa* (Oxford, 1960), pp. 290–291.

lative representation—a view which, in the words of Governor Sir Alexander Ransford Slater, depended "on the proof . . . of assent they command among the particular community from whom they emanate."[13] In a candid report to the Legislative Council on the government's strategy in formulating the 1924 constitution, Governor Slater elaborated this proposition as it applied to Chiefs: ". . . I was and am opposed to a suggestion which was put forward by the National Congress that the African representation of the Protectorate should not necessarily be paramount chiefs or subchiefs. If the principle of direct African representation of the Protectorate was to be conceded (as in my opinion it ought to be conceded) it necessarily followed, in my view, that the representatives must, at present at least, be paramount chiefs; under the tribal system no others would have adequate title to speak with authority."[14]

Over the long run, this policy proved to be the most important conservative feature of the Sierra Leone Constitution of 1924. As will be seen in later chapters, it was to play a major role in all subsequent constitutional changes down through the attainment of independence by Sierra Leone in 1961. Indeed, not only were subsequent constitutional changes significantly shaped by the special status given to Chiefs in Protectorate representation in 1924, but the whole process of postwar nationalist party development in Sierra Leone was equally influenced by it. Chiefs' status in the Legislative Council enabled chiefly institutions to absorb, and partly to control, the mainstream of postwar nationalist development, thereby reinforcing the over-all status of Chiefs in the new political system.

C. CONFLICT AMONG THE AFRICANS

When the political differences between elite Africans and the colonial oligarchy approach resolution through constitutional change, a distinct pattern of conflict within the African community becomes evident. This may be attributed, *inter alia*, to the

[13] *Sierra Leone Weekly News,* May 20, 1922, p. 9.
[14] *Legislative Council Debates, Session 1924–1925*, p. 221.

varied tribal, regional, administrative, and socio-economic factors that differentiate the African population under colonial modernization. Whatever its causes, the apparent homogeneity of interests within the African community, as against those of the colonial oligarchy, disintegrates when basic constitutional change is in the offing. The African community fragments into distinct categories, each defining its relationship to the constitution-making process in terms of its particular position in colonial society.

Although the educated elite of the Protectorate, as represented by the CEA, generally supported the elective franchise for the Colony elite, they insisted that it be accompanied by a policy to redistribute colonial resources in order to rectify the comparative backwardness of the Protectorate. As the CEA put it:

Without the Protectorate there never would have existed the Colony of Sierra Leone. Considering there were four Denominational Secondary Schools, and numerous Elementary and Intermediate Schools existing in the Colony previous to the establishment of the Government Model School, we should think it would have been a far more successful and beneficial scheme to Sierra Leone, if the money spent on the buildings and up-keep of this school had been expended on a scheme for compulsory elementary and intermediate education in the Protectorate . . . We . . . ask, to what purpose is that waste? We have always read with interest, the various reports of the Proceedings of the Legislative Council published now and again in the *Sierra Leone Weekly News,* but we do not remember coming across any Bill regulating the education of Protectorate Aborigines. Why is the thorough education of the Protectorate Aborigines neglected, if the Colonial Africans really considered them their kith-and-kin, and expected them to take their places amongst them in matters concerning the welfare of Sierra Leone in general? . . . After all these shall have been accomplished, and the Protectorate can literally march with the Colony in every sphere of life then, but not till then, will a new era dawn on Sierra Leone, and . . . Colonial African and Protectorate Aborigines will join heads and shoulders together to confer seriously on the question of Elective Franchise.[15]

The Colony elite, on the other hand, accepted the principle of direct legislative representation for the Protectorate but rejected the CEA's claim that Protectorate interests had not been hitherto

[15] *Sierra Leone Weekly News,* September 9, 1922, p. 8.

represented in the legislature. This was argued forcefully in an editorial in the *Sierra Leone Weekly News* which was the authoritative voice of the Colony middle class: "... On the principle that the educated section in any community does represent the views and interpret the feelings and aspirations of the illiterate or uneducated, we think this has hitherto been done, so far as the scope of nominated unofficial members of Council has allowed." The Creole middle class also rejected the CEA's articulation of Protectorate interests through a separate organization, because it implied that Protectorate Africans had interests peculiar to them and divided the over-all African position vis-à-vis the colonial oligarchy. As the editorial put it: "We shall welcome any proposal that will secure a wider or better representation of every section of the Dependency, particularly as some of the Chiefs are now able to stand by their interests and those of the people over whom they bear rule. But we shall be sorry if this is done as a set-off to the interest of those in the Colony. The progress of this Dependency will verily be stunted if its people are regarded as distinct and of divided interests. After all, the Hinterland could not have existed as a factor in the Government without the Colony . . ."[16] Another spokesman of Colony interests, Mr. A. Tuboku Metzger, a lawyer and Vice President of the SLNC in 1924, maintained that the SLNC would endorse the CEA's demands "without a dissentient voice" but only on condition that "the educated Aborigines will identify themselves with the Congress movements and explain its uplifting purpose to every Paramount Chief and Sub-Chief."[17]

The Creoles, it should be noted, had every reason to ally with the Protectorate leadership. They, after all, had innumerable economic interests in the Protectorate and had long sought to protect these interests through a direct political foothold in the Protectorate system. But these very Creole interests in the Protectorate were themselves a major cause for the Protectorate leaders' op-

[16] *Ibid.,* July 15, 1922, p. 9.

[17] Metzger, "The Proposed Reconstruction of the Legislative Council," *Sierra Leone Weekly News,* September 23, 1922, p. 5.

position to the SLNC, especially the Chiefs who frequently played havoc with the political impotence of Creole businessmen in the Protectorate, exploiting them at will. It is noteworthy, however, that in March 1925 a small group of liberal educated Protectorate Africans in the CEA joined with several members of the Creole intelligentsia to form the Sierra Leone Aborigines Society (SLAS). The aim of the SLAS was to establish "intercourse among all classes of Aborigines [i.e., all Sierra Leoneans], to further their interests . . . and to promote the welfare of the Aborigines."[18] But the SLAS proved a short-lived organization, and it was not until after World War II that a similar effort by liberal Africans in the Protectorate and the Colony to overcome the conflict between the two regions was attempted, and with some success.

Apart from the issue of the uneven development between the Colony and Protectorate, the most important factor that prevented the educated group in the CEA from allying with the SLNC was the latter's stubborn opposition to the appointment of Chiefs to the Legislative Council. Although a minority among the CEA members, who formed the SLAS in 1925, seemed inclined toward the SLNC position, the main body of the CEA could not possibly accept it. Their kinship ties to traditional rulers was a restraining factor. More significantly, their political influence rested largely upon Chiefs' status as the only legitimate political leaders in the eyes of the hinterland populace.

There were three reasons for the SLNC's opposition to Chiefs as members of the Legislative Council. Two of them related directly to the Chiefs' political role in the local colonial administration; the other concerned the apprehension of the conservative elements among Creole leadership that any form of Protectorate representation, through Chiefs or otherwise, would ultimately destroy the Creole ascendancy in the Legislative Council.

First, the SLNC argued that Chiefs were so closely linked to local colonial administration that, as members of the Legislative

[18] *Sierra Leone Weekly News*, March 14, 1925, p. 5.

Council, they could not be expected to act as free and independent agents. They could do no more than rubber-stamp proposals put before the Council by the government. Furthermore, the government, concerned with guaranteeing that Chiefs would not act as independent agents in the council, provided that Provincial or District Commissioners would sit in the legislature concurrently with Chiefs. This further convinced the SLNC leaders that Chiefs were incapable of acting for themselves as members of the legislature. As A. J. Shorunkeh-Sawyerr, a supporter of the SLNC, put it during the debate on the 1924 Constitution: "The power wielded in the Protectorate by the District Commissioner is great; in the Protectorate, the District Commissioner is a Governor: being such a Governor, it seems to me that to bring him here . . . is simply to muzzle the chiefs as to their real feelings and wishes . . . I am concerned that chiefs should come to this Council, but they should come under healthy auspices."[19]

Secondly, the SLNC maintained that, as applied to Paramount Chiefs, the government's own criterion for selecting legislative representatives as pronounced by Governor Slater (namely, selection would "necessarily depend on the proof that is forthcoming of the degree of assent they command among the particular community from whom they emanate") left much to be desired. At the very time of the debate on the Constitution the relations between Chiefs and peasants were seriously strained in several sections of the Protectorate, owing to the abusive exercise by Chiefs of their tax authority and their customary rights to tribute and labor. Mr. Shorunkeh-Sawyerr accordingly urged that "the Government should have taken steps by legislation to produce harmony between chiefs and people before deeming the chiefs fit to represent the people, and not only the people but their brother chiefs."[20]

Yet none of the arguments proferred by the SLNC persuaded either the main body of Protectorate educated leadership or the

[19] *Legislative Council Debates, No. II of Session 1923–1924* (Freetown, n.d.), p. 38.

[20] *Ibid.,* p. 36. On the poor relations between Chiefs and their subjects at this time, see *ibid.,* pp. 37, 40.

colonial government to oppose Chiefs as members of the Legislature.[21] Defeated on this crucial issue, the Colony leaders resorted to a final argument. They stated that since the Legislative Council was instituted originally as the Legislature of the Colony of Sierra Leone, whose citizens were *British subjects*, it was *ultra vires* to appoint any Protectorate African whatsoever to sit in the legislature. The main question of law in what was a rather intricate legal argument, was based upon the Foreign Jurisdiction Act of 1890, which provided, *inter alia*, that British-protected persons were aliens under the Act; as such they could not legislate for British subjects.[22]

This argument, clever though it was, was basically just so much legal hair-splitting on the part of Creole lawyers, verging on sharp practice. The Legislative Council had, after all, legislated for the Protectorate ever since 1913, though the citizens of the Protec-

[21] It is noteworthy that after Chiefs had served in the Legislative Council for several years, there was a small amount of dissatisfaction with their performance among some educated Protectorate Africans. One such African, a resident of the Southern Province, made the following criticism of Chiefs in the legislature in a letter to the *Sierra Leone Weekly News:* "Since these Chiefs have been nominated by the Government, in no instance have I known Government to convene an assembly of the influential Chiefs and the other principal natives of their provinces to ascertain their views and opinions on the various Ordinances and rules that have been passed since their appointment . . . [Chiefs] have no choice but to back the Government who are their Patrons for the honour conferred on them. They are afraid to hold contrary views from their Commissioners who recommended them for the post . . . When there were no Chiefs in the Council, the Colony Members used to safeguard our interests better than our Chiefs now do in Council . . . In the *Weekly News*, I read a series of articles of the account given of their Stewardship by the Urban and Rural Members to their constituents. Can we call those Protectorate nominees of the Government to do likewise? Decidedly not. And we have no right to call them in-as-much as they were not elected by us. The world is moving and we must adjust ourselves to its progressive movements." *Sierra Leone Weekly News*, August 31, 1929, pp. 4, 13.

[22] *Legislative Council Debates, No. V of Session 1923–1924* (Freetown, n.d.), pp. 3–8; E. S. Beoku-Betts, "The New Legislative Council from a Constitutional Standpoint," *Sierra Leone Weekly News*, August 23, 1924, p. 8. Beoku-Betts remarked in this article that "from a constitutional point of view an anomaly has been created, for so long as the Protectorate remains such, the Paramount Chiefs are aliens and not British subjects; and it is contrary to the fundamental principle of the British Constitution for aliens to legislate for British subjects: they owe no allegiance to the King and it is a moot point whether they can properly take the oath of allegiance . . ."

torate had not been declared *British subjects*.[23] The Creole lawyers who supported the SLNC were not, of course, unaware of this; they merely rationalized it as, in the words of Mr. Beoku-Betts, "a sort of convenience." At the same time they maintained that for British-protected persons to legislate for British subjects could not, in Beoku-Betts' words, be "a convenience" or "justified by any law or precedent."[24]

Shorunkeh-Sawyerr, the most flexible and able of the Creole lawyer-politicians, went beyond this argument and proposed that the legal anomaly of protected persons legislating for British subjects be resolved by bestowing subject status upon the former. Though he did not say so, Shorunkeh-Sawyerr was aware that his proposal, if adopted, would mean the annexation of the Protectorate by the Colony. As Shorunkeh-Sawyerr put it during a debate in the Legislative Council in May 1924: "The Honourable and learned Acting Attorney General says that this Council has for many years past been legislating for the Protectorate and he does not see why some natives of the Protectorate should not be allowed to do so now. I have no objection to that; my motion is not levelled against the natives of the Protectorate coming here. If it is His Majesty's will to bring in the natives of the Protectorate to legislate for the Colony nobody can say 'No'; all I say is make them homogenous with the Colony natives in status."[25]

---

[23] Cf. *Sierra Leone Protectorate Order-in-Council, 7th March 1913*, sec. 5. "It shall be lawful for the Legislative Council for the time being of the Colony of Sierra Leone, by an Ordinance or Ordinances to exercise and provide for giving effect to all such power and jurisdiction of His Majesty at any time before or after the passing of this Order has acquired or may acquire in the said territories or any of them."

[24] Beoku-Betts, "The New Legislative Council from a Constitutional Standpoint," p. 8.

[25] *Legislative Council Debates, No. V of Session 1923–1924*, p. 15. Mr. Shorunkeh-Sawyerr's proposal was put before the legislature on May 21, 1924, in a motion which read as follows: "That whereas under the pending reconstitution of this Council, persons nominated thereto from the inhabitants of the territories described as the Protectorate of Sierra Leone in the Sierra Leone Protectorate Order in Council, 1913, will, in the exercise of their rights and privileges as members thereof, legislate inclusively for the Colony, and that whereas doubts appear to exist as to whether or not such inhabitants are to all intents and purposes aliens, and it is expedient that such doubts should be disposed of, this

Shorunkeh-Sawyerr's proposal was by far the most ingenious argument adduced by Colony interests during the constitutional debate. If accepted by the government, the Colony middle class would have gained rights of participation in the Protectorate's political system. As already noted, such rights were considered extremely important by Creole merchants, businessmen, petty traders, and landowners who found their activities in the Protectorate subject to the selfish caprice and erratic whim of Chiefs and tribal authorities, without much hope of political or legal redress. European and other expatriate entrepreneurs, on the other hand, had the power and authority of the colonial system to serve their interests.

One notable instance of the disadvantages experienced by Creole business groups working in the Protectorate occurred in Bo Chiefdom in 1929. Nearly a hundred Creoles were summarily evicted from commercial and agricultural land they had long occupied, under agreement with earlier Chiefs, because they refused to pay a settlers' fee in the amount required by the ruling Paramount Chief Kamanda Bunge (or Bongay). A number of them were brought before the District Commissioner's Court by Chief Bunge, and damages were awarded against them amounting to £300.[26] It was for more adequate protection against precisely this sort of treatment that, as the constitutional debate progressed, the SLNC and its supporters emphasized the absence of reciprocity involved in the government's proposal for Protectorate representation in the Legislature. This representation, after all, entailed the right of qualified protected persons resident in the Colony to

---

Council do present its dutiful petition to His Majesty the King praying that such inhabitants be declared to be British subjects by an Order in Council to be made under the Foreign Jurisdiction Act, 1890, or otherwise." *Legislative Council Debates, No. V of Session 1923–1924*, p. 3. Shorunkeh-Sawyerr's motion was opposed by the government, and he subsequently withdrew it before the Council could vote on it. If it had been accepted by the government, the motion would have saved Sierra Leone some bitter political experiences in the postwar era.

[26] *Sierra Leone Weekly News*, March 30, 1929, pp. 8–9; *ibid.*, April 6, 1929, p. 8.

vote for the three elected unofficial African members under the 1924 Constitution.[27]

Shorunkeh-Sawyerr's annexation proposal would have provided reciprocity for Creoles in legal and political rights in the Protectorate. It would have also, no doubt, provided a more rapid political and economic integration of the Colony and Protectorate systems. But, to Shorunkeh-Sawyerr's chagrin, his proposal was rejected by the government; Governor Slater held that "there is no necessity for declaring the inhabitants of the Protectorate to be British subjects."[28] As a result, there ensued a fast polarization of the interests of Sierra Leonean elites within their respective political divisions. It reached its high-water mark during the postwar debate on new constitutional changes in 1947–51 and would have split the political system asunder but for the intervention of the colonial government, which now recognized the need to mediate, rather than manipulate, the differences between the Colony and Protectorate interests.

Though his proposal failed, Shorunkeh-Sawyerr was correct in asserting, in its defense, that "whether annexation is accepted now or not the ultimate step of policy that will be adopted will be the annexation to the Colony of the surrounding territories, and someday when it will happen it will be said that Mr. Shorunkeh-Sawyerr had prophesied it." But this event did not occur until over a quarter of a century later; meanwhile the situation that ensued between Colony and Protectorate interests was more

[27] Beoku-Betts, "The New Legislative Council from a Constitutional Point of View," *Sierra Leone Weekly News*, September 6, 1924, p. 9. During the 1929 controversy regarding the rights of Creole merchants in Bo, the *Sierra Leone Weekly News* remarked editorially that: "There seems no reason why the natives of the Protectorate should have the important right of deciding who should represent us, when we have no status in the Protectorate, and no right even indirectly of influencing the appointment of their representatives. It is a known fact that Sierra Leoneans [i.e., Creoles] who go to the Protectorate are regarded as Settlers with no rights, political or otherwise. They cannot take part in the election of chiefs or other Tribal Rulers, and . . . their right to properties has been cut down to a minimum. In spite of this, and with the unrestricted right of the 'natives of the Protectorate' to own lands in the Colony, there is the right to be registered as a voter and to vote at an election of representatives for the Colony. This is unfair and should be remedied." *Sierra Leone Weekly News*, August 17, 1929, p. 8.
[28] *Legislative Council Debates, No. V of Session 1923–1924*, p. 13.

nearly foreseen by another Creole member of the 1924 Legislative Council, E. H. Cummings, a medical doctor. He declared, in defense of Shorunkeh-Sawyerr's proposal: "The motion is not controversial, it aims at putting things right once and for all and to bring peace and harmony in the Council and to prevent anything being raked up against their [i.e., Protectorate Africans] sitting as members thereof. We are not legislating for the present only but for the future as well."[29] As will be seen in Chapter 10, a lot was indeed "raked up," including the SLNC's arguments against the 1924 constitution, during the four-year debate on the postwar proposals of the government for the establishment of an unofficial, African majority in the Legislative Council.

D. CONCLUSION

The above account of intra-African conflict over the 1924 constitution in Sierra Leone suggests several important conclusions about the role of such conflict in colonial constitutional change. Insofar as Africans exhausted their attention and energies on their own differences, the general conflict situation between Africans, as a community, and the colonial oligarchy was in a way pushed to the background. As a result, the colonial oligarchy's perception of this general conflict situation (which, it should be recalled, is ultimately the basic conflict situation underlying constitutional change) was distorted or refracted, resulting in a lessening of the oligarchy's apprehension that basic constitutional change in favor of African interests might entail harmful or uncontrollable consequences. The presumption underlying this lessening of the colonial oligarchy's apprehension must have been that, given the intra-African conflict, basic constitutional concessions would more likely than not keep the African community divided. This presumption was, in fact, essentially correct, for, as we have seen, this was precisely how the constitutional changes in

---

[29] The controversy about Protectorate annexation is recorded in *Legislative Council Debates, No. V of Session 1923–1924*—with Mr. Shorunkeh-Sawyerr's prophecy on p. 10, Dr. Cummings' on p. 11, and the official negative reply on p. 13.

1924 were received by the feuding African interests. The presumption also functioned as a sort of self-fulfilling prophecy for the colonial oligarchy: the colonial government shaped the framework of the 1924 constitution in a manner that facilitated the reforms being absorbed along lines of fission within the African elites. Thus it is evident that intra-African conflict was functional to constitutional change.

Another conclusion to be drawn from our account is that intra-African conflict over constitutional issues operated disproportionately in the interest of Chiefs, the least politically assertive of the African groups. By virtue of their strategic role in local colonial administration, Chiefs paradoxically benefited from being opposed by the Colony elite, inasmuch as the colonial government reacted by ensuring them a key position in the new constitutional arrangement. Consequently, the Chiefs, naturally wary of a too rapid pace of political change, employed their constitutional status to spread the process of change over a longer period of time. This in turn enabled them to expand the modern sources of their influence and power, while simultaneously buttressing as best they could their traditional authority. In this way, the Chiefs gained a favorable vantage point which in the postwar period facilitated their claim for a permanent status in the constitutional structure of Sierra Leone. As will be seen in later chapters, Chiefs first sought the establishment of a quasi-legislature in the Protectorate itself, called the Protectorate Assembly, which was instituted in 1946. They then obtained wider representation in the Legislative Council, and the combination of these two legislative positions inevitably enabled Chiefs to shape a major part of postwar politics in Sierra Leone.

CHAPTER 8

Constitutional Change and African Interests, 1924-1945

The Sierra Leone Constitution of 1924 was only a small step toward self-government. But it did provide a new framework for the development of African interests. The articulate African groups were now more favorably situated both to stimulate further constitutional change and to advance their social position. The post-1924 period was mainly concerned, therefore, with the effort of such groups to exact as much advantage as possible from the new African constitutional status in the central government.

A. THE COLONY MIDDLE CLASS

Representatives of the Colony middle class increasingly used their new constitutional status to oppose government policies that neglected the development of their own social group. During debate on the government budget, for instance, these representatives not only continued their old policy of questioning government's use of funds to increase salaries, allowances, and other perquisites of European officials, but they did so in a more militant and stickling manner, emphasizing the need for such expenditures to go to the African community. As part of the new constitutional situation of the post-1924 period, the colonial government was attentive to such African criticisms and took them

139

into account when circumstances suggested it wise to do so.[1] At an earlier period the government had been quite brief in its reply to similar African criticisms in the Legislature.

In addition to protesting against higher expenditures on European salaries and allowances, the Creole representatives complained about the appointment of more Europeans than Africans to civil service posts, the slow promotion rate of African civil servants, the poorer conditions of employment for African civil servants, and related matters.

In 1934, for example, an elected Colony representative criticized the government for discriminatory treatment of African civil service posts that were held in abeyance. "I say without fear of contradiction that the post of Africans held in abeyance exceeds that of Europeans by a long way; further, in the case of Africans, the filling of the posts held in abeyance merely means the promotion of some officer already in the Service, whilst in the case of Europeans it means the appointment of some new officer in the Service . . . Some of the European offices are superfluous to the establishment and when they were abolished the Service did not suffer, whilst as regards African appointments, even when they are abolished the work is performed by junior officers, and it does happen that although we are told that these are clerks supernumerary to the establishment, yet still the payment of overtime has been abolished and these men have had to do extra work and to work overtime when ordinarily they would have worked only during the normal hours of work."[2]

The Colony representatives were equally concerned that Africans gain appointment to senior posts in the civil service. Apart from the large personal emoluments attached to these posts, they brought Africans nearer to the policymaking machinery of colonial government than any other posts open to them. Whatever advances Africans gained in the Legislative Council short of an unofficial African majority, they still lacked influence over the

---

[1] *Legislative Council Debates, No. II of Session 1926–1927* (Freetown, n.d.), p. 37.
[2] *Legislative Council Debates, No. I of Session 1934–1935* (Freetown, 1935), p. 103.

premier policy-making body, the Executive Council. Senior civil posts would at least bring Africans within range of influencing this body at the point of executing its policy.[3]

Besides the issue of African civil servants, the Colony representatives were keen upon securing direct government assistance to the business elements among the new elite. On some occasions the demands for such assistance were merely limited to business undertakings in which the African legislators were themselves active. For instance, Mr. Cornelius May, a nominated unofficial member and editor-owner of the best newspaper in West Africa at this period—the *Sierra Leone Weekly News*—sought the exemption of printing paper from import duties. May argued, in a manner common to most businessmen seeking government aid, that newspaper publishing was "not a paying concern and . . . it assists in the diffusion of knowledge and consequently the administration . . ."[4]

Normally, however, the African legislators requested assistance for African businessmen as a group. They insisted that government use its tariff, lending, and other economic powers to assist African businessmen in the same way that it aided expatriate concerns. The most informed plea of this sort was made during the 1943–44 session of the Legislative Council when Mr. (later Sir) E. S. Beoku-Betts, a wealthy lawyer, urged government to assist African private enterprise:

Whatever schemes Government may initiate, they should not be of such a nature as to exclude any endeavour on the part of individuals or groups of individuals for private enterprise. I am referring particularly to Africans. It has been the practice to give the outside world the impression that as a people we have no initiative, we are not industrious, in fact we are lazy. But anyone examining this question with an open mind will find that in the main many an opportunity has been thwarted in several ways, e.g., for want of capital and to compete with European firms with unlimited capital and Government itself is not quite free from criticism in this regard . . . I bring before

[3] Cf. *Legislative Council Debates, No. II of Session 1927–1928* (Freetown, n.d.), pp. 6 ff; *Legislative Council Debates, No. I of Session 1934–1935*, pp. 101–102.

[4] *Legislative Council Debates, No. III of Session 1924–1925* (Freetown, n.d.), p. 33.

Your Excellency the case of the late Dr. Abayomi Cole who lived to the great age of 92 years . . . He was enterprising. Besides agricultural products, he manufactured Tobacco in this country, cured it, and his was pronounced amongst the best brands obtainable at the time. Dr. Abayomi Cole also produced Brandy, and the Chief Justice of the day declared it the best brandy he had ever tasted. He also manufactured Sugar and Soap. But what happened? A ban was placed by Government on these enterprises and Dr. Abayomi Cole had to close down and go over to Liberia, abandoning his Farm . . ., his Sugar Cane Plantations, besides extensive property in Mabang and elsewhere in the Protectorate. Next . . . I refer to the late D. B. Curry [who] manufactured lots of local foodstuffs and also ventured into chocolate making, selling them at a penny a bar, locally. That was enough to stir a great firm in England like Cadbury's to send representatives out here to see what Curry was doing, and following their report, Cadbury's produced chocolate which they placed on the market here at halfpenny a bar. How can we compete with a millionaire firm? . . . Here again is another instance of local enterprise. The Freetown Mineral Waters Company which is a purely African concern. That Company, in the early days, was tossed about a bit by the winds but by its own efforts is fairly stable now . . . Yet the Freetown Cold Storage Company [an expatriate concern] has enjoyed a subsidy from this Government of over £10,000, whereas the Freetown Mineral Waters Company, composed of peoples of this country (I am a member) has not enjoyed such a privilege: rather than that the Director of Agriculture did his best for the Company to be bought over, or close down. There has been no encouragement for us as a people to carry on Industries.[5]

Despite the persistence and fervor of the demands for greater government contribution to the advancement of the African elite, the post-1924 colonial hierarchy was still unready to satisfy them. In the sphere of the Africanization of senior civil service posts, for instance, very little progress was made in the post-1924 period. The same was true for the enhancement of the economic status of elite Africans. In the late 1930's and early 1940's, however, the colonial government did make two concessions which to some extent compensated for the dissatisfaction the African elite experienced in other spheres.

In November 1938 the government agreed to the establishment

[5] *Legislative Council Debates, No. I of Session 1943–1944* (Freetown, 1944), pp. 54 ff. See also *Legislative Council Debates, No. I of Session 1934–1935,* pp. 93–94, 101–102.

of a Standing Finance Committee of the Legislature, which was to consist of two official members (the Colonial Secretary and Treasurer) and all the unofficial members (seven Africans and three Europeans). The Committee thus became the first organ of central colonial government to have an unofficial majority as well as an unofficial African majority. As regards the Committee's powers, the Governor, Sir Douglas Jardine, observed that in proposing the establishment of the Committee he "had a two-fold object in view, first, to enable the unofficial members to keep a stricter check on supplementary expenditure after the budget is passed and, secondly, to maintain a closer contact between Government and the public during the long intervals between [legislative] sittings." Inasmuch as the Colony elite had demanded participation in colonial financial policies ever since 1920, the Governor was correct in characterizing the Standing Finance Committee as "a distinct move forward in the constitutional advancement of this Colony . . ."[6]

The second constitutional concession was the appointment in 1943 of two Africans to the Executive Council, the policy-making organ of colonial government. In recognition of the significance of this decision to Sierra Leone as a whole, the African members of the Council were chosen from both the Colony and the Protectorate: Mr. J. Fowell Boston, an African lawyer, represented the Colony, and Paramount Chief A. George Caulker represented the Protectorate.[7]

B. WAGE-LABORERS AND TRADE UNIONS

Although the 1938 and 1943 constitutional changes were basically concessions to the African elite, they were partly granted as a reaction to the growing needs of other politically effective segments of the population. The wage-laborers, for example, by the late 1930's had registered some advance in trade-union organization. By 1940 there were seven registered trade unions in

[6] For the composition of the Standing Finance Committee as well as Governor Jardine's remarks, see *Legislative Council Debates, No. I of Session 1939–1940* (Freetown, 1940), pp. 5–6.
[7] *Legislative Council Debates, No. I of Session 1943–1944*, p. 10.

Sierra Leone and eleven by 1942.[8] A series of labor laws marked the colonial government's response to this development. These laws included the Trade Unions Ordinance, No. 31 of 1939 that established machinery for the registration of unions; the Trade Disputes (Arbitration and Enquiry) Ordinance, No. 14 of 1939 that provided for arbitration of strikes and related disputes; and the Workmen's Compensation Ordinance, No. 35 of 1939 that established conditions for payment of compensation to injured workers.[9]

The colonial government was especially cognizant of the rising political militancy among urban laborers which was described in the official labor report for 1939–40 as "undoubtedly an undercurrent of discontent amongst workers generally." Strikes, of course, were a feature of this discontent: there were several major strikes in 1938 and 1939 and eleven in 1942.[10] Apart from representing a threat to Sierra Leone's contribution to the metropolitan power's war effort, the strikes reflected the emergence of a radical "Left" in the country's politics. Such violent labor troubles as the Mabella Works strike in 1939 at the Sierra Leone Coaling Company were connected with the Marxist Sierra Leone Youth League (SLYL) and its affiliated organ, the Sierra Leone Trade Union Congress.

The leader of the SLYL, Mr. I. T. A. Wallace-Johnson, a Colony Creole, was Socialist by conviction and had studied in the Soviet Union during the early 1930's. Formed in early 1938, the SLYL demonstrated a capacity to attract wage-laborers in the urban center and in the hinterland towns; within a year of its formation it claimed some 7,000 members.[11] Professor Macmillan vividly portrayed the position of the SLYL in the late 1930's, though he overstated its impact upon the political conflict between Colony and Protectorate interests: "It is a new phenomenon that Freetown for a year or more has been greatly stirred by the activities

[8] *Sierra Leone Labour Report, 1939–1940* (Freetown, 1941), p. 2; *Report on the Labour Department, 1943* (Freetown, 1944), p. 2.

[9] *Sierra Leone Labour Report, 1939–1940*, pp. 1–4. See also Michael Scott, *An Outline of Sierra Leone Trade Union Law* (Freetown, 1960).

[10] *Sierra Leone Labour Report, 1939–1940*, p. 3; *Report on the Labour Department, 1943*, p. 2.

[11] I. T. A. Wallace-Johnson, *Trade Unionism in Colonial and Dependent Territories* (London, 1946), pp. 24–25.

144

of a so-called Youth League. Night after night the Wilberforce Hall has been crowded to the doors and windows by those assembled to consider and foment grievances, and though the subjects of protests and demonstrations have by no means always been well chosen or well founded, the ventilation of constitutional or labour grievances has begun to bridge the old deep cleavage between the Creoles and the peoples of the Protectorate. Creole leaders, in short, not uninfluenced by the 'ideologies' of the new age, are coming into their own as the natural leaders of discontent wherever it may happen to show itself."[12]

Faced thus with an emergent Leftward-oriented nationalist group whose support rested essentially among wage-laborers, the colonial government appeared more inclined to accommodate some of the moderate post-1924 demands of the more established Colony elite. The constitutional concessions of 1938 and 1943 reflected this, and they bolstered the African middle class against competition from radical new leaders whose support came from wage-laborers and the urban poor. Here again was partial demonstration of the proposition that as the process of colonial development required constitutional reform, the colonial authorities granted such reform in a manner disproportionately favorable to those African elements which at any given period were likely to exert a moderating influence. The colonial government soon strengthened the established Creole elite's position further by proscribing the SLYL and interning its leader for the duration of World War II. It also brought the trade unions under closer supervision. These actions resulted in the virtual collapse of the political influence of radicalism, and in the postwar period the SLYL proved a mere figment of its prewar self.

C. THE PROTECTORATE TRADITIONAL ELITE

Like the Colony elite, the literate Paramount Chiefs in the post-1924 legislature utilized their new constitutional status to advance the interests of educated Africans. They were less open,

[12] W. M. MacMillan, "African Development," in C. K. Meek, et al., Europe and West Africa (London, 1940), p. 76.

less militant, perhaps, but their aims differed little from those of the Colony.

Posts for Protectorate Africans in the civil service, more schools, roads, health and medical services for the Protectorate, higher salaries for Chiefs, and African participation in the organs of decision-making in the Protectorate were among the issues Paramount Chiefs raised in the legislature. The Chiefs were especially keen about espousing the needs of the Protectorate educated elite. During the 1943–44 session Paramount Chief Albert G. Caulker, the best educated chiefly member and a representative of the Southwestern Province, was firm in his support of the large Protectorate clerical group in government service: ". . . There is still room for improvement to be made in [the Railway] Department. I observe that so many Third Grade Clerks, Second Class Station-Masters and Station Clerks have been drawing their maximum rates of pay for over 10 years, and without any prospects of bettering their position. These officers do the greater bulk of the work. I therefore feel that consideration should be given to them to encourage them. As to the post of Chief Clerk in that Department this seems lost and out of the question. One thing I notice, and I must say it. The Africans are always used to work and to build up the revenue and during that time they are considered qualified; they can do any work. But the moment the Government has got the required funds they start to look askance at these Africans; criticisms begin, they are not considered qualified; Europeans are appointed to come and eat up the revenue. I do not think that is in conformity with British justice."[13]

There were two important reasons for the tendency of Chiefs to advance the interest of the Protectorate educated elite. First, by the 1930's the older generation Chiefs, most of them illiterate, were dying off. They were increasingly replaced by better-educated men with experience in modern institutions. Besides attending the best schools in the Protectorate, many of the new Chiefs worked as merchants, civil servants, or clerks in European firms before assuming traditional office. They were thus basically assimilated to the standards and needs of the educated elite and

[13] *Legislative Council Debates, No. I of Session 1943–1944,* pp. 62–63.

accordingly reflected the interests of this elite. Second, those Chiefs who were still illiterate had, by virtue of their new position in the constitutional structure of Sierra Leone, an expanding need for the skills and knowledge of the educated elite. To note one important instance of this, throughout the 1930's and 1940's the first Protectorate medical doctor, Dr. (later Sir) Milton Margai (who served as a Medical Officer in the Protectorate during these years), was frequently called upon by older Chiefs for technical and political advice.[14] It was, incidentally, this long tenure as confidential adviser to Chiefs that gave Dr. Margai their devoted and unswerving support during his postwar ascent to the leadership of the nationalist movement.

Paramount Chiefs were not, of course, oblivious of their own interests, however much they attended to those of the Protectorate educated elite. In the mid-1930's the establishment of Native Administrations caused a closer supervision of Chiefs' political activities by the central government: restrictions were put upon their travel outside their Chiefdoms, traditional selection of Chiefs was more closely regulated, and financial affairs reduced to closer scrutiny. Both the educated and illiterate Chiefs disliked some or all of these features of the N.A. system, and the criticism of them by their spokesmen in the Legislative Council occasionally overreached the accommodationist manner expected of Chiefs.[15] For instance, at the 1943–44 session of the legislature, Paramount Chief Caulker declared: "We want the government to give us a free hand in our own affairs . . . If we are not fit for self-government, let the Government give us a trial . . . There is something going on in the Protectorate which is not known down here and probably may not [be] known even to the Secretary for Protectorate Affairs . . . I would ask that Your Excellency should make it known to His Majesty's representatives in the person of District Commissioners to give due respect to Paramount Chiefs. Leaving aside the personality of the Chief, the title attached to the Chief as His Majesty's Friend deserves some respect. District Commissioners are still taking the Protectorate as it was many

[14] Interview with Sir Milton Margai, January 1960.
[15] *Legislative Council Debates, No. I of Session 1939–1940*, p. 5.

years ago; they seem to forget that there are men in the Protectorate just now who know when a thing is black from when it is white. District Commissioners are regarding Chiefs as they used to do in days of long ago. This is what has been pressing our minds and we have nowhere to voice it but except for this opportunity here granted to us."[16]

Mindful of the importance of Chiefs' role in colonial administration — and, from 1924 onwards, in the over-all constitutional structure of Sierra Leone—the government heeded these criticisms. The appointment of a Paramount Chief to the Executive Council in 1943 was, no doubt, not unrelated to Chiefs' dissatisfaction with features of the N.A. system. But the government did not stop here; for another result of the N.A. system, combined with Chiefs' new constitutional status, was to turn Chiefs' attention to the need for larger inter-tribal and inter-regional institutions within the Protectorate. This need was first pointed out to the colonial authorities in 1940 and the government's response was to convene, in that year, the first Chiefs' Conference, which met at Moyamba. By 1944 these Conferences had become annual institutions in ten of the twelve Districts of the Protectorate.[17]

As originally instituted, the Chiefs' Conferences had neither executive nor legislative tasks: delegates merely advised the government on a variety of problems affecting Chiefs and the Protectorate in general. But Chiefs took the advisory function of the Conferences seriously, and, when the opportunity arose, they moved to give the Conferences statutory recognition and quasi-legislative status. In 1944, Paramount Chief A. B. Samba, member of the Legislative Council for the Northern Province, expressed the "hope that Conferences will be encouraged to continue to function in the interest of Government and the people." He remarked further that this required "the full assistance and sympathy of our political officers . . ., facilities . . . to convene our meetings of the desired places and time, and . . . official recognition." At the end of 1944 the government responded to this

16 *Legislative Council Debates, No. I of Session 1943–1944*, pp. 76 ff.
17 *Ibid.*, p. 5, Appendix I; *Legislative Council Debates, No. I of Session 1944–1945* (Freetown, 1945), p. 3, Appendix I.

request, first by expanding the advisory role of the Chiefs' Conferences to include economic matters. A Regional Committee for Protectorate Development was formed, composed of one Paramount Chief for each District and of technical officers representing government departments, and empowered to discuss and advise upon the Protectorate's role in the postwar development plans.[18] Shortly after the end of the war the government agreed to institute the Protectorate Assembly, a quasi-legislative body composed mainly of Chiefs. As will be seen in Chapter 10, the Assembly was a major factor in shaping postwar political change in Sierra Leone.

D. THE AFRICAN ELITE DURING THE WAR

The fact that the African elite did not vigorously press their political demands during World War II provides an important insight into the nature of the colonial relationship in Sierra Leone, and perhaps elsewhere in West Africa. Instead of exploiting the position of the metropolitan system, which was experiencing its most serious crisis in national and international power, the Sierra Leonean political leaders voluntarily pronounced their support of Britain and her colonial government.

To some extent this occurred because the 1939 and 1943 constitutional changes proved relatively satisfactory to the Colony and Protectorate elites. It also reflected the fact that both elites were now acculturated to certain standards and norms of the metropolitan power and were thus capable of viewing Britain's war effort as equally their own. Related to this was the belief of the Sierra Leonean elite that Britain's defeat by the Fascist powers would result in a colonial system in no way as civilized or progressive as the British colonial relationship.

Thus at the outbreak of the war in 1939, Dr. H. C. Bankole-Bright, General Secretary of the SLNC and the most ardent nationalist in the Legislative Council, declared: "Sierra Leone, as

[18] Paramount Chief Samba's remarks appear in *Legislative Council Debates, No. I of Session 1944–1945*, pp. 90, 110; and information about the Development Committee is given in Appendix I of these *Debates*.

all other British possessions, has good reasons to pray for England at this hour of her trial, because the foundation of this Colony is based on the principle of protection for the weak. Britain goes to war to-day not for aggrandisement; she goes to war to-day not for speculation, not for greed . . . She has gone out—to use the words of the Prime Minister, Mr. Chamberlain, to the Polish people—for honour, for justice, for freedom of the world. The heart of Sierra Leone throbs to-day towards England the motherland . . . Unshaken in her loyalty, unswerving in her devotion, she will contribute her own quota, however small, towards the emancipation of England from the thraldom of this great revolutionary act . . . I have not the slightest doubt in my mind . . . that . . . Great Britain and her ally France will remove this menace and will march victorious . . ., so that in the reconstruction of the pending new world men will beat their swords into ploughshares and their spears into pruning hooks and there will be peace on earth and goodwill towards men." Dr. Bankole-Bright later submitted a motion which declared, in part, that "this Council representing the whole . . . of Sierra Leone affirms its unshakable loyalty to the British Throne, pledges its devotion, sympathy, and support to the British Empire in her present struggle for the protection of the weak against the strong . . ."[19] (The motion, incidentally, was seconded by the Colonial Secretary, which was probably an unprecedented act involving an official and the most radical member of the unofficial side.)

Furthermore, in defense of a motion by Mr. C. E. Wright, a member of SLNC and a nominated unofficial legislator, that the Sierra Leone government contribute £100,000 to the British Imperial War Fund, Paramount Chief Albert G. Caulker declared: "From my experience I think the people in the Protectorate have realized the benefits of the British Empire, perhaps more than the people in the Colony, because before the advent of the British Government our lives in the Protectorate were more miserable than one could be able to express . . . Time and again we come across other Africans, some of whom are members of our tribes,

[19] *Legislative Council Debates, No. II of Session 1938–1939* (Freetown, 1939), pp. 3–4, for both quotations by Dr. Bankole-Bright.

who come from other colonies such as the French Colonies; when we compare their experience of the rule of foreign administrations with ours under the British Government we feel that we are in Heaven so to speak. The British Government has no distinction of race, colour or creed, and the British law, the law of England, without doubt, I say, is next to the law of God. I am worried we are not able to do more than what we have done. But I say on behalf of my people I am sure we will do anything more that the Government thinks fit, just to help the Government and to help the Empire not to be beaten . . . By the grace of God it will not be long when His Majesty's Government will rule in peace throughout the world once more. And it is my firm belief that we shall still sing on 'Britannia rules the waves.' "[20]

Considering the context in which these pronouncements were made, they constitute impeccable evidence of the attachment of Sierra Leone's political leadership to the British colonial connection. The strength of this attachment, moreover, carried over into the immediate postwar era, resulting in a surprisingly moderate approach by the elite to the postwar decolonization of Sierra Leone. In 1948, for instance, Mr. O. I. During, a lawyer and, like Dr. Bankole-Bright, one of the more nationalist-minded of the SLNC members in the Legislative Council, projected twenty years as the period in which full self-government should gradually be attained. "I am sure," he said, "that in the space of some 20 years, there will be many men who have passed through the Legislative Council, who must have been educated in the way policy is got through and thereby facilitate what we know is the aim of the United Kingdom Imperial Government that as soon as we are so educated we will be able to take the reins of our country into our hands."[21]

This moderate approach to the question of self-government was found elsewhere in West Africa immediately after the war; it was not, in fact, until the 1950's, when the generation educated in the

[20] *Legislative Council Debates, No. III of Session 1939–1940* (Freetown, 1940), p. 9.
[21] *Legislative Council Debates, No. III of Session 1947–1948* (Freetown, 1948), p. 46.

1930's and 1940's assumed a larger role in political leadership, that this approach gave way to a more militant nationalism. The moderation of the older leaders did not mean, however, that they had lost sight of the basic goal of self-government or were in any way compromising that goal. For instance, in the midst of the war in 1943, Paramount Chief Caulker declared: "I hope the Sierra Leone Government has already drawn up plans to make this Dependency what it should be after the war in the spirit of the Atlantic Charter."[22] In November 1944 Dr. G. C. E. Reffell, an elected member of the Legislative Council and President of the SLNC, expressed the hope that "Britain's pledge be carried out, that of self-government eventually in each territory . . ."[23] O. I. During went so far as to propose the institution of an unofficial majority at the war's end: "That this Council is of the opinion that the time has come when the people of Sierra Leone should take a more effective part in the government of the country and in order to harmonise with the principle of democratic government which is the prevailing policy of His Majesty's Government respectfully request . . . that the Constitution of the Legislative Council be amended to provide for an unofficial majority . . ." He noted further that by an unofficial majority was meant African *control* of the legislative process: "I will not take my seat without mentioning . . . that Unofficial majority does not and could not mean without some sort of control."[24]

These demands, it should be emphasized, were motivated by a deep feeling of respect for the British colonial connection and for the democratic heritage which it represented. Unlike the more militant nationalist policies put forth by the younger generation who moved into political leadership in much of West Africa in the 1950's, the postwar proposals of the older leaders never even intimated doubt regarding the ultimate value of British rule. These proposals also, of course, assumed that the British authorities would reciprocate the unswerving support they received from Sierra Leone in the war by laying the basis for postwar decolo-

[22] *Legislative Council Debates, No. I of Session 1943–1944*, p. 65.
[23] *Legislative Council Debates, No. I of Session 1944–1945*, p. 67.
[24] *Ibid.*, pp. 116, 118.

nization.[25] The assumption was warranted. Proposals to commence decolonization of Sierra Leone were submitted by the colonial authorities in 1947, and the subsequent constitutional evolution of Sierra Leone was essentially in African hands. Though ultimate authority necessarily remained with colonial officials between the start of decolonization and its terminal point in 1961, African interests and the differences among them shaped most of the course of postwar advances.

25 *Ibid.,* p. 119.

CHAPTER 9

Postwar Advances, 1946-1951

A. THE PROTECTORATE ASSEMBLY AND THE PROTECTORATE ELITE

An important feature of the movement toward self-government during the period 1946–1951 was the creation of a Protectorate Assembly and other institutions which began to give the hinterland more political weight in Sierra Leone. These institutions initially disrupted relations between the Chiefs and the educated elite of the Protectorate, but in time the intervention of the colonial authorities rectified this situation. A united Protectorate elite was seen as a buffer against precipitous changes in the central government of Sierra Leone.

Underlying the creation of the Assembly in 1945–46 was the government's earlier decision to reject the Colony elite's proposal for an unofficial majority in the central legislature. The Governor, Sir Hubert Stevenson, had maintained that a framework for surmounting the political and social backwardness of the Protectorate must precede the introduction of an elected unofficial majority. The Colony, after all, was so much more advanced in this regard: the government felt it should do more to assist the Protectorate's capacity to compete with the Colony. Only when this was done would an unofficial majority be in order.

But the government emphasized that given an unofficial majority the Colony could not possibly expect to maintain its previous predominance in the legislature. As Sir Hubert Stevenson put it during a debate in the Legislative Council in November 1944: ". . . Let me remind the Council that over 90 per cent of the total population of Sierra Leone is in the Protectorate, and it cannot be denied that the vast majority of these people are in a backward state of political development . . . Let us consider what would be the practical effect of changing the Constitution of this Council on the lines indicated by the Honourable the First Urban Member's [O. I. During] motion. At present the representation of the Colony on the Legislative Council is disproportionately high, having regard to the enormously greater proportion of population in the Protectorate, which incidentally is the main source of wealth of Sierra Leone. If the composition of the Council were changed to provide for an unofficial majority, it would be essential to take this into account and to give the Protectorate a representation more in accordance with facts. It is my considered opinion that, pending the social development of the Protectorate . . ., it would be clearly premature to consider the constitution of an unofficial majority in this Council . . ."[1]

The following year the government promulgated the ordinance establishing a Protectorate Assembly. More than half of the forty-two Assembly seats were reserved for Paramount Chiefs (twenty-six in all), who were indirectly elected to the Assembly by Native Administrations and District Councils over which Chiefs exercised much influence. The remaining seats in the Assembly were held by officials of government departments (eleven seats), one representative of European and one of Creole business interests, one missionary representative, and two educated Protectorate Africans selected by Native Administrations.[2]

Initially, the Protectorate Assembly was mainly a way of bringing the Chiefs together, consolidating their prewar gains, and preparing them for a major role in postwar development. At the first meeting of the Assembly in July 1946, Paramount Chief Julius Gulama, the leading member of the Assembly, spoke enthusias-

[1] *Legislative Council Debates, No. I of Session 1944–1945* (Freetown, 1945), p. 120. Cf. Governor A. Ransford Slater's address in 1924 to the National Congress of British West Africa, *Legislative Council Debates, Session 1924–1925,* pp. 226–227.

[2] *Protectorate (Amendment) Ordinance, No. 27 of 1945,* sec. 7; *Protectorate Assembly, Proceedings of First Meeting at Bo, 23rd to 26th July, 1946* (Freetown, 1946), pp. 1–2. Assembly deliberations are hereafter cited in the following style: *First Assembly Proceedings.*

tically: ". . . Fellow Chiefs . . . whoever knew that there would be a meeting like this to-day? Our fathers and grandfathers who are now buried never did they dream that such a meeting would take place. Whoever thought that the Limba man and the Kono and all the tribes of the Protectorate could meet like this to-day, without exchanging swords? Whoever thought that all these tribes would meet together in one place and sit together in common? All these things have just been possible because of the treaty entered into by our grandfathers with the Government. Our fathers and grandfathers lying now in their graves will rejoice that such a meeting has taken place to-day."[3]

The Protectorate educated elite, however, had precious little to be enthusiastic about. Their prewar alliance with Chiefs was erroneously taken for granted by the colonial government when creating the Protectorate Assembly, whereas in fact a new generation of educated persons had come forth who desired a more direct and independent role in the Protectorate's political affairs. Thus, the two seats reserved for the educated elite in the Protectorate Assembly, dependent as they were upon the favor of Native Administrations, merely antagonized the educated Africans. The latter were also aggrieved over the large role the government gave to the Assembly in the 1947 proposals for reconstituting the Legislative Council.

Patronized by Paramount Chief Julius Gulama, who, despite his general enthusiasm for the Protectorate Assembly, recognized the need to keep Chiefs and the educated elite in alliance, the new elite formed the Sierra Leone Organization Society (SOS) in July 1946 in order to express their approach to postwar development. From its inception, the SOS criticized the influence of Chiefs in the Protectorate Assembly, the postwar local government system, and the central legislature. For instance, in a memorandum to the British government in 1947, the SOS resolved: "That the suggestion in His Excellency's Memorandum [on reconstituting the Legislative Council] to confine Protectorate representation to members of the Protectorate Assembly does not give the franchise to

[3] *First Assembly Proceedings*, p. 29.

the common people of the Protectorate who are taxpayers and are entitled to even more representation . . . than the natural rulers of the country . . . That the suggestion under consideration denies the franchise to the literate class of Protectorate peoples, some of whom have had opportunities for higher education . . ."[4] The appeal, however, went unnoticed by the authorities, and in a subsequent memorandum of November 1948, the moderate tone of the SOS's 1947 appeal gave way to a note of bitterness. It charged the government for discriminating against the educated elite: "[The Government] has never nominated the 'Progressive and younger element' outside the Chiefs' class to sit in the Legislative Council." It rejected outright "the present monopoly over Protectorate representation which Chiefs hold in the District Councils, the Protectorate Assembly, the Legislative Council and the Executive Council." It proposed in an uncompromising tone that "definite provisions should be made for the inclusion of the new progressive and literate element into the membership of the new Legislative Council . . . Each province should be granted the privilege of electing at least two persons from among this class to represent their interest in the Legislative Council. These elected members should automatically become members of the Protectorate Assembly."[5]

By 1949 there were few prospects of bridging the growing gap between Chiefs and the Protectorate new elite; and there was surely little evidence indicating the restoration of their relationship to what it was in the prewar era. One mitigating factor, however, was the persistent friendship between Dr. Milton Margai, who was Deputy President of the SOS and a founding member, and the leading Paramount Chiefs, especially Paramount Chief Julius Gulama, who was Honorary President of the SOS. This relationship deterred Chiefs and the new elite from pushing their differences to the point of no return and ultimately proved

---

[4] "Memorandum of the Sierra Leone Organisation Society"; text in *Sierra Leone Weekly News*, October 18, 1947, p. 3.

[5] Albert Margai and F. S. Anthony, *Memorandum to the Secretary of State for the Colonies on the New Constitution, Sessional Paper No. 48 of 1948* (Freetown, ca. November 1948) (typescript)—cited hereafter as *Memorandum on the Constitution.*

to be the link which guided them back to an effective association within the Sierra Leone People's Party (SLPP) under Dr. Margai's leadership. Before this occurred, however, it was the colonial government who was decisive in halting the deteriorating relationship between the two Protectorate groups just short of the abyss.

The colonial government was, after all, instrumental in shaping the close ties between these groups in the prewar era. It was, therefore, no surprise that it should use its influence in the immediate postwar years to save its carefully constructed edifice from utter failure. Sir George Beresford-Stooke, who succeeded Sir Hubert Stevenson as Governor of Sierra Leone in 1947, was particularly keen on restoring harmony between the Chiefs and their educated competitors; but unlike his predecessors, his inclination was toward a balance which tilted somewhat in favor of the latter. In a confidential dispatch to the Secretary of State for the Colonies in January 1949, the Governor queried the traditional preference for Chiefs. Referring to a recent proposal in the Legislative Council, providing for appeals from Native Courts to the Supreme Court—a proposal that the Protectorate Assembly unanimously rejected—the Governor observed: "It stands to reason that with the spread of education and the growing number of Protectorate natives with experience of the British judicial system there will be increasing dissatisfaction with the somewhat arbitrary proceedings of Native Courts. On the other hand, the majority of the Paramount Chiefs must be expected to oppose strongly any measure which would, in their view, weaken their established position. Here in particular is a case where the opinion of the educated classes in the Protectorate may well be in direct conflict with that of the Paramount Chiefs, and where, if the voice of the Chiefs is to be accepted as the true voice of the people, discontent and disaffection against the whole political and administrative system may be expected sooner or later to lead to open defiance of the existing order."[6]

[6] *Despatch of Sir George Beresford-Stooke to Secretary of State, Rt. Honourable A. Creech Jones, 4th January, 1949* (typescript copy, Sierra Leone Government Archives.)

Indeed, as the Governor was keenly aware, violence had broken out in several parts of the Protectorate since 1946. Riots took place in the southern Mende areas in 1948, 1949, and again in 1951. Five years later, because of oppressive tax-collecting by Chiefs, similar disturbances occurred in many parts of the Protectorate, leading to £750,000 worth of property damage. The new-elite groups who formed the SOS in 1946—nearly all of them Mende—were very much aware of such outbreaks and hoped that the way was being paved for basic political change. Sir George Beresford Stooke ascribed even more importance than they did to displays of defiance. Fearing for the security of the colonial regime, he remarked in his dispatch of January 1949 that "recent events elsewhere have shown only too clearly how rapidly political thought and political organization can develop in West Africa."

With the security of a postwar regime undergoing fundamental change in mind, then, the Governor urged upon the Secretary of State the need to widen the basis of political participation for the Protectorate masses in general and for the articulate new elite in particular. "When framing a new Constitution," he wrote, "particular attention should be paid to the necessity of providing adequate opportunity for expression of the opinion of the common people in general and the educated classes in particular . . . It would be a mistake to overlook the claims to representation put forward by the educated classes in the Protectorate . . . The Chief Commissioner has told me that under the [proposed] new Constitution, as the proposals now stand, it is unlikely that commoners would be elected to the Legislative Council from more than two out of the [twelve] districts. The reason for this is that the District Councils [acting as electoral colleges for Legislative Council elections] are largely dominated by the Paramount Chiefs who, holding as they do both executive and judicial powers, are in a position to exert very considerable influence."[7]

The Governor was not, of course, proposing the demise of Chiefs' participation in the Protectorate system. Rather he was seeking,

[7] *Ibid.*

159

as indicated earlier, a more realistic balance between chiefly and new elites, albeit slanted in favor of the latter. The purpose of this balance, moreover, was the more effective integration and articulation of the wider mass forces seeking expression—forces whose momentum, if not controlled, would spell insecurity, inefficiency, and general malaise for the colonial regime. The Governor was perceptive enough to know that the more effective articulation of these mass forces was, under current conditions of colonial change, inconceivable without some role played by Chiefs. (The educated elite was also cognizant of this, as shown by the role given Chiefs in the SLPP from 1951 onwards.) The Governor consequently remarked in his dispatch to the Secretary of State for the Colonies that "it must be recorded . . . that some Paramount Chiefs are educated and progressive, and well equipped to play a proper part in the Councils of government."

Sir George, however, did not remain governor long enough to unify the Protectorate elites. It was left to Sir George's successor, Mr. R. O. Ramage, C.M.G., to impress upon the Chiefs the significance of a close relationship, or what Ramage called a "combination" between themselves and the educated elite. In his address to the Protectorate Assembly in October 1950 (some six months before the enactment of the first postwar Constitution for Sierra Leone) Governor Ramage declared: "The new constitution will represent a big step forward in the history of Sierra Leone . . . If it is to achieve its purpose, it will be essential to adapt traditional customs and practices to modern requirements. Traditionally the old men were the repositories of wisdom. They still are, but the younger men, thanks to education, also have their wisdom. It is essential that these younger men should be given an adequate opportunity to take part in government, whether in District Councils or elsewhere. If they are not given this opportunity, the result will be a feeling of frustration amongst them; and instead of the combination of old and younger wisdom being used for the progress of Sierra Leone, both may be wasted in mutual antagonisms. To achieve the best results will call for patience on both sides. Patience by the older men for the novel ideas of the younger, who may seem to want to change everything in a hurry; patience by the younger men for the ideas of the older who may seem reluctant to change anything at all. By patience and combination it will however be possible to obtain the best of both wisdoms and the result will be ... the orderly progress desired by all."[8]

Faced with the government pressure implicit in Governor Ramage's advice, the occurrence of peasant disturbances in the southern Provinces, and the opposition of the new elite who were peering at the possibility of lending leadership to the agitated rural populace, the Chiefs took close and immediate notice of the Governor's fatherly suggestions. By the end of 1950, following a series of consultations between the more progressive Chiefs and Dr. Milton Margai, the Protectorate Assembly augmented the representation of the new elite to six seats. In early 1951 the progressive Chiefs, now fully in accord with Dr. Margai on the course of constitutional development, joined the new elite in forming the SLPP. The consequences were foreseeable: the combination of Chiefs and the Protectorate new elite in the SLPP was to dominate political development in Sierra Leone for the next decade.

B. THE CONSTITUTIONAL PROPOSALS OF 1947

The outline of the postwar proposals for constitutional reform has already been presented. It is now necessary to consider the details of these proposals and their impact upon the Protectorate-Colony struggle for power.

The first postwar proposals were published in August 1947; their main provision was the establishment of an unofficial majority in the legislature.[9] The new Legislative Council would be composed of sixteen unofficial members as against eight officials, including the Governor, who remained President of the Council. In addition, there was to be an African majority within the unofficial majority: fourteen African members and two Europeans.

---

[8] Seventh Assembly Proceedings (Freetown, 1950), pp. 1–2.

[9] Despatch from Sir Hubert Stevenson to the Secretary of State for the Colonies, 13th October, 1947. Text of this Despatch is found in Proposals for the Reconstitution of the Legislative Council in Sierra Leone, Sessional Paper No. 2 of 1948 (Freetown, 1948), pp. 1–5. The latter is cited hereafter as Reconstitution Proposals.

And the total membership of twenty-four was also in favor of Africans—fourteen as against ten Europeans.

The Executive Council, however, was not to be affected by these changes in the legislature; it remained an official body save for its two nominated African members. Yet the Executive Council, in certain crucial spheres of its traditional relationship to the Legislative Council, was unlikely not to experience some diminution of its authority. For instance, the principle of unofficial nomination to the legislature by the Governor's favor, which was in practice exercised by the Governor in consultation with the Executive Council, was all but discarded under the 1947 proposals. All but one of the fourteen African members of the expanded Legislative Council would be elected either on direct franchise or through electoral colleges. Similarly, though the Governor remained President of the Legislative Council under the 1947 proposals, he would no longer "have an original or casting vote," which, like his exercise of the right of unofficial nomination, he invariably exercised on advice of the Executive Council. Thus the legislature could expect a large measure of independence from the Executive Council in this regard, for "when upon any question before the [Legislative] Council the votes are equally divided, the motion should be declared to be lost." The African majority in the proposed Legislative Council could, therefore, prevail on any issue around which it could muster the necessary votes.

Although these provisions of the 1947 Constitutional proposals represented a major step toward African self-government, there were still provisions which harked back to earlier colonial conservatism. Despite the application of the electoral principle to the fourteen members of the African unofficial majority, only four of these were to be elected on direct franchise and they were to represent Colony constituencies. Of the remaining unofficial members, who were to represent the Protectorate, nine were to be elected by the Protectorate Assembly and one would be nominated by the Governor from among the Assembly members. The overwhelming influence of Chiefs in the Assembly necessarily meant that the majority of the unofficial members in the Legislative Council would be of a very conservative cut.[10]

Yet, there was no gainsaying the real advances entailed in the 1947 Constitutional proposals. The different reactions of the Protectorate and the Colony leadership to these proposals were testimony to this. The Protectorate leaders, initially the Chiefs alone and by 1950 the new elite as well, openly embraced the proposals, seeing in them a whole range of new possibilities for the political and social advancement of the Protectorate. In particular, they saw in the 1947 proposals the first real opportunity to redress the Protectorate's long-standing disadvantages vis-à-vis the Colony. As Paramount Chief Bai Koblo, a leading spokesman for Protectorate interests in the postwar Legislative Council, observed during a debate on the 1947 proposals: "The old system is about to be finished and in this reconstitution paper is dawning a new day . . ."[11] In a later debate on the proposals in December 1948, Bai Koblo proceeded to specify at length the factors in the Protectorate's more backward standing vis-à-vis the Colony that would be rectified under the new Constitution:

We have in the Protectorate awaited the righting of the anomalous situation by which the Colony has enjoyed a larger elected representation in this Assembly. The slight majority which we are prepared to accept at the present time should not lead the inhabitants of the Colony to believe that we are easily satisfied. This is only the beginning of the process of the Protectorate coming to its own politically . . . I shall now proceed to mention a few of the reasons why we in the Protectorate do indeed need this majority to safeguard our interests in the future.

Education—Despite the growing need of the Protectorate for schools and teachers in order to remedy the deplorable fact that only about 4 per cent of the children of school-going age are able to attend, yet previous Legislative Councils have continued an unfair distribution of the funds for any educational development, by spending in the Colony

---

[10] All the provisions so far mentioned are given in *Reconstitution Proposals*, pp. 3–4. It should be noted that the new franchise for the Colony was still short of universal but was surely an advance over the limited franchise instituted in 1924.

[11] *Legislative Council Debates, No. III of Session 1947–1948* (Freetown, 1948), p. 30.

almost twice the money spent in the Protectorate. If the plans for the development of education in the Protectorate . . . are to be allowed to develop in the direction of placing priority to schemes in the Protectorate, then we need a Protectorate majority of sufficient size that proper budgetary allowances will be guaranteed.

Medical—Only the persistent reminder from the Protectorate members and an over-ruling voice seems to be able to attract their attention to the ordinary plans for the great needs of the Protectorate for medical care. We intend to use our majority to exert proper pressure to help relieve this situation . . . I want to state that I make no apologies for openly stating that we intend to use our majority to safeguard our interests whenever and wherever necessary.[12]

In contrast to the optimistic Protectorate reaction to the 1947 proposals was the despondent mood of the Colony response, which soon shaded off into implacable bitterness. The despondent stage of the Colony leaders' response was characterized by a rather shrewd attempt to capitalize on the fission within the Protectorate leadership at the time of the 1947 proposals. At the end of 1947 the Colony interests, under the leadership of Dr. H. C. Bankole-Bright, the General Secretary of the SLNC, demanded that three additional seats be given the Colony (bringing the total to seven) and that literacy be required of all Paramount Chiefs who stood for election to the Legislative Council. The Protectorate chiefly leaders accepted the first demand, with the proviso that three additional seats be granted the Protectorate as well; but they roundly opposed the literacy demand, as the Colony leaders must have imagined they would. The literacy proposal, after all, struck at the very nature of political influence in the Protectorate, based as it was upon Chiefs and the institutions they controlled. By 1947 only 20 per cent of the 200 or so Paramount Chiefs were literate, although 50 per cent of the Chiefs in the Protectorate Assembly were literate.[13] The colonial government itself had taken these realities into consideration when is-

---

[12] *Legislative Council Debates, No. I of Session 1948–1949* (Freetown, 1949), pp. 70–71.

[13] *Report of the Select Committee Appointed by His Excellency . . . to Consider Proposals for a Reconstituted Legislative Council in Sierra Leone, Sessional Paper No. 7 of 1948* (Freetown, 1948), p. 2; *Third Assembly Proceedings* (Freetown, 1948), pp. 9–11.

suing its proposals for constitutional reform: "It would be unwise initially to exclude potentially useful [chiefly] members on the grounds of their inability to pass a literacy test in English."[14]

The literacy proposal, then, clearly hit a sensitive chord in the structure of political influence in the Protectorate, and before its impact had spent itself—as there was little doubt it would—it momentarily ruffled relations among the Protectorate groups. The new elite in the Protectorate was already itself at odds with the colonial government and the Chiefs over the second-class status it was allocated in postwar development and accordingly welcomed the literacy proposal. "It is most alarming," remarked an SOS memorandum to the Secretary of State for the Colonies in 1948, "that neither the Protectorate Assembly, nor the special committee which considered the proposals for the new constitution, nor the Acting Governor, could arrive at a definite decision on this matter of literacy . . . merely on the ground that, if literacy qualifications [are] imposed, it would cause annoyance to a few illiterates who would for mere sentimental reasons want to be elected into the Legislative Council, whilst in reality they would not profit by the deliberation nor benefit the country by their presence in Council, since they would not contribute to the discussion . . . We therefore humbly pray that literacy qualifications be imposed."[15]

Among the Chiefs, the Colony's literacy demand, as already noted, was virtually rejected out-of-hand. But before even the Chiefs, displaying a growing heterogeneity of interests between their literate and illiterate members, could take this position, the literacy demand struck a momentarily divisive note. A rather sharp debate ensued in the Protectorate Assembly which revealed signs of a slight fissure in the hitherto unified chiefly political front. On one side was the small group of progressive and educated Chiefs led by the rather urbane Paramount Chief Julius Gulama of Moyamba District which had 56 per cent literacy among its Chiefs, the largest such rate in the Protectorate. They supported the literacy qualification. On the other side was the

[14] *Reconstitution Proposals,* p. 4.
[15] Margai and Anthony, *Memorandum on the Constitution.*

majority of illiterate Chiefs whose main spokesmen in the debate were Paramount Chief Sahr Siama of Kono District (80 per cent illiterate Chiefs), Paramount Chief Kai Tungi of Kailahun District (56 per cent illiterate Chiefs), Paramount Chief A. C. Demby of Bo District (61 per cent illiterate Chiefs), and Paramount Chief Kai Samba of Kenema District (75 per cent illiterate Chiefs).

The majority faction in the Protectorate Assembly opposed the Colony's literacy demand and, indeed, opposed any discussion whatever of the matter by the Assembly, fearing the discussion would exacerbate the differences among Chiefs. "I do not think we need hold any discussion on that [literacy issue]," declared Paramount Chief Mana Luseni of Pujehun District (which had 76 per cent illiterate Chiefs), "but leave it to the District Councils and the Assembly to do whatever they see fit at any time of election. Discussion may lead to a bar to illiteracy which might create ill-feelings; but this will be avoided if the position is left as it is and electors decide to elect whoever they like, whether literate or illiterate." When the issue came to a vote, the conservative faction prevailed: the motion by Paramount Chief Gulama to accept the literacy proposal was defeated, twenty-one votes against and seven in favor.[16] Furthermore, the subsequent movement, under stimulus of the colonial government, toward unification of the Chiefs and the new elite, eventually brought the latter to discard its earlier approval of the literacy proposal.

The Colony elite's failure to rally any durable Protectorate support around the literacy proposal led it toward an obstinately antagonistic outlook on nearly all features of the 1947 proposals. And this occurred despite several gestures by the government to placate Colony interests, including the rejection in late 1948 of the Protectorate Assembly's resolution opposing the literacy qualification for membership of the Legislative Council. It was clear beyond doubt that defeat stared the Creoles in the face; but as is not unusual for such groups who have had long-standing advantages, they seek to deny defeat by ritualizing the values and

---

[16] *Third Assembly Proceedings*, pp. 18–22. Literacy figures for Chiefs may be calculated from data in *Sierra Leone Protectorate Handbook, 1947*, pp. 3–17.

positions associated with their previous hegemony. Accordingly, in September 1948 a rather motley gathering of Creole political groups—led by the SLNC and including the Combined Rate-payers' Association, the West End (Freetown) Political Group, and the Sierra Leone Socialist Party—dispatched an idiosyncratic petition to the Secretary of State for the Colonies.[17] The petition dealt reverently with literacy as the *sine qua non* of representative government, rejecting out-of-hand what it called the colonial government's "plea that the illiterates should not be discouraged from entering the Legislative Council . . ." Then, as if to re-enact the Colony-Protectorate conflict over the 1924 Constitution, the petition reiterated the SLNC's argument of twenty-four years earlier that British-protected persons were in law unsuited for membership in the Legislative Council. "From a constitutional point of view," the petition observed, "a legislative council in the Colony with a majority of foreigners—as British protected persons are in the Commonwealth, is contrary to the whole conception of British citizenship. British citizens have the right that they shall be governed only by such persons as are of the same status as themselves . . . By the suggested set-up of Protectorate majority, persons who are not British subjects would be empowered to make legislation that may seriously affect the rights of British subjects. So long as Sierra Leone continues to be divided into Colony and Protectorate . . ., the people of the Protectorate cannot govern the people of the Colony even by a manipulation such as is proposed to be done by the new constitution."

The British government, of course, rejected the petition. But this did not deter the conservative Creole groups' ritualization of their defeat. They persisted in sundry petty attacks upon the postwar constitutional reforms for another decade, long after the 1947 proposals were eventually enacted in 1951. Priggishly derisive articles against Protectorate leaders filled the pages of the conservative Creole newspapers; further petitions and delegations

[17] *Memorandum Presented through the Sierra Leone Government to the Rt. Honourable Arthur Creech-Jones His Majesty's Principal Secretary of State for the Colonies . . . by the Political Organizations of The Colony . . . on the Subject of the Reconstitution of the Legislative Council of Sierra Leone* (mimeographed; Freetown, 1948).

were dispatched to the Colonial Office in London; a lawsuit against the 1951 Constitution was initiated by the Positive Action Party, an ultra-conservative Creole group, and carried ultimately to the Privy Council, where it was dismissed; and obstructionist tactics of all sorts were employed by Creole members of the Legislative Council.[18] In the latter case, on one occasion the Creole legislators moved the dissolution of the SLPP Executive Council by the colonial authorities on grounds that all groups in the Legislative Council were not represented in it. In view of the fact that a party system of representatives had already been established when the motion was put before the Legislative Council—its mover, incidentally, was Dr. Bankole-Bright—the hypocrisy and peevishness of it all was evident. As Paramount Chief Bai Farima Tass II, member for Kambia District and a minister in the first SLPP Cabinet, put it, the motion was "but child's play. It is just like what the native man commonly says that when a father is hungry he tells his wife to cook very quickly because the children are hungry."[19]

During the high point of the Colony's ritualistic antagonism to the constitutional proposals, the Protectorate leaders remained both passive and unconciliatory. They knew that it was simply a matter of time before effective political power in Sierra Leone was theirs; meanwhile they would permit the conservative Creoles to rant and rave but would offer no concessions to them. The deadlock between the two groups, however, disturbed the colonial authorities, who endeavored to bring the Creole leaders to their senses. In late 1949 the government warned the Creole leaders that their tactics were provoking among the Protectorate leaders "a growing impatience at the delay in setting up a new Legislative Council with an unofficial majority" and intimated that certain minor concessions might be made if they would cease

[18] For derisory articles, see the *Evening Dispatch* of December 3, 1949, p. 2, and January 19, 1950, p. 2. The *Dispatch* was edited and owned by Dr. H. C. Bankole-Bright, who founded the National Council of the Colony of Sierra Leone in 1950 as the leading Creole party. Creole petitions are reported in the *Sierra Leone Weekly News* of September 30, 1950, p. 1, and February 17, 1951, p. 6.

[19] *Legislative Council Debates, No. I of Session 1951–1952* (Freetown, 1952), p. 286. Cf. *Legislative Council Debates, Session 1951–1952*, Vol. II (Freetown, 1953), pp. 114–121.

their attacks on the 1947 proposals.[20] But, as we have said, the Creoles were less concerned with the political reality they confronted than with ritualizing the values and positions associated with their past ascendancy. As with primitive peoples, ritualization of life's circumstances becomes life (reality) itself. For the Creoles their ritualization was such a false reality—that is, it was an illusory buffer between their self-evaluation and the harsh world of political reality; it was superficially satisfying like all such buffers, and thus died hard, leaving the Colony unable to return to reality unassisted. In early 1950 the colonial government accordingly began what was to be a long series of blows which would ultimately assist the Creoles back to reality. It announced that "deadlock or no deadlock . . . we cannot afford to stand still any longer. We must go forward . . ."[21]

This announcement marked the beginning of the end for the long-standing Creole political advantage. In September 1950 the Protectorate leadership declared that it would seek immediate enactment of the constitutional reforms as originally proposed by government in 1947. This declaration was made in the course of an address delivered by Dr. Milton Margai, now the undisputed leader of the Protectorate groups, to the Protectorate Assembly, and it marked a turning point in the Colony-Protectorate conflict. It is not amiss to quote Dr. Margai's address at length:

Sierra Leone, which has been the foremost of all West African Colonies, is still saddled with an archaic constitution with official majority. The reason for this backwardness is evidently due to the fact that our forefathers, I regret very much to say, had given shelter to a handful of foreigners [ie., Creoles] who have no will to cooperate with us and imagine themselves to be our superiors because they are aping the Western mode of living, and have never breathed the true spirit of independence . . . We are very much unfortunate to have with us in this country a handful of foreigners whose leaders, whatever one may do, can never bring themselves to wipe off the superiority complex, and they imagine themselves more like Europeans than Africans, which is indeed a very sad state of affairs; and moreover they have never im-

[20] *Legislative Council Debates, No. II of Session 1949–1950* (Freetown, 1950), pp. 3–4.
[21] *Ibid.*

pressed us as being sincere in their actions toward us. If they would have their own way, they would prefer the old constitution to continue indefinitely because they have five men to represent them. Furthermore their arguments have been so unreasonable that to think of opening up the question will only result in prolonging our agony and unhappiness for want of proper representation . . . Feelings have run so high on both sides that no useful purpose will be served by sitting with them in a committee just now. After we shall have all calmed down we shall all be in a better frame of mind to remodel what we have accepted . . . If the 30,000 non-natives in the Colony should attempt a boycott, I make no hesitation to assure the Government that all of the seats on the Colony side would be occupied by our countrymen. We mean to push ahead and we are in no way prepared to allow a handful of foreigners to impede our progress.[22]

Although Dr. Margai's pronouncement was the first public statement of the Protectorate's intention to proceed forthwith to work the proposed constitutional arrangement, the colonial government was already aware that Protectorate leaders had reached this position by mid-1950. It had accordingly requested the British Colonial Office in May 1950 to approve a modified version of the original 1947 proposals. In June 1950 the Secretary of State for the Colonies informed the Sierra Leone government that "arrangements will now be made to prepare the necessary constitutional instruments, so that the new constitution can be brought into force early next year."[23] These instruments were finally agreed upon on April 9, 1951; the main instrument, the Sierra Leone (Legislative Council) Order in Council, was promulgated on November 19, 1951, by the Governor's Proclamation, Public Notice No. 106 of 1951. By this Order in Council the Sierra Leone Constitution of 1924 was revoked and a new constitutional framework was instituted around the principles of representative government, including political independence as the terminal point of colonial political change.

---

[22] *Seventh Assembly Proceedings*, pp. 28–31.
[23] *Reconstitution of the Legislative Council of Sierra Leone, 1950, Sessional Paper No. 2 of 1950* (Freetown, 1950), p. 4.

CHAPTER 10

Decolonization and Self-Government, 1951-1961

A. THE MEANING OF DECOLONIZATION

The context of political change during decolonization is qualitatively different from that of any preceding period. The constitutional structure, consisting of two parallel systems—the colonial and the emergent African-controlled regime—is explicitly in favor of African interests. A tacit agreement prevails to the effect that full constitutional powers will soon rest in African hands. In the social sphere as well, the process of decolonization tacitly recognizes that an African elite will replace the colonial oligarchy as, in Nadel's words, the "standard-setting group" in the modern social system.[1]

With regard to economic and financial matters, however, the process of decolonization does not necessarily imply African predominance. Decolonization, in fact, is not infrequently accompanied by an expansion of certain crucial aspects of the expatriate role in African economic and financial institutions. Cognizant of their own limitations in modern economic and financial capacity, the new African elite rely perforce upon expatriate interests of one sort or another in order to fulfill their plans for the economic development and diversification of their countries. Thus, despite the progressive transfer of political power to the African elite during decolonization, they seldom employ it to uproot the vestiges of

---

[1] S. F. Nadel, "African Elites," *International Social Science Bulletin,* Vol. III, No. 3 (1956), 415 ff.

expatriate economic control. The best they can hope for is to expand regulatory control over expatriate economic activities.

This sort of interaction produces a form of accommodation by the African elite to the decolonizing procedures pursued by the colonial regimes.[2] Indeed, throughout decolonization there is an apparent identity of interests between the African elite and the colonial oligarchy; and within limits this identity of interests shapes the process of constitutional reorganization preparatory to independence.

B. CONSTITUTIONAL STRUCTURE OF DECOLONIZATION

In general, the constitutional reorganization of Sierra Leone between 1951 and 1961 entailed marginal adjustments between the colonial authorities and the African elite. These adjustments centered upon such technical matters as the timing of African assumption of leading political roles, safeguards to be provided by a future independent Sierra Leone government for expatriate interests, and the nature of the bureaucratic framework within which these interests would continue to function. At no point in the course of effecting these adjustments were there any substantive differences between the colonial authorities and the African elite. What differences there were paled into insignificance in face of the basic identity of interests between these groups.

The constitutional basis of the identity of interests between the colonial oligarchy and the African elite was laid down in 1951 when the Legislative and Executive Councils received an African majority. This marked the beginning of a progressive and relentless movement toward the transfer of power. Within one year the Governor proposed that African members of the Executive Council assume ministerial portfolios. In announcing this proposal, the Governor remarked that it was "the inevitable consequence of the introduction of an unofficial majority in the Legislature."[3] Initially,

[2] Cf. Martin Kilson, "African Political Change and the Modernization Process," *Journal of Modern African Studies* (December 1963).

[3] *Ninth Assembly Proceedings* (Freetown, 1952), p. 3. Cf. *Legislative Council Debates, Vol. I of Session 1952–1953* (Freetown, 1954), pp. 229. See also pp. 208–209.

the African members of the Executive Council were granted responsibility for only the administrative side of the government departments entrusted to them; responsibility for policy-making was not extended until 1953, at which time the leading African minister, Sir Milton Margai, was named Chief Minister and later (1956) Premier.

Although an African cabinet was established in 1953 with policy-making authority for a limited range of executive functions, the colonial authorities held out for the retention of the expatriate department heads falling under the authority of African ministers. These expatriate officials also continued membership in the Legislative Council, though not in the Executive Council, and had virtually concurrent responsibility with African ministers for defending policy of their departments in the Legislature. The reason for this arrangement was simply the need to maintain a reasonable level of technical and administrative proficiency in the central departments while African ministers found their footing and while an African bureaucracy was being formed. As the Governor, Sir George Beresford-Stooke, explained the matter in his official proposal to the Colonial Office for appointing African ministers: "I recommend that there should be for the present no change in the constitution of the Legislative Council, and that the [expatriate] Directors of Medical Services, Education and Agriculture should continue to sit. While [African] Ministers would be responsible for introducing into the Legislative Council all questions concerning subjects coming within their portfolios, it would for the time being be an advantage to have the assistance of these Directors who should be able to make useful contributions to the debates, particularly in the elucidation of professional and technical points."[4]

In other spheres of the central governing bureaucracy, especially with regard to the civil service, the judiciary, finance, and defense and foreign affairs, effective authority for policy-making

[4] *Assumption of Ministerial Portfolios, Sessional Paper No. 1 of 1953* (Freetown, 1953), p. 1. Sir Milton Margai supported the Governor's proposal and went so far as to advocate that some officials be given portfolios in his cabinet. See *Legislative Council Debates, Vol. I of Session 1952–1953*, p. 229.

and administration was retained by the colonial government until two years before the grant of independence. As regards the public service, the Governor retained ultimate responsibility for it and was unapologetic in his defense of this decision. He informed the Colonial Office in 1953 that "on this question I need not say more than it is widely recognised that the preservation of a loyal, contented and efficient Civil Service depends to a great extent upon keeping the Service free from political interference [by African ministerial government and party system]." Yet the colonial authorities recognized the stage of decolonization for what it was—namely, an arrangement preparatory to the transfer of power. It was accordingly necessary to accommodate a measure of African responsibility for the public service; a statutory Public Service Commission was therefore created, chaired by a senior expatriate official, "with a strong and impartial [mixed] membership," and empowered to oversee the Africanization of the civil service in conjunction with the Governor.[5] Seven years later, in 1960, the chairmanship of the Commission was given to an African, Mr. A. J. Momoh, and the membership fully Africanized.

A rather different arrangement was fashioned to handle the departments of justice and finance during decolonization. The expatriate heads of these departments retained not only administrative control at the establishment of African ministerial government in 1953 but also full policy-making responsibility. It was not until 1958, three years prior to the transfer of power, that this situation was materially altered. In that year it was agreed that the Attorney-General, an expatriate official, would no longer sit in the Executive Council and that his policy-making function in judiciary matters would be assumed by the African Prime Minister, Sir Milton Margai. However, the expatriate Attorney-General continued to sit in the Legislature "for the purpose of explaining legal technicalities and such like matters," and he continued his executive responsibility "for the initiation, conduct and discontinuance of criminal proceedings, as it is in no wise desired that these should become political functions." This arrangement lasted until 1961 when an African became Minister of Justice.

[5] *Assumption of Ministerial Portfolios, Sessional Paper No. 1 of 1953,* p. 2.

Finance and foreign affairs equally remained the executive responsibility of the Governor and his advisers until shortly before independence. In 1958 an African, Mr. M. S. Mustapha, was appointed Minister of Finance but with only administrative authority, or what Governor Sir Maurice Dorman described as "full responsibility for control of Sierra Leone's financial affairs . . ." Executive responsibility, on the other hand, was reserved for an expatriate Financial Secretary whose duties were described by the Governor as "the principal financial adviser to the Government . . ."[6] This arrangement proved one of the few cases during decolonization where rather sharp disagreement occurred within the SLPP government regarding the process of constitutional reorganization; it was considered utterly inconsistent to appoint an African Minister of Finance and simultaneously retain an expatriate as principal financial adviser. In 1959 the issue was resolved by making the expatriate Financial Secretary the Permanent Secretary to the Minister of Finance.

Finally, the responsibility for foreign affairs and defense remained with the Governor until 1960 when an African Minister of External Affairs, Dr. John Karefa-Smart, was appointed. As with the other sectors of the central bureaucracy, there was no difficulty in convincing the SLPP leadership of the need to reserve powers over foreign affairs and defense in the Governor's hands. There was little doubt, after all, that the colonial authorities could pursue the emergent state's foreign interests and protect its territorial integrity far better than the African regime could. The financial burden of these undertakings was far beyond the ken of the SLPP government; in 1959–60 some 70 per cent of Sierra Leone's military establishment, including internal security forces, was supported by subvention from Britain.[7] The British government also was responsible for training the African officer corps, and at independence the armed forces remained largely under the command of British officers.

[6] Governor Dorman's statements about the Attorney-General and the Ministry of Finance appear in *Exchange of Despatches on Further Constitutional Change, Sessional Paper No. 2 of 1958* (Freetown, 1958), pp. 5–6.

[7] *Sierra Leone Government Estimates of Revenue and Expenditure, 1959–1960* (Freetown, 1959), p. 34.

C. CONCLUSION

Unlike the precipitous decolonization publicly demanded by African nationalists, the constitutional reorganization of Sierra Leone's government preparatory to the transfer of power entailed little conflict between the African elite and expatriate officials. It was largely a matter of transferring executive functions in an orderly way and ensuring continuity in administration. The Europeans desired to maintain certain financial and military interests under the post-colonial regime, and the African political elite recognized this as legitimate.

The identity of interests between the African elite and expatriate groups was carried over into the post-colonial period in Sierra Leone in a number of ways. In April 1960 the British government agreed to assist Sierra Leone with matters of defense, development, and civil service through a grant of £7 million.[8] Though the post-colonial era inevitably produces complicating situations for the maintenance of the identity of interests between the African elite and expatriate groups, there are few reasons to doubt that it will remain a part of the political landscape of most African states.

[8] *Report of the Sierra Leone Constitutional Conference, 1960* (Freetown, 1960), pp. 7–8.

The Rt. Hon. Sir Milton Margai, Chief Minister of Sierra Leone, 1951–1953, Premier, 1953–1958, Prime Minister, 1958–1964. (Photo courtesy of the Embassy of Sierra Leone, Washington, D.C.)

The Hon. Albert Margai, Prime Minister of Sierra Leone. (Embassy of Sierra Leone, Washington, D.C.)

Sir Milton Margai campaigning on behalf of A. B. Pailla, SLPP candidate in the Freetown West Constituency during the 1962 election. Sir Milton rarely mounted the platform at rallies. (**Sierra Leone Daily Mail.**)

The Hon. I. T. A. Wallace-Johnson, founder and leader of the Sierra Leone Youth League, 1938–1949, and leader of the Radical Democratic Party, 1958–1961. He is seen here at a rally of the All People's Congress in the Freetown West Constituency during the 1962 election campaign. Seated at left is Mrs. Stella Ralph-James, a well-known political figure among Sierra Leone women. (**Sierra Leone Daily Mail.**)

Paramount Chief Julius Gulama, Kai-yamba Chiefdom, Moyamba District, 1928–1950. He was a member of the Protectorate Assembly at Bo, 1946–1949, and the only Chiefly patron of the Sierra Leone Organization Society, 1946–1949. (Sierra Leone Ministry of Information.)

The Hon. Dr. H. C. Bankole-Bright, leader of the National Council of the Colony of Sierra Leone, 1950–1958. (Sierra Leone Ministry of Information.)

The Hon. Dr. John Karefa-Smart, President of the Sierra Leone Organization Society, 1946–1949, member of SLPP Cabinet, 1957–1964. (Sierra Leone Ministry of Information.)

The Hon. Siaka Stevens, deputy leader of the People's National Party, 1958–1961, leader of the All People's Congress since 1961. Here he is appearing at a mass APC rally in the Freetown West Constituency in 1962. **(Sierra Leone Daily Mail.)**

Paramount Chief Fula Mansa Bimbe Koro II, Yoni Chiefdom, Tonkolili District, and Madame Ella Koblo Gulama, Paramount Chief in Kaiyamba Chiefdom, Moyamba District, campaigning in Tonkolili West Constituency on behalf of Dr. John Karefa-Smart, SLPP candidate, seen behind Madame Gulama on left. (**Sierra Leone Daily Mail.**)

Mrs. Constance Cummings-John, founder of the Federation of Sierra Leonean Women and one of the three leading women in Sierra Leonean politics. The meeting shown here was held by the SLPP to instruct the public in voting procedure in the Freetown Central Constituency, which Mrs. Cummings-John contested and lost in 1962. (Mrs. Constance Cummings-John.)

Private home of the late Paramount Chief Bai Farima Tass II, Kambia District. (M. Kilson.)

D. Jalloh, Propaganda Secretary of the UPP, campaigning in a slum settlement in Freetown West. **(Sierra Leone Daily Mail.)**

Madame Nancy Koroma, Mende Tribal Headman in Freetown, who is one of the leading women in Sierra Leone politics. (M. Kilson.)

The Hon. Tamba S. Mbriwa (arrow), President of the Kono Progressive Movement and the Sierra Leone Progressive Independence Movement, speaking to an SLPIM meeting in Sefadu, Kono District. (**Sierra Leone Daily Mail.**)

Part IV -

Postwar Local Government and Political Change

CHAPTER 11

Populist Forces in Local Political Change

Social change was very much intensified during World War II, resulting, among other things, in a diminution of the local populace's allegiance to traditional institutions. This weakening of traditional allegiances was greatest among young school-leavers, some cash-crop peasants, and rural wage-earners; and though these groups were often unclear about the use of their new self-consciousness, they stimulated postwar "populist" pressures for political change.

In describing local political pressures as "populist," I do not suggest that they were part of a systematic egalitarian political ideology. I simply mean that they represented the lower reaches of provincial society; they came nearest to reflecting the political feelings of what we may call the masses—the little people.

Pressures for change in local political institutions were first asserted by the so-called "young men" among the rural populace. The term "young men" was often used in the reports of colonial officials to describe two types of politically assertive groups within the rural and town-dwelling hinterland population. One group consisted simply of the more or less youthful members of the population who, during World War II and after, increasingly severed their ties with traditional society through a certain amount of education and through work experiences in the money economy. As such they became a disturbing factor in the local political system. The Chief Commissioner characterized this group in his annual report for 1948 as follows: "The Commissioner, Northern

179

Province . . . commented on the increasing number of 'dead-end kids,' boys who had just left school and have neither the education for clerical jobs nor the desire to remain on the land. To them the bright lights of Bo, Makeni and Port Loko [all hinterland towns] were a dangerous attraction. The District Commissioner, Kabala, also reported that the high dowry being demanded by Yalunka fathers was driving young men out of the district. Some of them presumably drifted into the urban areas, where love hovered with less confined wings."[1]

The other element among the "young men" was comprised of adult males in the age range 25–35 years who were past "adolescent rebellion" but who were increasingly involved in and dependent upon the modern market. Some were small-scale cash-crop farmers who, though spending most of their life in the traditional setting, were broadening their contact with the modern system. Others were independent traders in hinterland towns, and some were wage-laborers employed in small expatriate firms, in government services, or on cash-crop farms owned by Africans.[2] A number of persons among these groups were ex-servicemen who returned to their hinterland homes after World War II but were not easily integrated into the old way of life. It was this second category of "young men" who spearheaded the postwar pressures for local political change.

A. CAUSES OF POPULIST POLITICAL PRESSURES

One feature of the local political system against which populist pressures were directed was the corrupt, extortionist, and generally inefficient behavior of traditional rulers who controlled Native Administrations. This behavior was fundamental to the Chiefs' astute manipulation of traditional authority in ways that maximized their power in the modern sector of colonial society.

[1] L. W. Wilson, *Annual Report on the Sierra Leone Protectorate for the Year 1948* (Freetown, 1950), p. 3—cited hereafter as *Protectorate Report* by year.

[2] For an excellent account of the postwar position of traders in a northern Sierra Leonean hinterland town, see Vernon R. Dorjahn, "African Traders in Central Sierra Leone," in Paul Bohannan and George Dalton, eds., *Markets in Africa* (Evanston, Ill., 1962), pp. 61–88.

As the District Commissioner of Kailahun District put it in 1948, this situation reflected the desire of Chiefs "to have their cake and eat it—on no account do they wish to pay for it."[3] The Chief Commissioner's report for 1947 described the corrupt and abusive practices of Chiefs at length and noted their disturbing influences among the local populace:

In Bongor Chiefdom [Bo District], where the Paramount Chief was deposed in April, 1947, for practices contrary to the interests of good government, the Native Administration has been a dismal failure. As a result of extortion and the infliction of illegal fines and levies the Native Administration court fell into disrepute, and illegal private courts sprang up. Under such conditions development of any kind was impossible and there is reported to be little hope of making a fresh start until an honest and efficient Chief is elected. Other examples are not wanting and it is clear that if one object of policy must be to reduce the number of chiefdom units, another must be to raise the standard of chieftainship . . . There is always a temptation for Paramount Chiefs to recoup themselves by illicit means. Finding themselves unable to support the pomp and circumstances to which they feel themselves entitled, they are all too apt to see a ready way out of their difficulties in the imposition of illegal levies, the holding of surreptitious courts, or the use of forced labour. Whether from a sense of loyalty to the chiefdom, or from fear of the consequences, sufferers from such abuses are generally slow in coming forward with complaints until their grievances burst bounds and disgruntlement becomes so widespread that only drastic action can cure the ill . . . Two [other instances of corruption] which came to light during the year must be mentioned. In Lower Bambara Chiefdom in Kenema District [one of the wealthiest in the area] a Commission of Enquiry had to be appointed to investigate a long list of alleged malpractices by the Paramount Chief . . . In Bagru Chiefdom in Moyamba District, a large crop of allegations of extortion by the Paramount Chief under cover of Poro Customs was under investigation when the year closed.[4]

Similarly, in the Chief Commissioner's report on Provincial Administration for 1948 it was observed that in Port Loko District, Northern Province, Chiefs viewed their Native Administrations "as their personal property during their lifetime," and some "seemed shamelessly preoccupied with lining their pockets." The

---

[3] Wilson, *Protectorate Report for 1948*, p. 7.
[4] Hubert Childs, *Protectorate Report for 1947* (Freetown, 1949), pp. 7–8.

181

report further remarked that "this attitude on the part of chiefs, though regrettable, was not in any way surprising. They were in the position of feudal rulers suddenly introduced to a money economy. The temptation to capitalize feudal services was more than many of them could resist, any more than their predecessors in other countries had been able. And, as in other countries, a corresponding difficulty was that the majority of their subjects still expected the chiefs to perform many of the functions of feudal rulers, particularly in regard to hospitality."[5]

Related to the abusive and corrupt practices was the authoritarian character of the Native Administrations. The colonial authorities were not unaware of this feature of Native Administrations, and they endeavored to correct it in order to ensure law and order in face of the social changes generated by World War II. The Chief Commissioner's report for 1947 described the position of Chiefs in Native Administration as that of "a petty autocrat." The report also recorded the following observations of Provincial and District Commissioners on the nature of this autocracy:

[Provincial Commissioner, Southeastern Province] reports that at meetings of Tribal Authorities it is rare for a member to express any view contrary to that of the Chief, and that when he does so it is usually indicative of bad relations between the two. The conception that there must be "one word" with the Chief is so ingrained that great difficulty is found in explaining even to the more educated Chiefs that a difference of opinion or an independent point of view is not a matter of complaint, and that free discussion can be a source of strength rather than of weakness . . . A District Commissioner in the Southwestern Province refers to the members of Tribal Authorities in his district as "Yes-men" who dare not oppose the wishes of the Paramount Chiefs.[6]

It was, then, within this thoroughly corrupt, inefficient, and autocratic system of local government that populist pressures for political change emerged. Soon, however, pressure was applied from the top as well as the bottom. As we will see in the next

[5] Wilson, *Protectorate Report for 1948*, p. 6.
[6] Childs, *Protectorate Report for 1947*, p. 8.

two chapters, the colonial authorities themselves recognized the need to reform Native Administrations so as to avert the more riotous forms of populist pressures.

B. NATURE OF POPULIST POLITICAL DEMANDS

Though basically modern in purpose or inspiration, populist demands for local political change were not precise about the institutional form the desired change should take. This, of course, was not surprising insofar as the rural masses lacked both the knowledge and experience necessary to formulate details of institutional change. Nor was it always clear that populist political pressures were directed against the traditional authority structure as such, seeking its destruction as a legitimate political institution. Given the ambivalence of most rural Africans toward the chiefly groups, they were unable to push grievances against traditional authority to the point of outright revolution. Many populist demands went no further than to request the removal of a particular Paramount Chief or Section Chief but not the displacement of his office as such.[7] Furthermore, the groups who spearheaded popular protest not infrequently asserted their demands within a traditional framework. Thus in his annual report for 1948 the Chief Commissioner observed that "when 'young men' made complaints of a general nature they had usually obtained the approval of their headmen before coming forward in public."[8]

Despite the traditional framework of projecting populist demands, what discontented groups asked for had, as already noted, a basically modern character. For instance, when Native Administrations gave the appearance of widening their basis of representation by nominating younger men who were related to traditional ruling families in replacement of older men, the populist groups

[7] Childs, *Protectorate Report for 1951* (Freetown, 1952), p. 2.

[8] Wilson, *Protectorate Report for 1948*, p. 7. The use of some traditional mode was a characteristic feature of peasant political expression throughout colonial Africa and reached a high point of organizational development in Ghana between the two World Wars, as I shall show in a forthcoming study entitled "Chiefs, Peasants, and Politicians: Grass-roots Politics in Ghana, 1900–61."

considered this unsatisfactory and demanded that commoners be selected.[9] In general, the populist groups favored a sort of modern-based functional representation of commoner elements in the Native Administrations, such as representatives of traders, cash-crop farmers, wage-laborers, and so on. By 1952 representation of this sort had been instituted in a number of Native Administrations; the District Commissioner for Bonthe District, Southwestern Province, noted in his report for 1952 that "the inclusion of workers' representatives as members of the Tribal Authorities was found on the whole to be a success, and a few chiefdoms started to appoint representatives of traders as well."[10]

Another important feature of the populist pressures upon local government was that they were seldom directed toward the colonial government or European dominance as such. They used neither the language nor symbols normally associated with the anti-colonial nationalist expression of the urban elite. Even the riotous acts often associated with populist demands were not directed explicitly against the colonial authorities. Although such acts invariably entailed widespread damage to property, it was seldom the property of European expatriate groups but was more frequently the property of Chiefs that was damaged. This feature of the populist pressures was commented upon by the Chief Commissioner in his report for 1949–50: "A number of generalisations with regard to these events can be made. In the first place the disorders which occurred were in every case chiefdom affairs and were in no way directed against Government or against authority in general. This is an important fact which needs to be kept continually in mind. The disturbers of the peace repeatedly showed by their conduct that they had no wish to quarrel with Government and were animated by no ill will towards the [European] Administration."[11]

This observation, however, might be challenged. Into the riotous

[9] *Ibid.*, pp. 7–8.

[10] Hubert Childs, *Annual Report on the Provincial Administration for the Year 1952* (Freetown, 1953), p. 10—cited hereafter as *Provinces Report* by year.

[11] Childs, *Protectorate Report for 1949–1950* (Freetown, 1952), p. 4.

forms of populist expression could be read a "hidden" or indirect anti-colonial feature. Insofar as Chiefs and other tribal authorities in the Native Administrations were the creation of colonial authority, any populist outburst against them was at least an indirect attack upon the colonial regime. What complicated this situation was that Chiefs and their Native Administrations were simultaneously both traditional and modern (i.e., colonial) as regards their authority and power. On the other hand, the populist groups who criticized Chiefs were themselves only peripherally involved in the modern sector of colonial society, still clinging to many traditional patterns. It was, then, reasonable that colonial officials would view the traditional factor that the populists and Chiefs had in common as the main source of any dispute between them.[12]

Furthermore, there was a natural tendency for colonial officials to look elsewhere than the colonial system itself for causes of conflicts between Chiefs and the local population. Indeed, for some British officials it was virtually inconceivable that *their* colonial system could itself be a cause of violent populist discontent. Such discontent, they believed, stemmed more from a distortion by Chiefs of traditional political norms than from the particular manner in which colonial change affected the traditional system. Nevertheless, by 1952 the Sierra Leone government felt compelled to overcome these disputes by democratizing the system of local government. The Provincial Commissioner, Southwestern Province, said in 1951 that the government hoped its attempts at democratizing local government in that year would "calm the spirit of restlessness and rebellion which has been an

[12] Cf. Childs, *Protectorate Report for 1951*, p. 3. A similar situation prevailed in the central Gold Coast area of Ashanti in the postwar period. Professor Busia correctly attributed this political conflict between Chiefs and populist groups to colonial change but also delineated how the persistent traditional patterns were in a real sense involved. As he put it: "Some subsidiary charges also recur: that the chief has violated native custom; that he has broken the laws to which he assented on his enstoolment; that he does not add to stool property . . . With native custom in its present confused state it is always possible to find a custom that the chief has violated. For example, a chief who owned private [modern] property (houses and cocoa-farms) was said to have violated custom." K. A. Busia, *Position of Chiefs in the Modern Political System of Ashanti* (London, 1951), p. 214.

185

unfortunate feature in some chiefdoms during the past five years."[13]

A final feature of the populist responses in postwar society should be mentioned. It is assumed by many observers that such responses are essentially chaotic, aimless and atavistic in nature. To some extent this is true; as noted earlier, the groups who perpetrate violent acts in local African society have at best a precarious foothold in modern society and claim few of the skills for political action based upon a precise definition of goals.[14] Yet, on closer observation, the violent populist responses may *themselves* reveal something about the goals of their perpetrators. More specifically, by considering the objects of populist violence one may gain insight into both the goals of the populist groups and the causes of their violent behavior.[15]

Evidence for this proposition is found in official accounts of postwar populist disturbances in the Sierra Leone Protectorate. In nearly all instances of such disturbances the issues in dispute related directly to the way colonial change affected relations between Chiefs and the rural populace. The autocratic position of Chiefs in the Native Administration system was often singled out as a main object of populist criticism. This is evident in the following account of riots in the Southern Provinces during 1948–50:

The Baoma Chiefdom [Bo District] disorders took place in November, 1948. In the early months of 1949 more than one hundred persons

[13] Childs, *Protectorate Report for 1952*, p. 9.

[14] It would seem that only among the more skilled wage-laborers in such places as the hinterland mining towns does one find a specific populist definition of goals. One such instance in Sierra Leone was a strike in 1950 by the African United Mine Workers' Union in the iron-ore mining towns of Marampa and Pepel, Northern Province. Strikers burned "the house of the African personnel officer and committed various other acts of hooliganism and violence," but the goals involved were quite clear: the union wanted the British iron-ore firm, the Sierra Leone Development Company, to negotiate in all matters affecting the workers with their own elected representative and Secretary General, Mr. Siaka Stevens, who was himself a former mine worker. See "Report of the Board of Inquiry into the Causes and Circumstances of the Stoppages of Work at the Works of the Sierra Leone Development Company, Ltd., October, 1950, at Marampa and Pepel" (mimeographed; Sierra Leone Government Archives), pp. 11 ff., 19 ff.

[15] Cf. Karl Marx's analysis of workers' anti-machine rebellion in *Capital* (New York, 1936), pp. 466–468.

were committed for trial before the Supreme Court for their part in these disorders . . . There seems to be grounds for thinking that the apparent success of the malcontents in Baoma Chiefdom in securing the removal of a Paramount Chief who had become obnoxious to an important section of his people may have caused persons elsewhere who felt themselves to be laboring under similar injustices to seek their remedy in the same way . . . More serious was the situation which was building up throughout 1949 in Kailahun District against the administration and conduct of the Paramount Chief of Luawa Chiefdom, the biggest Chiefdom in the district with headquarters at Kailahun. When all attempts to reach a settlement failed it became necessary for a Commission of Inquiry to be held . . . into the conduct of the Paramount Chief . . . The decision that he was to be deposed was . . . not in time to prevent an outbreak of rioting involving about 5,000 people at Kailahun on the 30th of October, 1950. The cause of the riot was a rumour that the Paramount Chief had been upheld [by colonial government] and was to be reinstated in the chiefdom. The extent and violence of the rioting, which spread from Kailahun to outlying towns and villages in the chiefdom . . ., [entailed] casualties and considerable damage to property.[16]

In other instances the populist groups concentrated upon tax policies as the object of their grievances. Sometimes they cried out against the general maladministration by Chiefs and tribal authorities. These were the main objects of widespread populist riots in Pujehun District, Southeastern Province, in 1951, as revealed in the following account:

Trouble started in January with a number of complaints against the Paramount Chief. An inquiry was held at Bandajuma, the headquarters town of [Sowa] chiefdom, in February by the Acting Provincial Commissioner who found that the Chief had been responsible for certain acts of maladministration but that these were not of so serious a nature as to merit deposition. In accordance with well-established native custom he ordered the Chief to pay compensation. Certain other directions were given which it was hoped would remove the discontent, but instead of this, on the 3rd of March, only two days after the Acting Provincial Commissioner's decision, an armed attack was made on the Paramount Chief's house at night. This was repelled by the force of Court Messengers [Police] held at Bandajuma, but the occurrence

[16] Childs, *Protectorate Report for 1949–1950*, pp. 4–5; Childs, *Protectorate Report for 1951*, p. 2.

showed how uncompromising was the opposition to the Chief. This was further confirmed on the 15th of March when an attempt to collect house tax in the chiefdom, in accordance with a tax programme which had long been announced and which it was not thought appropriate to postpone on account of these events, was met by blunt refusal by a number of villages to pay unless the Chief was first deposed. This attitude was accompanied by a campaign of intimidation making it virtually impossible to secure support from the moderate people in the chiefdom, or to obtain evidence against those who had instigated or taken part in the attack on the Chief's house. In these circumstances . . . four of the principal agitators, who had declined even to discuss a settlement except on their own terms, were ordered to leave Pujehun District . . . This measure did not have the result of restoring the Chief's authority . . . Further attempts were being made to arrest the others when events came to a climax on the 2nd of June with an attack on Bandajuma by rioters from outlying villages estimated to number about 300 men . . . This necessitated the most vigorous police action . . . Altogether 101 persons were committed on serious charges for trial before the Supreme Court, and many others were dealt with summarily in the Magistrate's Court and by the Native Court. It was thus shown that violence would not be tolerated, but a large part of the chiefdom remained stubbornly hostile to the Paramount Chief who, for his part, decided that his best course was to leave the chiefdom . . .[17]

In late 1955 and early 1956 tens of thousands of peasants and rural and town wage-laborers participated in riots which a commission of inquiry described as "mass disobedience to authority in the matter of tax collection . . ."[18] From the Northern Province District of Kambia to the Southeastern Pujehun District a populist groundswell against taxes resulted in great violence. An additional object of this populist reaction was the modern property

[17] Childs, *Protectorate Report for 1951*, p. 3; Childs, *Protectorate Report for 1952*, p. 5.
[18] Sir Herbert Cox, *Sierra Leone Report of Commission of Inquiry into Disturbances in the Provinces, November 1955 to March 1956* (London, 1956), p. 15. Taxes and related financial maladministration were a common cause of populist claims against traditional rulers in other African territories. Busia noted innumerable instances of this in the particular form of populist-chief conflict that surrounded the "destoolment" episodes in Ashanti. "Nowadays the most common cause [of destoolments] is that of 'misappropriating stool funds.' This has become a prominent charge against chiefs since the 1920's . . . The charge now regularly appears in every destoolment case." Busia, *Position of Chiefs in the Modern Political System of Ashanti*, p. 214.

accumulated by Paramount Chiefs as well as lesser rulers. The rioters burned or otherwise destroyed Chiefs' automobiles, transport vans, modern houses, and sundry other property; they also destroyed tons of crops and maimed or killed Chiefs' livestock. The property damage done in these riots was conservatively estimated by the commission of inquiry at £750,000; but "that is exclusive of the damage to trade in the affected areas."[19]

In view of these instances of the objects of populist violence, it is evident that they were all related to specific features of local administration that proved unjust or unduly burdensome to the masses. Thus (1) corrupt tax administration was at the root of much of the modern wealth accumulated by Chiefs; and (2) abusive exercise of customary rights to tribute and communal labor was a source of Chiefs' large surpluses of cash crops. It was only when the colonial government rectified these features of local administration, mainly through the extension of democratic reforms to the rural masses, that a more orderly mode of local political change was possible. As already indicated, the colonial government was not unaware of this, and throughout the 1950's it proceeded to reform the whole system of local government.

C. ELITE-MASS RELATIONSHIPS AND POLITICAL CHANGE

Ultimately, the importance of local populist pressures depended upon the way they affected the politics of the urban-based nationalist elites. In general, the more radical nationalist groups like the People's National Party and the United Progressive Party supported the populist forces in the hope of using them in the contest for political office. For the radicals, populism widened the basis of political appeal in rural areas, providing them their first opportunity for penetrating the local power structure hitherto dominated by traditional rulers. The SLPP, on the other hand, which was intimately associated with the chiefly ruling strata, opposed populism and sought to suppress all populist initiatives for political change.

[19] Cox, *Inquiry into Disturbances in the Provinces*, p. 15.

189

This policy was forcefully initiated by Dr. Milton Margai, leader of the SLPP, at the 1952 meeting of the Protectorate Assembly, a Chief-dominated body. During the course of a debate on populist riots, Dr. Margai proferred the following motion: "Be it resolved that this House expresses its entire disapproval of the frequent outbreaks of lawlessness in some parts of the Protectorate and urges the Government that after going very carefully into the complaints made constitutionally and through the proper channel to take the firmest action possible against any person, or group of people, who attempt to take the law into their own hands." In defense of the motion—which was carried unanimously—Dr. Margai remarked: "This motion is due to the fact that it is quite evident that there has been a lot of lawlessness in some parts of the Protectorate . . . Some people naturally feel that by threatening the Government or organising themselves into a group and using threats they will be able to force the hands of the Government to do what is not right. We as a body, a duly constituted body of elected representatives, should really stand and voice out our opinion that we do not like such methods . . . I stress firmly that we should register our strong disapproval of such action taken by some of our lawless people, and ask Government to adopt the firmest measures to quell these things."[20]

As Dr. Margai was well aware, his insensitive response to populist demands was precisely what his chiefly allies required as a condition of their support of the SLPP. His motion for suppression of populism was immediately supported by Paramount Chief Bai Koblo, a well-educated and wealthy Chief from Port Loko District who was an early supporter of the SLPP. "I rise to support this motion in all its entirety," he informed the Protectorate Assembly, "for the simple reason that it has been thought by some people in the Protectorate that they can use intimidation to secure their own ends . . . In some districts our economic advancement has been fettered to a great extent through outbursts organized by revolutionists [populists], and it is time that the Government should take firm measures to put these hooligans under control.

[20] *Ninth Assembly Proceedings* (Freetown, 1952), p. 31.

We cannot prosper as a people if lawlessness is tolerated . . . We are all handicapped when our economic advancement, which was calculated to put Sierra Leone on a firm footing, is set back. Setbacks in various districts are due to these outbreaks . . . I feel that the motion as it stands is proper, and I endorse it wholeheartedly and crave the support of all members in this House to see that this attempted lunacy is controlled by government once and for all."[21]

Thus, the dominant nationalist elite groups were adamantly opposed to populist pressures for political change. The SLPP had no hesitation whatever about the outright suppression of populism. Even the differences it had with the colonial regime—none of which, incidentally, was ever fundamental—did not perturb the SLPP's policy of alliance with colonial authority in quelling populist outbursts. The SLPP, in fact, was more prone to use coercion in face of populist claims than was the colonial authority. Moreover, this situation recurs in the post-colonial period in Sierra Leone and other African states in the form of the closing of ranks among factions of the new elite to create the authoritarian single-party regime. The party, having usurped the field of political action, becomes the guarantor against precipitous and unwanted populist demands; it constitutes, in effect, a veritable dictatorship of the black bourgeoisie.

D. CONCLUSION

In view of the above it is evident that, nationalist myths to the contrary notwithstanding, there is no necessary harmony of interests between African elite groups and mass elements during colonial political change. No doubt there were periods when a relative harmony of interests between these groups prevailed. But analysis of the different way in which colonial change affected elites and masses at different periods strongly suggests the unlikelihood of any automatic or universal harmony of interests among these groups.

[21] *Ibid.,* p. 32.

191

Far more than has been recognized by some observers of African political change, there are numerous circumstances in which the African elite may well have a greater harmony or identity of interests with colonial authorities or expatriate groups than with the common people. This is particularly the case during decolonization, whenever the people challenge the authority of the governmental and social systems. These are after all, the systems the new elite aspire to control once colonial authorities transfer power to them. Populist behavior, in their reckoning, could hardly be permitted to threaten the transfer of this power.

CHAPTER 12 -

Postwar Native Administration

A. GOVERNMENT INITIATIVE IN POLITICAL CHANGE

The postwar populist agitation was a matter of much concern to the colonial government. In his opening address to the Sierra Leone Legislative Council in December 1951, Governor Beresford-Stooke declared the government's resolve to quell populist violence. "Violence will not be tolerated," he remarked, "and the Police and Court Messenger Forces are authorised to take the most vigorous steps to deal with the undisciplined young hooligans who disturb the peace in this manner, and with those who instigate and encourage riotous behavior. Defiance of discipline and authority can lead only to anarchy. I sincerely trust that this disease will spread no further in the Protectorate . . . The people must realise that the organization of society which we call civilisation requires not only the imposition of discipline and respect for authority, but also a large measure of self-discipline. I can think of nothing which will more effectively thwart all our plans for the social, economic and political development of this country than the abandonment of discipline and the defiance of duly constituted authority."

But the Governor was quite aware that quelling populist outbursts with police power was no solution to the situations that produced them. He thus implored the Native Administrations and Chiefs to "move with the times, like the rest of us," and declared the government's concern that "tribal authorities should be made fully representative of all sections of the Community . . ."[1]

[1] *Legislative Council Debates, No. I of Session 1950–1951* (Freetown, 1951), pp. 5–6.

193

Within less than a year of the Governor's admonition to Chiefs to move with the times, the Tribal Authorities were reconstituted to provide a ratio of one member for every forty taxpayers.[2] Although this change stopped short of democratizing the method of selecting members of Tribal Authorities, it established the principle that the Authorities expressly represented a body of local taxpayers. This principle was later expanded as a result of the tax riots in 1955–56. Six months after these riots a joint executive order of the Governor and the Minister of Local Government, then Albert Margai, reconstituted the Tribal Authorities as follows:

(a) The Paramount Chief, Acting Chief or Regent Chief, speakers, section chiefs and section speakers and any other customary officials who by virtue of their office are included in the present Tribal Authority List.

(b) The headmen of towns of twenty or more taxpayers.

(c) One representative for every twenty taxpayers in any town additional to the first twenty.

(d) One representative of neighbouring villages of less than twenty taxpayers where such villages agree to group into units of not less than twenty taxpayers.[3]

Apart from the reconstitution of Native Administrations along representative lines, the government initiated two additional policies toward a more effective organization of local administration. One was that of extending central government supervision over Native Administration; the other was that of rationalizing the units of Native Administration through a policy of amalgamation.

1. Supervision of Native Administration

Under the Tribal Authority Ordinance of 1946 the powers of the Provincial and District Commissioners to intervene in the affairs of Native Administrations were greatly enhanced. The Provincial Commissioner, for instance, was given full discretion to issue any order required for the maintenance of good govern-

[2] Sir Herbert Cox, *Sierra Leone Report of Commission of Inquiry into Disturbances in the Provinces, November 1955 to March 1956* (London, 1956), p. 170.

[3] Letter CCP 618A (182) of 9.2.56, Ministry of Education and Local Government; quoted in *ibid.*

ment in any Chiefdom, and the Tribal Authority was obligated to enforce such an order. He was also authorized to intervene at any phase of the customary procedure for selecting Chiefs, in order to avert the protracted turmoil that the customary procedure often entailed. This authority entailed the right to initiate the election of a Chief and if, in his judgment, such election did not proceed satisfactorily, the Commissioner could request the Governor to appoint a Chief of his choice.[4]

As regards the District Commissioner, who was the agent of central government in closest contact with Native Administrations, it was considered necessary to strengthen his powers of intervention by inquiry into any aspect of the affairs of Chiefs and Native Administrations. Before World War II the right of government intervention into chiefly affairs was reserved to the Governor-in-Council; but this was too cumbersome for the manifold problems of postwar administration. Accordingly, under Section 29 of the Protectorate Ordinance, 1946, the District Commissioner was granted "power and authority to inquire into and decide as hereafter provided any matters within his district which have their origin in poro laws, native rites or customs, land disputes, including land disputes arising between paramount chiefs, or any other disputes which if not promptly settled, might lead to breaches of the peace." In pursuance of these powers the District Commissioner could use Chiefs as assessors "if he thinks fit," but "the decision shall rest exclusively with the District Commissioner, and no decision shall be deemed invalid, if any, or all, of the assessors so summoned shall not be present throughout the whole of the inquiry."[5]

2. Amalgamating Administrative Units

The amalgamation of unviable Chiefdom of Native Administration into more efficient ones was a major postwar policy of the Sierra Leone government. It was hoped in particular that larger and more efficient Native Administrations would alleviate widespread corruption by Chiefs and the populist violence which it produced. Corruption was especially common in the small and

[4] *Tribal Authority Ordinance, 1946*, sec. 10.
[5] *Protectorate Ordinance, 1946*, sec. 9.

financially weak Native Administrations where, as the Chief Commissioner of the Protectorate remarked in 1947, the Chief "who finds himself unable to live in the pomp and circumstances to which he considers he is entitled [resorts] to the imposition of illegal levies, to holding surreptitious courts from which the revenue does not reach the Chiefdom treasury, or to the use of forced labour for farms and the like."[6]

The government undertook to amalgamate Chiefdoms usually upon the death or resignation, often under populist pressures, of a Paramount Chief. By the mid-1950's the amalgamation policy could claim a fair measure of success. In the Northern Province, for instance, there were ninety-three Chiefdoms in 1947 (forty-four of which were organized Native Administrations), but the number was reduced to fifty-three by 1953, and "all of them organised Native Administrations."[7] In the more politically turbulent southern provinces no comparable success was achieved, though several important amalgamations were obtained, especially the case of Sowa Chiefdom in Pujehun District. In 1951 large areas in the Southeastern Province were on the brink of widespread violence because of populist disturbances in Sowa Chiefdom, whose political life had long been unsettled owing to the social changes attendant upon the diamond-mining industry.[8] Small in area, population, and financial resources, amalgamation was seen as the resolution par excellence for Sowa Chiefdom's unstabilizing political influences. After two years of delicate negotiations involving the Paramount Chiefs of Sowa and three neighboring Chiefdoms (Peje Chiefdom and Panga-Kabonde Chiefdom in Pujehun District and Wunde Chiefdom in Bo District) it was decided to partition Sowa among these Chiefdoms.[9]

---

[6] "Provincial Administration Annual Reports, 1947" (unpublished MS; Sierra Leone Government Archives, n.d.), pp. 5–6.

[7] Hubert Childs, *Provinces Report for 1953* (Freetown, 1955), p. 17.

[8] Hubert Childs, *Protectorate Report for 1951* (Freetown, 1953), pp. 2–3.

[9] Sowa Chiefdom had an area of 100 square miles and a hut tax revenue of £334 in 1952; Peje Chiefdom had an area of 195 square miles and a hut tax revenue of £276; Panga-Kabonde Chiefdom had an area of 160 square miles and £886 revenue; and Wunde Chiefdom had an area of 140 square miles and £432 revenue. *Provinces Handbook, 1952* (Bo, 1952), pp. 2, 5. See also Childs, *Provinces Report for 1953*, p. 17.

The success of the postwar amalgamation policy did not, however, prove as helpful in producing more efficient Native Administrations as the government expected. There were of course some improvements in the expenditure pattern of Native Administrations as a result of the larger, amalgamated units; but in general it was apparent that the unproductive use of Native Administration revenue was more a matter of the position of Chiefs in local administration than of anything else. Little could be hoped for in the way of more productive uses of local revenue as long as Chiefs held the central position in local government.

B. DECLINE OF THE NATIVE ADMINISTRATION SYSTEM

One cannot overemphasize the extent to which the political ethos basic to Chiefs, with its view of government as a means for maintaining the status quo and benefiting those who prevail therein, hindered the performance of Native Administrations. In Sierra Leone and elsewhere in colonial Africa this ethos was deeply ingrained in the behavior of the traditional elite. It persisted, moreover, despite evidence of not inconsiderable social change among these leaders.

In 1947 only 18 per cent of the Paramount Chiefs in Sierra Leone were literate, but by the mid-1950's the proportion augmented to nearly 40 per cent. The effect of this change upon the petty tyranny and corruption of Native Administrations, however, was virtually nil. Administration, indeed, was not infrequently at its worst in Native Administrations ruled by fairly well-educated Chiefs. Commenting on the widespread populist disorders, entailing considerable property damage, in the southern provinces in 1951, the Chief Commissioner remarked that a "particularly regrettable feature of these events is that the Paramount Chiefs who figured in them were in almost every case the product of secondary school education." He then proceeded to lament the shallow impact of Western education upon the traditional conception of leadership and use of public office: ". . . It is evident that there has been something lacking in their approach to their duties and responsibilities, and perhaps in the educational training which

197

they have received. The privileges of education, the obligations of leadership, and the whole idea of public service seem to be less understood than they should be, and it is for consideration whether more could not be done in the schools than at present to teach the meaning of these things and of the qualities of restraint, and justice, and unselfishness."[10]

By the mid-1950's evidence from all sources indicated that Native Administrations, on any reasonable reckoning, were still inadequate for providing local services in a developing society. Although the colonial government had submitted Native Administrations to closer supervision and had weeded out many unviable Chiefdoms through amalgamation, it did not undertake the basic reorganization of Native Administrations in a manner that would alleviate the backward-leaning influence of Chiefs upon their functioning. Nor was the attempt to democratize the N.A. system by broadening its basis of representation adequate as a means of reorganizing Native Administrations. Accordingly, the observation of Lucy Mair upon the role of Chiefs in local administration throughout British Africa in the 1950's was applicable with special force to Sierra Leone: "In general the experience has been that those Chiefs who have been subjected to no stronger pressure than the ambience of enlightened ideas have shown little interest in the expenditure of revenues for public purposes in the modern sense."[11] It was no surprise, then, that the Chief Commissioner recorded in his report on provincial administration for 1956 a pattern of expenditure by Native Administrations precisely the same as that before World War II.[12]

More recent data on the finances of Native Administrations is for the year 1960. Table 14 gives the financial position of a small Chiefdom in the Northern Province; the administrative head consumed 55 per cent of revenue, and 44 per cent of the administrative expenditure went into the salaries of hereditary officials. Though the small size of the Bonkolenken Chiefdom undoubtedly

[10] Childs, *Protectorate Report for 1949–1950* (Freetown, 1951), p. 4.

[11] Mair, "Representative Local Government as a Problem in Social Change," *Rhodes-Livingstone Institute Journal* (March 1957), pp. 4–5. Cf. E. A. Waldock, *Provinces Report for 1954* (Freetown, 1956), pp. 12–13.

[12] Hubert Childs, *Provinces Report for 1956* (Freetown, 1958), p. 22.

TABLE 14

Revenue and Expenditure in Bonkolenken, a Small Native Administration, 1960

Revenue		Administration head	
		Emoluments	
Local tax	£4,391		
Government grant	997	Paramount Chief	£ 600
Court fees and fines	600	Speakers	280
Interest to P.O.S.B.		Sub-chiefs	176
account	23	Village Heads	220
Land rents	67	Court President	250
Market dues	20	Clerks	261
Societies	10	Messengers	909
Building permits	10	Inspector of N.A.M.F.	20
Swearing	10	Sitting fees	192
Rural development grant	227	Registrar	6
Total	£6,355	Town Crier	6
		Rent Allowance—Clerks	48
		Other charges	
		Entertainment	78
		Uniforms	70
Expenditure		Stationery	40
Administration	3,496	Transport	250
Medical and health	342	Prisoners' diet	20
Miscellaneous	1,818	Contingencies	10
Works	75	Assessment committee	50
Extraordinary	250	Chiefdom committee	10
Total	£5,981	Total	£3,496

Source: *Chiefdom Estimates, Tonkolili District, 1960* (Magburaka: District Commissioner's Office, 1960).

contributed much to the Native Administration's unproductive expenditure, this pattern of expenditure was equally a result of the role of Chiefs as such. This is seen more clearly from Table 15, which gives the 1960 financial record of the comparatively large Luawa Chiefdom in Kailahun District, Southeastern Province. Here as in the smaller Native Administrations nearly one-half of revenue was claimed by administrative expenditures (41 per cent in this instance) and the salaries of hereditary officials amounted to 53 per cent of these expenditures. Apart from these salary charges of Chiefs on Native Administration revenue, sizable funds never reached the Chiefdom Treasury, because, as

TABLE 15

Revenue and Expenditure in Luawa, a Large Native
Administration, 1960

Revenue		Administration head	
Chiefdom tax	£ 10,108	*Emoluments*	
Government grant	610	Paramount Chief	£ 1,360
Court fees and fines	2,500	Speakers	600
Market dues	500	Sub-chiefs	430
Societies	25	Village Heads	404
Building permits	20	Court President	378
Swearing fees	120	Clerks	713
Reserve	500	Messengers	1,463
Rents	195	Court officials	480
Interest	75	Registrar	10
Subsidies	3,463	Gaoler	80
Total	£ 17,616	Market Keeper	180
		Assessment committee	70
Expenditure		*Other charges*	
Administration	7,168		
Education	2,095	Entertainment	125
Medical-health	1,982	Uniforms	135
Works	200	Equipment	100
Extraordinary (mainly		Transport	600
rural and town		Prisoners' food	30
improvement)	2,234	Contingencies	10
Miscellaneous (mainly			
District Council			
precept)	4,251		
Total	£ 17,930	Total	£ 7,168

Source: *Chiefdom Estimates, Kailahun District, 1959–1960* (Kailahun: District Commissioner's Office, 1960).

the Chief Commissioner remarked in his 1951 report, "all Paramount Chiefs received various (unrecorded) fees and allowances."[13]

Comparative data on the postwar finances of Native Administrations elsewhere in Africa further support the argument that
the position of Chiefs was the basic cause of the unproductive use
of local revenue. Ursula Hicks has recently demonstrated, in a

[13] Childs, *Protectorate Report for 1951*, p. 13.

comparative study of postwar local government in Africa, Asia, and the West Indies, that as the taxable population and over-all scale of a local government unit expand, the administrative expenditure head usually decreases in proportion to more directly productive expenditure.[14] This generalization applied to those local government units conceived explicitly as modern administrative bodies, free of ties to the traditional authority structures. But as regards the units of local government that were formed out of traditional authority structures under indirect rule, Hicks found her generalization wanting. For instance, in Northern Nigeria she discovered that "on the whole . . . there is little evidence of any definite relation between size and outlay on administration." The reason she adduced for this was the "exceptional uniformity of local organization, and this is reflected in a considerable degree of homogeneity of administrative outlay." The main element in the "exceptional uniformity of local organization" in Northern Nigeria was the Chiefs; and in the data given by Hicks on the administrative expenditures of the Native Administrations for the period 1956–57, they consumed between 30 per cent and 47 per cent of revenue.[15]

More recent data on Northern Nigeria for 1960 support Hicks' argument. In the average-size Gumel Native Administration, Kano Province, the administrative head claimed 42 per cent of ordinary expenditure (as against 9 per cent for public works, 2 per cent agriculture, 7 per cent health, 15 per cent education, and so forth); 46 per cent of the administrative expenditure went to Chiefs' salaries. In the Kano Native Administration, the largest and wealthiest in Nigeria, the administrative expenditures claimed 36 per cent of total expenditure in 1960 (i.e., £429,395 out of £1,214,618); the emoluments of Chiefs represented 75 per cent of these expenditures (i.e., £324,177 out of £429,395), or 27 per cent of the total expenditure.[16]

[14] U. K. Hicks, *Development from Below* (Oxford, 1961), pp. 242–250.
[15] *Ibid.*, p. 246.
[16] *Native Administrations Estimates, 1959–1960, Kano Province* (Kaduna, 1960), pp. 2–3, 54 ff.

C. CONCLUSION

The colonial authorities in Sierra Leone never lost sight of the basic dilemma confronting them in local administration, and throughout the postwar era they endeavored, short of uprooting Chiefs altogether, to resolve it. There was patently no prospect of resolution within the framework of the N.A. system, as our account has demonstrated. The colonial government accordingly established a second tier of local government called District Councils, which were formed initially as advisory bodies in 1946. Since then they have coexisted with Native Administrations, and their development into full-fledged executive bodies has been characterized by a fierce competition with Native Administrations.

As will be seen in the next chapter, District Councils had a difficult go at relegating the N.A. system to the rubbish can of history where it belongs. One reason for this was the doctrinaire and nearly pathological obsession of British colonial authorities with the theory of indirect rule. Another reason, equally related to the inability of the colonial authorities to escape the limitations of indirect rule, was the system of party politics in which Chiefs gained a firm foothold in the postwar era.[17] Thus the Native Administrations continued to exist down through Sierra Leone's attainment of independence in 1961 and will be a part of the political landscape of Sierra Leone for some time to come.

[17] See chapters 14–15.

CHAPTER 13

The Politics of District Councils

A. ESTABLISHMENT OF DISTRICT COUNCILS

At the close of World War II the Protectorate was reorganized into three provinces (there were four before the war), each administered by a Provincial Commissioner who was in turn subordinate to the Chief Commissioner, the main executive officer in provincial administration. The Chief Commissioner was headquartered in the provinces, at Bo, where his office served as the focal point of postwar planning for Protectorate development. All technical and administrative agents of central departments concerned with the postwar development plans were concentrated at the Chief Commissioner's headquarters; the Commissioner was responsible for coordinating their activities and integrating them with the tasks of local government bodies.[1]

District Councils were created in 1946 initially as a means of widening the basis of local consultation with regard to the development plans. Under the Protectorate Ordinance of 1946 the Councils, one in each of the twelve Districts, were empowered to advise on any matters brought before them by the Governor or the Chief Commissioner and to make recommendations "on matters affecting the welfare of the people [and] to suggest, where any such advice or recommendations involved expenditure, the source or sources from which the funds necessary to meet such expenditure can be derived . . ."[2]

Although District Councils were intended ultimately to replace

[1] Hubert Childs, *An Outline of the Ten-Year Plan for the Development of Sierra Leone, Sessional Paper No. 4 of 1946* (Freetown, 1946), esp. pp. 21–22.
[2] *Protectorate Ordinance, 1946*, sec. 5.

Native Administrations in the sphere of local-government services, the colonial authorities were reluctant to let them develop outside the purview of the latter's influence. Paramount Chiefs were accordingly made ex officio members of the District Council, and, in the absence of the District or provincial Commissioner who was to chair Council meetings, the Chiefs could "elect one of their number to preside."[3] Another category of members was provided to represent commoner interests in each Chiefdom; but inasmuch as they were to be selected by Tribal Authorities, they were largely under the control of Native Administrations.

As established under the Protectorate Ordinance of 1946, District Councils continued until 1950. By this time it was evident that the Councils required renovation if they were to play a more active role in local development and to satisfy local pressures for more services and more representation. Under the District Councils Ordinance, No. 17 of 1950, four additional members were added to the Councils to represent popular interests. The Councils were also empowered to execute a small range of social services, which were initially financed by a voluntary precept upon Native Administrations.[4] In 1954, however, the government decided, on the advice of an inquiry into local government finance, to make the precept mandatory.[5] Under the Local Tax Ordinance, No. 23 of 1954, it was provided that "each District Council shall . . . declare by resolution the amount, to be called precept, which each Tribal Authority within the area of its jurisdiction is to pay to it out of the local tax collected from each taxpayer in respect of the forthcoming year."[6] The amount of precept each Council received was left to negotiation between it and the Native Administrations. In 1955 the precept ranged between 40–55 per cent of

[3] Ibid., sec. 8.

[4] See District Councils Ordinance, No. 17 of 1950, secs. 4, 8, 14.

[5] Cf. H. W. Davidson, Report on the Functions and Finances of District Councils in Sierra Leone (Freetown, 1953), pp. 21–24; Address of His Excellency the Governor, Sir George Beresford-Stooke, K. C. M. C. on the Opening of the First Session of the Legislative Council, 1951 (Freetown, 1951), pp. 4–5.

[6] Local Tax Ordinance, No. 23 of 1954, sec. 20. For the details of the consolidation of existing taxes into a single local tax, see J. M. Wann, "Report of Local Tax Enquiry Committee, 1957" (unpublished MS; Freetown: Ministry of Internal Affairs).

the local tax; in 1956, following the tax riots, the precept was standardized on order of the Governor at 44 per cent of the local tax.[7] Apart from the precept, District Councils received grants for specific purposes from the surplus funds of the Sierra Leone Produce Marketing Board and the Protectorate Mining Benefit Fund.

B. POSITION OF CHIEFS IN DISTRICT COUNCILS

As we have seen, Paramount Chiefs were ex officio members of the local Councils at their inception in each of the twelve Districts, and they retained this status when the Councils were reorganized under the District Councils Ordinance of 1950. When the structure and functions of the Councils were further reorganized in 1954, the Chiefs effectively employed their influence to guarantee themselves a firm position in the District Council system. The first major change in the Councils in 1954 was the enactment of the Local Tax Ordinance which made the precept mandatory. In addition to this, the Tax Ordinance exempted Chiefs from all local taxation, whereas under the Chiefdom Tax Ordinance of 1937 they were taxable. The 1954 Tax Ordinance also removed the earlier criminal liability that the 1937 Tax Ordinance placed upon Chiefs to pay all taxes they collected into the Native Administration Treasury.[8] In view of the Cox Commission's findings in 1956 regarding the widespread corruption by Chiefs in the administration of local taxes, it would seem they obtained the removal of criminal liability in order to facilitate corruption. What enabled the Chiefs to obtain these favorable provisions in the 1954 Tax Ordinance was their strong position in the organization of the SLPP and their control of 25 per cent of the seats in the SLPP-dominated legislature. They also had the backing of the colonial government who, though increasingly wary of Chiefs, considered it necessary to cater to them while attempting to reform local government.

[7] Sir Herbert Cox, *Sierra Leone Report of Commission of Inquiry into Disturbances in the Provinces, November 1955 to March 1956* (London, 1956), p. 255.
[8] *Local Tax Ordinance, No. 23 of 1954,* sec. 15.

Apart from the advantages Chiefs obtained under the 1954 Tax Ordinance, two additional ordinances, which were amendments to the original District Council Ordinance of 1950, gave Chiefs further advantages in the District Council system. Under the District Councils (Amendment) Ordinance, No. 9 of 1954, the District Commissioner's right to preside over the meetings of Councils was significantly qualified; he now presided only if the Councils failed to elect one of their own members as President—who was invariably a Paramount Chief—and he no longer sat in the Councils unless he held the presidency, whereas under the 1950 District Council Ordinance the District Commissioner was given ex officio membership.[9] The Amendment Ordinance also transferred virtually all the powers of the Chief Commissioner in regard to District Councils—especially his powers to approve or reject their estimates of expenditure and revenue—to the SLPP Minister for Local Government, Albert Margai, who was a grandson and nephew of Paramount Chiefs.[10] The Amendment Ordinance did make a concession to popular interests by adding another non-chiefly member to the Councils; but, as in the case of the 1946 Protectorate Ordinance and 1950 District Councils Ordinance, this member was to be selected by the Tribal Authorities and was thus controllable by the Chiefs. It was not, in fact, until the aftermath of the tax riots of late 1955 and early 1956 that popular representation through direct elections was finally given to District Councils, though Paramount Chiefs remained ex officio members and continued to dominate the presidency of most Councils.

The final change in the organization of District Councils enacted in 1954 concerned their executive functions. Under the District Councils (Amendment No. 2) Ordinance, No. 26 of 1954, the Councils' executive functions, hitherto concerned with the provision of water supply, roads, health and agricultural services, were expanded to include the authority "to acquire any type of building material and . . . dispose of the same to any Tribal Authority . . . within the District, or to any person normally resident within the District, in such manner and on such terms and conditions as the

[9] *District Councils (Amendment) Ordinance, No. 9 of 1954*, sec. 5.
[10] *Ibid.*, sec. 4.

District Council may think fit." The ordinance also empowered the Councils "to lend money to any Tribal Authority . . . or to any person ordinarily resident within the district . . ., subject . . . to the conditions that money so lent is to be used in the construction of a specified building within the district . . ."[11] These new economic powers of District Councils were subsequently (in 1955) embodied in a Building Materials Scheme which was provided for by a special set of rules enacted by the SLPP government. The scheme, financed by the SLPP government to the amount of £300,000 by 1961, provided loans for the purchase of corrugated iron sheets, nails, lumber, and other building materials. It was administered by District Councils but through the agency of Tribal Authorities; for example, under the District Councils (Pujehun District) (Building Scheme) Rules, 1958, it was provided that "the Council will not consider any application under the Scheme which is not recommended by the Tribal Authority having jurisdiction over the area in which the applicant is normally resident . . ."[12] An account of the execution of the scheme will give some insight into the uses of political influence in local government.

C. SOME USES OF LOCAL POLITICAL INFLUENCE

1. The Building Materials Scheme

Chiefs were favorably situated to dominate the execution of the Building Materials Scheme. Besides the statutory provision in the rules governing the scheme that applicants for loans be processed through Tribal Authorities, the Chiefs had influence over the other members of District Councils because many of them, like the SLPP leaders in the central government, were the direct kin of Chiefs. Similar kinship ties to Chiefs were found among many of the executive officers of District Councils, and these ties were not infrequently of more moment than the obligations these officers were expected to adhere to as civil servants.

---

[11] *District Councils (Amendment No. 2) Ordinance, No. 26 of 1954,* sec. 2.
[12] *District Councils (Pujehun District) (Building Scheme) Rules, 1958,* sec. 6. These rules were the same for all District Councils.

Finally, though the colonial government was by now awake to the need to remove Chiefs from any executive role whatsoever in local government, reducing them to ceremonial chores, the decolonizing stage of constitutional dyarchy had progressed too far for its counsel to be heard. Local government was now largely the concern of the SLPP government, and Chiefs were a considerable force in the SLPP. The outcome of the Building Materials Scheme was predictable.

By 1961 the scheme had consumed some £300,000 in central-government grants, and a major part of the recipients of loans under the scheme were either Chiefs themselves, kin of Chiefs and lesser hereditary officials, or commoners with untarnished loyalty to Chiefs.[13] Nepotism, then, was the main yardstick for deciding who would benefit from the scheme, with questions regarding the applicants' need or ability to repay the loan receiving little or no consideration whatever. The result was widespread defaulting of repayment of loans and interest by recipients. In Koinadugu District, for instance, there were 144 recipients by 1958 who collectively had repaid barely 10 per cent of £9,678 borrowed; in Bombali District the sum defaulted was £10,000 in 1959; and in Bo District the defaulting caused Council a £7,895 debt to the United Africa Company, an expatriate firm from whom the Councils purchased materials on credit.[14]

This experience was more or less common for all District Councils, and in 1958 the Minister of Internal Affairs, Sir Milton Margai, ordered the Councils to sue in court for repayment. Furthermore, District Commissioners were urged to employ their influence and office to effect repayment; the Commissioner in Bombali District, in an address to the Council in 1959, "pointed out to all Paramount Chiefs present, the importance of their co-operation with the Council Staff in collecting these debts . . . The District Commissioner also advised members to be discreet in their choice of members of the various Committees responsible for carrying out the

13 Interview with executive officers, Moyamba District Council, March 1960.
14 *Minutes of the Koinadugu District Council, 26th–27th June, 9th December 1957* (Kabala, 1957), pp. 4–5; *Minutes of the 26th Meeting of Bombali District Council, 13th–16th November, 1959* (Makeni, 1959), p. 1; *Minutes of the Bo District Council, 26 February, 1959* (Bo, 1959), p. 3.

affairs of the Council."[15] In Kenema District, where defaulters under the scheme were very numerous, the Council implored the Native Administrations to bear responsibility for effecting repayment of loans: "Since the Paramount Chiefs and Tribal Authorities recommended the people to whom the building material loans scheme was extended, and . . . much difficulty is being experienced in collecting these loans, the Native Administrations in which these defaulters are should pay the loans, and collect back from the debtors the amounts owed by them."[16]

Despite these efforts to recover loans, very few were ever repaid. In view of this peculation the scheme should have been called to a halt and written off as an ill-conceived use of government resources. But, alas, no such response was forthcoming from the SLPP government. The scheme continues to operate and is a manifest attestation to the SLPP's considerable dependence upon Chiefs and their retainers in local society. The government's support of the scheme also attests to its rather immature approach to local development; the funds put into the scheme would have been better spent on expanding agricultural production and improving technique. For example, the country's staple food, rice, was in short supply during the late 1950's, and local needs were met by importing large quantities. But, then, the requirements of politics and those of development are seldom the same; in the new African states the former are likely to take precedence for some time to come.

2. Advance Payments to Office-Holders

The District Councils' policy of granting financial advances to councillors, staff, and other groups was another realm for the exercise of local political influence. The amount of any particular financial advance varied according to the person seeking it, as well as the Council's own financial status, though this was not always a consideration.

---

[15] Minutes of the 26th Meeting of Bombali District Council, p. 1.

[16] Minutes of Finance Committee of Kenema District Council, 27th August 1959 (Kenema, 1959), p. 1. See also Minutes of the Finance and General Purposes Committee of Bombali District Council, 15th January 1960 (Makeni, 1960), p. 1.

Paramount Chiefs often received the largest advances. For instance, in 1955 the Kenema District Council advanced its President, a Paramount Chief, £900 to purchase a car for personal use unrelated to his duties as President.[17] Similarly, the President of the Tonkolili District Council, also a Chief, obtained an advance of £800 in 1955 to purchase a van for his private business. In this instance the Chief let his loan go unpaid for three years, during which period he was deposed by the colonial government on recommendation of the commissioners who inquired into tax riots of 1955–56. When the Paramount Chief, Bai Bairoh II, finally heeded the Council's request to settle his debt, an arrangement was worked out whereby one of his several modern houses was let to the Council at £180 per annum, the Council withholding payment until the debt was cleared.[18]

Other councillors besides Chiefs exploited the Councils' policy of granting financial advances, and so did the executive staff who were recruited through the Public Service Commission. For example, in 1955 the Koinadugu District Council advanced its Secretary £680 to purchase a car; while the Kenema District Council advanced its Treasurer £740 for the same purpose in 1957 and advanced its Provincial Education Secretary £300.[19] In the latter case the recipient won a legislative seat in the 1957 General Election and two years later became a Minister in the SLPP government, but the £300 advance was never repaid.[20]

Besides defaulting on such advances, both councillors and the executive staff not infrequently utilized the advances for purposes other than that for which they were granted. An instance of this was recorded in the Auditor's report on the accounts of Moyamba

[17] *Minutes of the Finance Committee of Kenema District Council, 20th October 1955* (Kenema, 1955), p. 1.

[18] *Minutes of the Finance and General Purposes Committee of Tonkolili District Council, 30th June 1958* (Magburaka, 1958), p. 1.

[19] *Minutes of the Finance Committee of Kenema District Council, 15th August 1955* (Kenema, 1955), p. 3; *Minutes of the Finance and General Purposes Committee of Koinadugu District Council, 28th May and 1st June 1957* (Kabala, 1957), p. 2.

[20] *Minutes of the Finance Committee of Kenema District Council, 27th August 1959*, p. 2; *Report of the Director of Audit on the Accounts of the Kenema District Council for the Year Ended the 31st of December 1959* (Government Notice 900 of 1959).

District Council for 1958; advances to the executive staff totaled £1,206 (other advances, including some under the Building Scheme, exceeded £6,000), and one advance of £300 to a Paramount Chief was used as he saw fit. Wrote the auditor: "It was mentioned in . . . the last Report that £315.15s.10d. was due from a Works Officer who was dismissed in 1957 and that amounts of £300 and £167 were due from two Paramount Chiefs. There was no recovery from the Works Officer during the year. The loan of £300 was made in 1955 for the purchase of a motor car. I am given to understand that no motor car was purchased and the whole amount should therefore have been repaid. According to the accounts of the Council, however, there had been no repayment by the 31st December, 1958 . . ."[21]

The grant of financial advances did not stop with councillors and executive staff. They were granted as well to sundry low-level personnel like clerks, messengers, and typists; and even influential local groups came in for a share. One instance of the latter was the subject of a circular from the British Permanent Secretary, Ministry of Internal Affairs, opposing the Tonkolili District Council's decision to advance funds to schoolteachers for the purchase of radio sets at £18 each. "The Finance Committee should be aware," he remarked, "that the Council is indebted to Central Government to the extent of £3,389 in respect to school materials and £7,000 plus accrued interest thereon in respect of Building Materials Loan Scheme. I . . . therefore . . . suggest the Council may re-consider the plan to give advances to purchase Radio sets."[22]

The upshot of allocating local-government funds as if they were a sort of private credit agency was the immobilization or loss of sizable sums. In view of the fact that the revenue of District Councils has never been adequate to the social services required by the local populace, this particular exploitation of local resources constituted a grossly irresponsible use of political influence. Much

[21] *Report of the Director of Audit on the Accounts of the Moyamba District Council for the Year Ended the 31st of December 1958* (Government Notice 882 of 1958).

[22] *Minutes of the Finance Committee of Tonkolili District Council, 14th–15th August 1959* (Magburaka, 1959), p. 3.

of this state of affairs, however, is probably unavoidable and is likely to persist as a feature of local politics and government in Sierra Leone and elsewhere in Africa. The politically influential groups in local areas have precious few resources available to them, and those they do have are subject to fierce competition. Combined with the central political elite's dependence upon the politically influential in local areas, very little can be expected in the way of a more rational utilization of local resources.

D. AN EVALUATION OF DISTRICT COUNCILS

In general, District Councils in Sierra Leone represent a more modern (rational) system of local government than Native Administrations. Whereas the latter invariably expend 50 per cent and more on personal emoluments of Chiefs and other hereditary officials, the District Councils' administrative costs are normally between 15–20 per cent of revenue. For example, the Kailahun District Council spent 70 per cent of the revenue on such productive services as education, public works, and agriculture in 1955.[23]

Yet the functioning of District Councils is far from adequate; they exhibit many weaknesses, most of which are basic to modern local government throughout West Africa. Inefficiency and inability to follow a plan weaken the Councils. Funds allocated by central government for specific purposes are frequently expended, without authority of the granting agency, on quite different functions. For example, the grants of the Sierra Leone Marketing Board, which are meant to facilitate agricultural production (especially cash crops), are spent on education or, in many instances, on erecting and maintaining costly offices for District Councils. Poor expenditure control has also characterized the allocation of contracts by District Councils. In 1958 the Tonkolili District Council engaged an African road contractor who was less equipped than the Council itself; he lacked some of the most basic tools and required recourse to the Council's equipment in order to fulfill the contract.[24]

[23] *Kailahun District Council Financial Statements, 1955* (Kailahun, 1955).
[24] *Minutes of the Finance and General Purposes Committee of Tonkolili District Council, 30th–31st May, 3rd June 1958* (Magburaka, 1958), p. 2.

Furthermore, District Councils have tended to take on more functions than they can handle, and occasionally inappropriate or unnecessary functions are chosen. The absence of a systematic policy of priorities governing the assumption of functions by Councils has contributed to this problem. It also stems from the opportunistic manner in which Native Administrations have transferred their functions to District Councils. The assumption by Councils of additional tasks was underlined by the Cox Commission of Inquiry into the tax riots in 1955–56 as causing an increase of the precept and thus the local tax, which the Commission held as a basic factor in the riots. The Commission accordingly recommended that the Councils should be restricted in their assumption of new functions and their right of precept. The Commission's charge, however, was only partly correct; in a table appended to the Commission's report the rates of tax and precept do not correlate with the degree of rioting in the Districts concerned.

The Commission had erred in overlooking the fact that the Native Administrations themselves were responsible for the Councils' over-extension of functions. The Native Administrations were never keen on performing needed services for their taxpayers; as the opportunity presented itself, they invariably transferred obligations to the Councils. The Chief Commissioner remarked on this process in his annual report for 1953: "In general Native Administrations are still reluctant to take the initiative over the expenditure of the funds voted in their estimates, except in so far as payment of salaries is concerned. Even where some interest is displayed, there is too easy satisfaction with poor work by contractors and little sense of responsibility for ensuring that the taxpayers' money is spent to advantage . . . The absence of readiness to accept responsibility has . . . had the effect in some districts of causing Tribal Authorities to attempt to shift responsibility for difficult decisions on to the District Councils."[25]

To some extent, the transfer of functions was not a bad policy insofar as District Councils were basically more effective units for performing modern services. Several factors intervened, however, to limit this shift of functions from Native Administrations to

[25] Hubert Childs, *Provinces Report for 1953* (Freetown, 1955), p. 19.

213

District Councils, thereby preventing Native Administrations from being seen as redundant and unnecessary. First, the Cox Commission, as noted, wrongly blamed District Councils for the increase in the tax rate which contributed to the riots of 1955–56. This advice caused the colonial government to think that District Councils were the organizations to watch in order to regulate the rate of tax and precept. Second, the colonial government (as well as the SLPP government) actually considered Native Administrations as the more desirable unit of local government, though now appreciating their most obvious limitations.

Despite the postwar aim of modernizing local government, colonial policy-makers clung to much of the prewar view of local government as basically a matter of law and order. Not yet certain that District Councils could both perform modern services and secure order and stability in local society, the colonial government was simply reluctant to dispense with Native Administrations. Thus, in his report for 1953 the Chief Commissioner warned that the tendency for Native Administrations to shift functions to District Councils "is one which needs guarding against since it would be a mistake to permit the District Council, with its stronger financial resources, to usurp the rights and powers of the less powerful [financially] but *indigenous* authority. In particular, the Tribal Authority has radical responsibilities for the maintenance of law and order . . . and in regard to the disposal of all [indigenous] interests in land [this also basically a matter of law and order] . . . Any step which would have the effect of derogating from the full responsibility of the Tribal Authorities in favour of the District Councils for these fundamental matters is to be deprecated since the District Councils, by their nature as statutory bodies, are unable to command the family and tribal sanctions on which the social structure of the country is built *and upon which its continued stability depends. To let these things go by default could have far-reaching consequences.*"[26]

Revealing as Chief Commissioner Childs' statement was as regards the dogged persistence of the principles of indirect rule at this late stage of colonial change, it was incorrect in its reference

[26] *Ibid.*

214

to District Councils as financially better off than Native Administrations. Indeed, it was the financial superiority of Native Administrations that constituted the third barrier to a complete
transfer of their executive functions to District Councils. Native
Administrations were more than willing to burden the Councils
with as many of their responsibilities as the latter would accept;
but, alas, they would not grant the Councils a corresponding share
of the local finance. Without such finance the Councils could not
possibly handle adequately the functions they assumed, and the
Chiefs were quite aware of this.

By any reckoning of financial superiority, it is clear that throughout the 1950's the Native Administrations were the dominant
bodies. In 1953 the total revenue of some 150 Native Administrations was £405,801, as against some £242,216 revenue for District Councils, in 1956 the revenue of 141 Native Administrations
was £626,097, against £375,235 for District Councils. Furthermore, even if the Councils' precept upon Native Administration
revenue was excluded from the calculation (the precept was
£165,972 in 1956), the Native Administrations' total share of local
finance still remained greater than that the Councils received.[27]
This was equally so on a per-capita reckoning: In 1957 the most
populous Native Administration claimed only 49,000 persons,
whereas the most populous District (Bo District) claimed 250,000
persons. No District had less than 100,000, and most had more
than this.[28]

Thus, despite the large shift of Native Administration executive
functions to District Councils, combined with their responsibility
for larger areas and more people, the Councils have been denied
the requisite share of local finance. Although in their present
form the District Councils are far from model bodies, they are
much more capable of handling local services than Native Administrations. To this extent it would be the course of better government to have Native Administrations give District Councils
the funds they require.

[27] *Ibid.*, pp. 18, 40; Childs, *Provinces Report for 1956* (Freetown, 1958), pp. 21,
34.
[28] *Sierra Leone Protectorate Handbook, 1957* (Bo, 1958).

But the problem here, widespread in African local government, is less one of government than of politics. As I have argued elsewhere, the structure of party politics in Sierra Leone greatly hinders the rationalization of local government.[29] The central SLPP elite depend upon the support of Chiefs, in return for which the latter are permitted a large influence in local politics through the archaic N.A. system. As long as this political arrangement prevails, the District Councils will be unable to achieve a more effective measure of local government. But, then, politics is mainly about power and what power brings to those who hold it, and perhaps not very much else.

[29] Martin Kilson, "Sierra Leone Politics," West Africa (June 25, 1960), pp. 708–709.

Part V -

Party Politics

CHAPTER 14

Background of Sierra Leonean Political Parties

A. POLITICAL GROUPS BEFORE WORLD WAR II

Before World War II Sierra Leone was well in the forefront of political organization development in colonial Africa. Sometime in the mid-1850's a group of well-to-do Creole Merchants formed the Sierra Leone Mercantile Association (SLMA) which functioned as a quasi-political association on behalf of the trading community. Its main activity was to pressure the colonial government for favorable trade policies, and in 1863 a leading member of the SLMA, John Ezzidio, was appointed by the Governor to the Legislative Council.[1] Throughout the 1860's the SLMA was the main spokesman of articulate African interests and the colonial government invariably turned to it whenever the advice of these interests was required.

By the 1870's the SLMA had been superseded by the Sierra Leone Native Association (1872–1882), which in turn gave way to the Sierra Leone Association for the Improvement and Defence of Commerce, Agriculture, and Industry (SLA). The SLA, founded in 1884, had several unique features about it which were not associated with its predecessors. A few European merchants were included among its otherwise African membership and one of them, Herr Ernst Vohsen, German Consul at Freetown, was its first President.[2] The SLA was also more explicit in its political

[1] Christopher Fyfe, A History of Sierra Leone (Oxford, 1962), pp. 319–320.
[2] Sierra Leone Weekly News, January 24, 1885, pp. 2–3.

219

concerns; it held frequent public meetings in Freetown at which the attendance of the wider community was occasionally encouraged. A contemporary report of one such meeting remarked that "the Susus, Mandingoes, and Timanees mustered strong; the boatmen . . ., the labourers and porters . . ., the hawkers and petty traders . . . all were present."[3] A more activist policy in pursuit of larger trading areas for African and European traders also distinguished the SLA from the earlier associations. The SLA constantly informed the colonial government of the many impediments to trade in the Sierra Leone hinterland, as it did in a memorial to the Governor, Sir Samuel Rowe in 1885. The memorial complained "of interference in trade by chiefs and war boys in hinterland, and [of] forcing of persons in rural areas bordering hinterland into slavery." The memorial also opposed what was then the colonial policy of "noninterference" in the affairs of the hinterland; it considered this policy "as highly impolitic" and that it "increases the dangers of the situation," proposing instead a program of active governmental intervention leading eventually to annexation of the hinterland. As the memorial of the SLA put it: "That . . . greater freedom of action and authority be given to our Colonial Government to establish and maintain peace by force of arms, if necessary, under exigent circumstances in the surrounding countries from whence we receive fully nine-tenths of the total exports . . . That the highroads leading to and from the interior be protected by the appointment of Government Agents who shall be supported either by small detachments of the troops now stationed at Sierra Leone or by a large addition to the Armed Police Force of the Colony to give sufficient security to the native caravans and traders which come and go from the Settlement bringing and taking their merchandise."[4]

In 1896 the SLA's goal of annexation of the hinterland as the only means to advance and protect trade was obtained. The role of the Creole merchants in the establishment of the Sierra Leone

[3] *Sierra Leone Weekly News,* October 10, 1885, p. 2.
[4] *Sierra Leone Weekly News,* June 6, 1885, p. 3. See also inaugaural address of Ernst Vohsen, SLA President in *Sierra Leone Weekly News,* February 7 and 14, 1885, p. 3.

Protectorate became an important factor in the subsequent political relationship between the Colony and the Protectorate peoples. This was apparent in the Hut Tax War which broke out within two years of the promulgation of the Protectorate; many Creole merchants and their families were savagely murdered by warring Mende tribesmen. The subsequent constitutional development of Sierra Leone was heavily colored by these events, as we have already seen, as was also the evolution of modern political parties.

By the turn of the twentieth century the professional class began to supplant the merchants as the leading spokesmen for African interests in the Colony. As the professional class gained appointments by the Governor to the Legislative Council, it consolidated and advanced its new political status through incipient political party organization. The first such parties, all of which differed markedly from the earlier merchant semi-political associations, were called Ratepayers' Associations, which emerged in 1909 in response to the provision of the franchise for elections to the Freetown City Council.[5] Payers of the City Rate, most of whom were Creoles—though a few indigenous Sierra Leoneans resident in Freetown also paid the Rate—formed the basis of the Associations. They were usually educated persons, some highly so, who possessed the means to support a more sustained form of political activity than required of the earlier mercantile bodies. The institution of the franchise for the City Council necessarily entailed such activity from those who were interested in controlling it; for the City Council, within limits prescribed by the colonial authorities, was a decision-making body with financial and other resources at its disposal. The members and leaders of the Ratepayers' Associations were preeminent among that element in the urban population concerned with controlling the Council in their own behalf. Within a year of their foundation the Ratepayers' Associations clearly displayed what the conservative Mayor of the City Council called their "party-spirit," for which he

[5] The City Council was created by ordinance in 1893 but was not inaugurated until 1895. It consisted of an elected unofficial African majority of twelve members and three official members. For elections Freetown was divided into three wards which had about 3,000 eligible voters in 1909 out of a citywide population of 34,000.

had little patience. "I must," he declared, "condemn the party-spirit and antagonism for party purposes . . . which have manifested themselves during the year in Council meetings . . . It is like a desire to secure personal ends rather than . . . the interests of the City."[6]

Apart from their self-serving concerns, the Ratepayers' Associations assumed the wider social-service functions sometimes adopted by modern parties. They performed a variety of voluntary services in such fields as health, sanitation, and child care, and occasionally they lent their organization to colonial-government departments that functioned in these fields. For instance, in 1936 the government Medical Officer for the Colony noted in his annual report that "an invitation to co-operate (in government's health and baby week program) was sent to the Ratepayers' Association of the East, Central and West Wards of the City. The response was gratifying, and the West Ward Ratepayers held a special health meeting on the afternoon of the 2nd March at which a lecture was delivered by the Rev. S. B. A. Campbell on Hygiene and Sanitation, and at which the Medical Officer (Health) acted as Chairman. The meeting was well attended and great enthusiasm was shown. The Association also sent a bell-ringer around the town announcing Health and Baby Week to the people."[7]

Although the Ratepayers' Associations possessed the attributes of the modern political party they, like the earlier mercantile pressure groups, lacked an explicitly anti-colonial orientation. Political groups possessing both the characteristics of parties and of an anti-colonial nationalist movement did not appear until after World War I. Several important political groups of this sort emerged in this period, and were the progenitors of the post-World War II movement for national independence of Sierra Leone. Among them were the Committee of (Protectorate) Educated

[6] *Fifteenth Annual Minute of the Mayor of the City* (Freetown, 1910), p. 2. See also *Fourteenth Annual Minute of the Mayor of the City* (Freetown, 1909), pp. 3–4.

[7] W. Allan, "Report on the Health and Baby Week, 1936," in *Annual Report of the Medical and Sanitary Department for the Year 1936* (Freetown, 1937), p. 37.

Africans (CEA), the Sierra Leone Branch of the National Congress of British West Africa (SLNC), and the Sierra Leone Branch of the West African Youth League (SLYL). The last two were of more significance as anti-colonial nationalist groups, and we will therefore restrict our discussion to them.

The parent body of the SLNC originated in the Gold Coast in 1918; the Sierra Leone National Congress was organized two years later.[8] What marked the SLNC off from the earlier political groups was, as noted, its incipient effort to question and contest the legitimacy of colonial rule of African peoples. In the SLNC's constitution of 1923 it was proposed that "The aims of the Congress shall be to aid in the development of the political institutions of British West Africa under the Union Jack, so as to eventually take her place beside the sister nations of the Empire, and in time, to ensure within her borders the government of the people, by the people, for the people . . ."[9] The contest of the legitimacy of colonial government involved the SLNC in a range of political activities quite beyond those of the earlier political associations. To provide a reliable following and a mechanism for involving it in political activity, the SLNC established ties, often through overlapping leadership links, with a variety of voluntary associations like women's clubs, literary clubs, churches, teachers' associations, and incipient trade unions. When asserting its organized influence in behalf of alterations in the structure and purposes of colonial government, the SLNC utilized political techniques like public rallies, sent deputations to the Colonial Office, systematically pilloried the colonial government with petitions, organized protest marches in the streets of Freetown, and participated in elections to the Legislative Council. This last activity was possible because of the constitutional advance in 1924 which provided for the first election of African representatives to the colonial Legislature. Between 1924 and World War II the candidates of the SLNC, who were either doctors, lawyers, or wealthy businessmen, won three of the four elections to the Legislature. Apart from providing an outlet

[8] *Sierra Leone Weekly News,* December 7 and 14, 1918, pp. 9, 5.

[9] *Constitution of the National Congress of British West Africa* (Freetown, 1923), sec. 19.

for incipient nationalist demands, elected representation in the Legislative Council enabled the nationalist-minded elite to participate in a wide range of governmental activities hitherto beyond their ken. Throughout the 1920's and 1930's the colonial government, cognizant of the utility of elected African representatives, appointed the leaders of the SLNC to government committees concerned with such matters as slum clearance, education, and taxation.[10]

Other segments of the nationalist movement during the interwar years, however, remained outside any effective role in the colonial establishment. These elements were grouped around the Sierra Leone Youth League (SLYL), whose leaders came from a social stratum a cut or two below the professionals who headed the SLNC. They were mainly poorly trained teachers, clerks, letter-writers, small traders, and a few struggling journalists. Under the leadership of I. T. A. Wallace-Johnson, a journalist, the SLYL was formed in 1938 "on the principles of Collective Security for the oppressed section of the inhabitants of the country . . ."[11] In part, this radical orientation of the SLYL was a necessary strategy for a group that hoped to entice the town-dwelling masses in the Colony and Protectorate into the political arena as a counterweight to the established elite. And the strategy was relatively successful, for within a year of its formation the SLYL won a following of 7,000, most of whom were illiterate and semiliterate wage-laborers and cash-crop farmers.[12]

The radicalism of the SLYL was also related to the Marxist orientation of its Organizing Secretary, Wallace-Johnson, who had intimate ties with European Communist parties during the early 1930's and had spent a year or two studying in the Soviet Union. He returned to West Africa sometime in 1935, first to the Gold Coast where he founded the first branch of the West African Youth League and coedited a weekly newspaper with Nnamdi

[10] See, e.g., *Report of the Committee Appointed by His Excellency the Governor to Consider the Education Bill, Sessional Paper No. 3 of 1938* (Freetown, 1938); *Report of the Committee Appointed to Consider Workmen's Compensation Legislation in this Colony, Sessional Paper No. 9 of 1938* (Freetown, 1938).

[11] *Sierra Leone Weekly News*, August 13, 1938, pp. 8–9.

[12] *Sierra Leone Weekly News*, August 20, 1938, p. 4.

Azikiwe, and then to Sierra Leone in late 1937.[13] His first task was to found two newspapers, the *African Standard* and the *African Worker*, both of which became the official organs of the SLYL. The *African Worker*, subtitled "Being the Articulative Voice of the Toiling Masses," played a particularly important role in radicalizing the political responses of the SLYL's more articulate followers. Its Marxist-Leninist interpretations of colonial government also prompted the authorities to imprison Wallace-Johnson in 1940, and he remained in confinement until the end of the war. In the postwar years Wallace-Johnson discarded his earlier penchant for radical nationalism and joined the conservative, Creole-led National Council of the Colony of Sierra Leone, which was the postwar successor to the SLNC.

B. POSTWAR POLITICAL PARTIES

The colonial government's proposals for constitutional reforms, discussed in Chapter 9, influenced the postwar evolution of Sierra Leonean parties. The proposals provided for an African unofficial majority of fourteen in a Legislative Council of twenty-three members; ten of the African members would represent Protectorate interests, and four would sit for the Colony.[14] The articulate political groups in the Colony and Protectorate found themselves at odds soon after the announcement of these proposals, and their differences eventually formed the basis of the two major postwar nationalist parties.

1. The National Council of the Colony of Sierra Leone

The NCSL was formed in August 1950, following upon the failure of Colony groups to alter materially the substance of the 1947 constitutional proposals. It was almost exclusively a Creole

[13] Interview with I. T. A. Wallace-Johnson, June 1960. The Ghana National Archives possess some valuable materials on Wallace-Johnson's role in the Gold Coast Branch of the West African Youth League in the mid-1930's. See files entitled "Societies and Other Charitable Institutions," G.N.A. Accession No. 716/1956.

[14] *Proposals for the Reconstitution of the Legislative Council in Sierra Leone, Sessional Paper No. 2 of 1948* (Freetown, 1948).

affair. Its leaders were all Creoles: Dr. H. C. Bankole-Bright, General Organizing Secretary of the prewar SLNC, was President; C. D. Hotobah During, a lawyer and SLNC supporter in the pre-war Legislative Council, was Vice President; and C. M. A. Thompson, a Creole businessman, was General Secretary. Organizationally, the NCSL was an alliance of nearly a dozen political or semipolitical associations which were either predominantly Creole in membership and leadership (e.g., the Ratepayers' Associations, the Nova Scotian Maroon Descendants' Association, the Settlers' Descendants' Union, the SLNC) or were Creole in leadership but composed largely of Protectorate Africans resident in Freetown (e.g., the Artisan and General Workers' Union, the Maritime and Waterfront Workers' Union, the Sierra Leone Women's Movement).

As a Creole affair the NCSL's program was to counter any encroachment by Protectorate Africans upon the long-standing Creole supremacy in the modern sector of colonial life. "We object to foreigners [i.e., Protectorate Africans] preponderring in our Legislative Council," declared the NCSL's Election Manifesto issued in the 1951 elections to the Legislative Council.[15] The program was no doubt wrong-headed from the start, and as the NCSL persisted in it, it approached inanity. On July 29, 1952, Dr. Bankole-Bright, who gained a seat in the legislature in 1951, moved in the Legislative Council for the grant of immediate independence to the Colony: "That this Sierra Leone Government stands impeached by the Creole element of this Colony through their representatives in the Legislative Council who are members of the National Council of the Colony of Sierra Leone in that it has by its action brought into existence a cleavage between the people of this Colony and Protectorate . . . That in consequence of the present existing relationship this Colony through its National Council's representatives now ASK for its independence to control its own affairs . . ."[16]

---

[15] *Manifesto of the National Council of the Colony of Sierra Leone* (Freetown, 1951), p. 10.

[16] *Legislative Council Debates, Session 1951–1952* (Freetown, 1953), II, 121–128.

The NCSL's demand for independence for the Colony was rejected without debate by both the colonial and the SLPP government. But the leaders of the NCSL remained adamant in their opposition. They initiated a fierce campaign of invective and vilification against the SLPP in the local press, opposed nearly all acts of the Legislature irrespective of merit, and contested the legality of the 1951 constitution.[17] These actions were no more than the last struggles of conservative Creole society, which was facing its demise as a political force in Sierra Leone. The ultimate test came in the 1957 General Election. The NCSL contested all of the Colony seats; it gained none, and its candidates, including the venerable nationalist Dr. Bankole-Bright, lost their deposits.[18] A year later Bankole-Bright died, a bitter and defeated man. He was virtually penniless at his death, and his arch political opponent, Sir Milton Margai, contributed to the cost of his burial. The NCSL was a mere shadow of its former self after Bankole-Bright's death; it eventually dissolved and joined the SLPP-dominated coalition government in May 1960.

2. The Sierra Leone People's Party

The SLPP, whose importance has been emphasized in earlier chapters, was founded in April 1951, some eight months after the NCSL was organized. Like the NCSL, the SLPP was shaped in response to the postwar constitutional reforms. It was almost exclusively a Protectorate affair. The majority of the founding members wanted to call the party "The Protectorate People's Party," and only because Sir Milton Margai insisted that the party put forth an all-Sierra Leonean format were the words "Sierra Leone" included.[19] But the substance of the SLPP's program was almost wholly centered on the Protectorate; it sought to put an end to the long-standing Creole dominance in the central colonial government. "Dr. Bright should appreciate by now," declared the SLPP's main organ, the Sierra Leone Observer, in 1952, "that we

[17] See the Evening Dispatch, December 3, 1949, p. 2. This paper was owned and edited by Dr. Bankole-Bright.
[18] A. G. Simpson, Report on the Sierra Leone General Election, 1957 (Freetown, 1957), pp. 1–6.
[19] Interview with Sir Milton Margai, April 1960.

are determined to abolish the several disadvantages against us in the past to make decisive improvements in our educational and social institutions."[20]

Protectorate Africans predominated in the leadership of the SLPP. Sir Milton Margai, the grandson of a Paramount Chief and the first Protectorate African to graduate from Fourah Bay College, was the National Chairman and Parliamentary Leader; Paramount Chief Bai Farima Tass II, an educated and wealthy Chief from Kambia, was Deputy Leader; A J. Momoh, a retired senior civil servant and a founder in 1929 of one of the semi-political associations out of which the SLPP was formed, was Vice President; and Kandeh Bureh, the Temne Tribal Headman in Freetown, was National Treasurer. Sir Milton Margai, however, favored the grant of two posts to liberal Creole supporters of the Protectorate cause in the constitutional dispute. Thus the post of National General Secretary went to H. E. B. John, a Creole schoolteacher who was associated with the Protectorate Teachers' Union, and a second Vice Presidency was given to Laminah Sankoh. Sankoh had founded an organization called the People's Party in 1949 as a meeting ground in Freetown for liberal Creoles and Protectorate Africans.[21] When the SLPP was formed, he merged his small party with it and turned over to the SLPP a newspaper which he founded and financed, the *African Vanguard*.

Organizationally, the SLPP was a fusion party comprised of two semipolitical associations, the Protectorate Educational Progressive Union (PEPU) and the Sierra Leone Organization Society (SOS). The PEPU was first formed in 1929 as an improvement association but lapsed after several years' endeavor in providing scholarships for secondary education of Protectorate youths. It

---

[20] *Sierra Leone Observer,* May 17, 1952, p. 6.

[21] See Laminah Sankoh's two pamphlets, *The Root-Cause of Dissension between the Peoples of the Colony and Protectorate* (Freetown, 1951), and *The Two P's, or Politics for the People* (Freetown, 1952). Sankoh studied for the ministry in Britain and turned to politics after he was denied ordination service by an Anglican Bishop because he was black. This event caused him to leave the church altogether, and he discarded his Christian name, E. N. Jones, for the Temne name, Laminah Sankoh. For an account of his experiences in Britain, see K. Little, *Negroes in Britain* (London, 1947), pp. 257, 262–263; Bankole Timothy, "Laminah Sankoh Remembered," *Sierra Leone Daily Mail,* July 30, 1960, pp. 5, 10.

was reconstituted in 1946 "to perform the spread of education in the Protectorate and . . . pledged to work for the progress of these parts."[22] Although it had no explicit political aims, the PEPU was nonetheless a political organization in that it was founded by Chiefs, financed by them, and played some part in the postwar discussions of the role of Chiefs in local government.[23] Only one member of the Protectorate professional elite was associated with the postwar PEPU, Sir Milton Margai, who was its first Deputy President and who gained the post as a result of his long period as adviser to Chiefs while he was a medical officer in the Protectorate. Sir Milton was later to be the undisputed choice of Chiefs for the leading position in the SLPP.

The SOS, like the PEPU, was founded in 1946 as an improvement association. Its main purpose was to sponsor "a programme of self development aiming at raising the standard of living in the country in all its aspects . . ."[24] Unlike the PEPU, however, the SOS had political inclinations as well; in his inaugural address the SOS's President, Dr. John Karefa-Smart, declared the political aims of the association: "To tackle . . . political subjugation, and discover our hidden resources . . . and use them to lay down in our generation the foundation stones of a united, progressive, economically developed and free Sierra Leone."[25] The SOS also differed from the PEPU in that it was founded mainly by members of the professional elite, among whom, besides Dr. Karefa-Smart, were D. J. Manley (clergyman), Siaka Stevens (trade-union general secretary), Doyle Sumner (President of the Protectorate Teachers' Union and editor of its publication, *Vacco*), and T. M. Williams and F. S. Anthony (both teachers and officers of the Teachers' Union). Paramount Chief Julius Gulama, one of the thirty educated Paramount Chiefs among 211 who held office in 1946, was the only chiefly member of the SOS and was elected its Honorary President. Although the SOS had many differences

[22] *Sierra Leone Weekly News,* April 7, 1946, p. 6.
[23] *Minutes of the Moyamba District Council* (Moyamba, March 14, 1947), p. 1.
[24] *Constitution of the Sierra Leone Organization Society* (Moyamba, 1946), para. 7.
[25] *S.O.S.: The Bulletin of the Sierra Leone Organization Society* (October 1946), p. 6.

with Chiefs over the content of postwar constitutional reforms, as was discussed in earlier chapters, it was fully aware of the need to utilize Chiefs in its organizational work. All field organizers of the SOS were advised by its President, Dr. Karefa-Smart, to "begin by calling a meeting of the Tribal Authority and putting the aims of the SOS before them."[26] As will be seen presently, this principle of organization became an established feature of the SLPP's political activity and was the key to its success.

[26] J. Karefa-Smart, "How to Organise the S.O.S.," *S.O.S.: The Bulletin of the Sierra Leone Organization Society* (March 1947), p. 8.

CHAPTER 15

Power and Influence in Sierra Leonean Parties

A. LEADERS AND FOLLOWERS

The social attributes of political leaders and their followers or supporters are useful indicators of the nature of power and influence in political parties. In African parties, many of these attributes have been shaped by the historical pattern of colonial change. This is especially so for the tribal (traditional), occupational, and educational attributes of political leaders in Sierra Leone. The following discussion of leaders and followers is based on data gathered in 1960 and early 1961.

1. Traditional Attributes

One important traditional attribute of Sierra Leonean leaders concerns their tribal origins. In general the tribes that obtained most in the way of educational and commercial development under colonial rule contributed the largest number of political leaders. In 1961 the Mende, the best situated of the Protectorate groups in these respects, held six of the national posts in the SLPP, as against four held by Temne, three Creole, one Fula, and one Aku (Yoruba); they also held the crucial posts of Life President and Party Leader, both in possession of one man, Sir Milton Margai. The Mende also held 38 per cent of the SLPP's seats in the Legislature and a majority of the posts in the SLPP Cabinet, including the premiership. But whereas the position of the Mende in political leadership was helped by their compara-

tively large proportion of the population, the Creoles' comparatively large share of political leaders, as seen in Table 16, was
almost exclusively the result of their more advanced educational
and commercial status.

TABLE 16

Tribal Attributes of Sierra Leonean Legislators, 1960

		Number of legislators						
Tribe and population	% of pop.	SLPP	PNP	IPP	UPP	Appointed member	Total tribe	% by tribe
Mende (815,000)	36	15	3	—	—	—	18	35
Temne (620,000)	28	12	—	—	—	—	12	23
Creole (25,000)	1	5	1	3	1	1	11	22
Kono (164,000)	7	1	2	—	—	—	3	6
Kuranko (80,000)	3	2	—	—	—	—	2	4
Loko (80,000)	3	1	—	—	—	—	1	2
Sherbro (90,000)	4	1	—	1	—	—	2	4
Mandika (10,000)	0.4	1	—	—	—	—	1	2
Aku (5,000)	0.2	1	—	—	—	—	1	2
Total	82.6%	39	6	4	1	1	51	100%

Source: Population figures are estimates based on *Sierra Leone Protectorate Handbook 1959*
(Freetown, 1959), pp. 1–13; and M. Banton, *West African City* (London, 1957), p. 122. Total
population is 2,250,000.

Another traditional factor that has shaped political leadership
in Sierra Leone has been the kinship of leaders to chiefly families.
In 1960–61 some 35 per cent of the SLPP's national officers were
either sons, grandsons, or nephews of Chiefs (mainly Paramount
Chiefs), as was the overwhelming majority of SLPP ministers.
Among those possessing such kinship were such influential personalities as Sir Milton Margai, Prime Minister and Minister of
Internal Affairs; Albert Margai, who dissolved his opposition People's National Party and joined the SLPP Cabinet as Minister of
Natural Resources in 1961; A. J. Demby, Minister of Lands, Mines
and Labor; Dr. John Karefa-Smart, Minister of External Affairs
and Defense; Kandeh Bureh, Minister of Public Works; Doyle

Sumner, Minister of Communications; I. B. Taylor Kamara, Minister of Trade; and T. Ngobeh, Minister of Health. In addition to this, two Paramount Chiefs sat in the SLPP Cabinet as Ministers without Portfolio. The extent of the influence of chiefly kinship in determining political leadership is further demonstrated by Table 17. Candidates with chiefly kinship ties constituted 59 per cent of

TABLE 17

Candidates with Chiefly Kinship Ties in 1957 Election[a]

Party and candidates		Southwestern Province (21)[b]	Southeastern Province (20)	Northern Province (23)	Party total	Party %
SLPP	25	7	4	7	18	72
UPP	6	2	—	—	2	33
IND	33	5	10	3	18	55
Total	64	14	14	10	38	59%

Source: Table based upon Election Nomination papers, Ministry of Internal Affairs, and upon data gathered through a questionnaire and interviews.
[a] This table refers only to Protectorate constituencies.
[b] Figures in parentheses denote number of candidates per province.

all candidates who contested Protectorate constituencies in the 1957 General Election. It is equally notable that 84 per cent of the successful candidates possessed chiefly kinship ties.

Local government elections in 1959 also reflected the influence of chiefly kinship in the choice and success of party candidates. In Kenema District, for example, 54 per cent of the SLPP candidates either were sons of Chiefs or were educated persons holding traditional office. This persistent pattern of interlocking kinship ties between modern and traditional elite, evident from the very start of modern political organization in the Sierra Leone Protectorate in the 1920's, was, of course, a direct result of the preeminent role Chiefs played in colonial modernization. Chiefly families not only gained disproportionate advantages under colonial social change, but, more important, they were able to employ their strategic political position to reinforce these advantages and pass them on to the succeeding generation.

233

2. Occupational and Educational Attributes and Multiple Office-Holding

Although traditional attributes were significant in shaping political leadership in Sierra Leone, they were not sufficient influences in themselves. Access to leading roles in the modern political system also required a relatively high level of modern occupational and educational attainment. To some extent there was a close correlation between such attainment and rank in the old society. Thus the first persons to receive professional educational training in the Protectorate were normally the kin of traditional rulers, as were the first persons to gain senior posts in government service and in European firms. At any rate, high occupational and educational achievement was a prerequisite for political leadership roles, and in 1960–61 those who could be called political leaders ranked high in these respects. For instance, whereas the average rate of literacy for the country was between 5 to 10 per cent, some 30 per cent of the SLPP ministers had attained higher education, and 61 per cent secondary education. Similarly, 67 per cent of the opposition People's National Party members of the House of Representatives attained higher education and 33 per cent secondary education. Of the fifty-two African members of the Legislature in 1960–61 (one member was a European), 44 per cent were professionals, 23 per cent businessmen, and 23 per cent educated Paramount Chiefs who had held jobs in government service or European firms before becoming Chiefs.

When the attributes of traditional kinship to Chiefs and high occupational and educational attainment are combined in a given candidate, he is well placed for achieving simultaneously more than one political office. Sierra Leonean political leaders displayed a high degree of multiple office-holding in 1960–61; besides being members of the central Legislature they held office as district councillors, city councillors, and members of Native Administrations. Data for 1957 show that 64 per cent of the candidates (i.e., 77 out of 121) in the General Election held such positions before the election, as did 72 per cent of the successful candidates. There is, so it seems, a built-in tendency for a relatively small political elite

234

in African states to monopolize the major political posts at both the central and local level. To some extent this stems from the fact that most African states are small-scale political systems in the sense that they embrace small populations, ranging between two to seven million on the average, with some states like Gabon, Mauritania, Liberia, Dahomey, Togo having significantly less than two million population and several having more than seven million (e.g., Congo, Sudan, Tanganyika, Nigeria). But the main cause of multiple office-holding (which, incidentally, in the case of Ghana has gone beyond so-called contested political posts to include major posts in the bureaucracy, like the forty-seven government or quasi-government corporations which control a significant part of Ghana's economic life) would appear to be the monopolization on the part of a small number of persons of the traditional and modern attributes of political leadership we have discussed. Moreover, once power has been secured from the colonial oligarchy, this monopoly has often been reinforced by the establishment of the authoritarian single-party system. The obvious consequence of this development will be the formation of post-colonial oligarchical political systems whose elite, not unlike those in Latin America, will be self-perpetuating and will effectively dominate the decision making involved in the allocation of scarce resources. The rural masses—and to a lesser extent the town-dwelling wage-laborers—will be increasingly alienated from these political systems and forced to fall back on some facet of traditional or neo-traditional life for "meaningful" socio-political participation.

3. Leader-Follower Relationship

The manner in which the leader-follower relationship has developed in Sierra Leonean parties provides another index of the nature of power and influence in these parties. From their beginning the major postwar parties offered membership to all segments of the adult population irrespective of sex, tribe, religion, etc. All parties required a member to pay either an initial fee or an annual subscription or both. For example, the SLPP and the United Progressive Party (UPP), one of the major opposition parties since 1955, required only an initial fee of 1s. and 2s. respectively; the People's National Party (PNP), another important opposition party founded in 1958, required both an initial membership fee of 6d. and an additional 6d. annual subscription. The UPP and PNP, unlike the SLPP, also provided for membership by entire organizations, among which were, as listed in the UPP Constitution, "Trade Unions, Organizations of Professional Workers, Ex-Servicemen's Associations, Civil Service Associations, Co-Operative and Farmers' Organizations, etc. . . ."[1] The SLPP, however, was also linked to voluntary organizations of one sort or other, largely through interlocking leadership ties. As will be discussed in the next chapter, key leaders in the SLPP were simultaneously heads of sizable voluntary bodies like the Ex-Servicemen's Association, which had a membership over 3,000, and the Sierra Leone Women's Movement, which had a membership of 5,000 women traders, hawkers, seamstresses, etc. Though these organizations did not hold direct membership in the SLPP, they invariably brought many of their followers into the party or implored them to support it in general elections.

In general, Sierra Leonean parties do not actively pursue the enrollment of ordinary members, as do, say, the radical type of African parties like the *Parti Démocratique de Guinée* (PDG) which claimed 1,600,000 members in 1961 out of a total population of 3,000,000. Of the nearly 1,000,000 qualified voters in Sierra Leone in 1961 (out of a total population estimated at 2,250,000, though probably nearer 3,000,000 in fact), only 150,000 were reported as enrolled party members. This comparatively low party membership resulted from, among other things, the absence of a militant nationalist ideology on the part of the major party, the SLPP, the relatively small role of party machinery in the political process, and the tendency of Sierra Leonean parties to activate themselves only in periods of political crisis, after which they revert to relative inactivity. A political crisis of one sort or other was, in fact, invariably associated with the main effort of opposition parties to gain members.

[1] *Constitution of the United Sierra Leone Progressive Party* (Freetown, 1956), pp. 3–4.

The UPP, for instance, obtained the main body of its members during the tax riots in 1955–56, at which time the party's leader, Cyril Rogers-Wright, a lawyer-politician, freely placed his legal skills at the service of thousands of tax rioters who confronted the Magistrate's Court. Some peasant rioters so defended by Rogers-Wright responded by joining the UPP; others voted for the UPP candidates in the 1957 General Election in which the UPP gained seven seats in the Northern and Southwestern Provinces, the only Creole-led party ever to do so.[2] This crisis-based backing for the UPP was, however, merely a transitory gain. Its new peasant following had joined or supported the party only partly out of positive sympathy, being motivated more by a desire to discredit the corrupt system of Native Administration taxation that had plagued them for some thirty years. By 1958 most of the UPP's supporters in the Northern and Southwestern Provinces had left it; in some instances they had, indeed, requested that the pro-SLPP Chiefs whose corrupt administrations had sparked the tax riots be reinstated.[3] It would seem that such peasant ambivalence toward traditional rulers, evident throughout West Africa, constitutes a decisive factor in limiting the capacity of militant or radical parties (which in the Sierra Leone context the UPP was) to penetrate the rural populace.

The PNP also gained much of its membership in the context of a political crisis. The party arose out of a protracted struggle for leadership of the SLPP between Sir Milton Margai and his younger brother, Albert Margai, which reflected a more basic conflict between the older and younger men in the party. (Sir Milton Margai was 62 years old at the time, and Albert was 48 years old.) Upon his failure to wrest leadership from Sir Milton, Albert Margai formed the PNP in mid-1958, largely as an afterthought in which he was prompted by Siaka Stevens, a former minister in the SLPP government who shared Albert Margai's misfortune but was game for, and capable of, battle with the SLPP. In leaving the SLPP Albert Margai and Stevens carried

[2] See A. G. Simpson, *Report on the Sierra Leone General Election, 1957* (Freetown, 1957), pp. 1–6.
[3] Interview with District Commissioner, Kambia, March 1960.

many of the young supporters of the party with them, especially young clerks, teachers, professionals, and some skilled workers in the hinterland towns like Moyamba, Bo, Port Loko, Kenema, and Sefadu. These elements were never happy in their support of the SLPP, given its large dependence upon Chiefs, and seized the opportunity to realign when Albert Margai and Siaka Stevens formed the PNP. Furthermore, these elements later shifted their support to the All People's Congress (APC) which Siaka Stevens founded in mid-1960 after Albert Margai disbanded the PNP to rejoin the SLPP government as Minister of Natural Resources. Shortly thereafter the APC proved itself the most effective party ever to oppose the SLPP, gaining twenty-two of the sixty-four seats contested in the 1962 General Election.[4]

In addition to the voluntary associations—and we have mentioned only a few of them—Chiefs and the institutions they control have been even more important in obtaining a popular following for the SLPP.[5] Those peasants and casual wage-laborers in the provinces who supported or joined the SLPP did so largely because their Chiefs suggested or required it. Despite their not infrequent rebellious outbursts against chiefly rule, the bulk of the peasants continue to defer to chiefly dictates in matters of authority and politics. The SLPP Propaganda Secretaries responsible for organizing the provinces leave the major part of membership recruitment to Chiefs and Native Administrations.[6] The 1959 report of the SLPP Propaganda Secretary in Kenema District recorded the procedure involved as follows: "No sale conducted by me in this town; at the same time, I appointed Section Chief Alfred Pekawa of Baama, Secretary for Baama town only—the largest and most populous town in the Chiefdom. He was given 150 cards and I fully demonstrated how each card is to be issued

[4] Electoral Commission, *Sierra Leone General Election, 1962 Score-Sheet* (Freetown, 1962), pp. 8–12.

[5] For data on cooperatives, through which many cash-crop producers were linked to the SLPP through government aid, see *Sierra Leone Protectorate Handbook, 1961* (Freetown, 1961).

[6] Interview with A. H. Kabia, SLPP Senior Propaganda Secretary, December 1960.

238

out."[7] The report further noted that the staff of Native Administrations were utilized to distribute party cards.

One outcome of this method of recruiting members or supporters was a rather uninspired kind of participation in party activity. Even aside from the lack of adequate party machinery to stimulate member participation, it was unlikely that the people enrolled as party members through Chiefs' instigation would express a penchant for serious activity. An SLPP gathering in the rural areas is typically a rather contrived affair; several hundred peasants are herded by a Chief into a Native Court *barri* or some other traditional setting to welcome touring SLPP ministers and other leaders. The dancing, drumming, and singing in traditional idioms characteristic of these gatherings seldom amount to more than merrymaking—a kind of respite from the boredom of village life. A more politically meaningful experience for the rural populace came only in anomic outbursts of one sort or other.

It is notable that though this pattern of member participation has been characteristic largely of the caucus-type parties like the SLPP or the Northern People's Congress in Nigeria—parties, that is, which are linked to the wider populace through the intermediary agency of chiefly bodies—it is increasingly being reverted to by the mass-type parties, or rather what were mass-type parties during the mature period of anti-colonial nationalism, like the *Parti Démocratique de la Côte d'Ivoire,* the PDG, and the Convention People's Party (CPP) in Ghana.[8] Once the elite who used the mass-type party to obtain political office succeeded, the tendency has been for them to preempt the process of bona fide political participation by the populace, turning the party instead into a callous instrument of political control (including oppression) and social order. This has often involved a reversion to traditional and chiefly-centered agencies of public gatherings of all sorts, though strictly under the ruling party's auspices. In

[7] S. M. Kone, *SLPP Propaganda Secretary's Report on Kenema Election, October, 1959* (typescript; Freetown, 1959).

[8] For an excellent study of a mass party, see A. Zolberg, *One-Party Government in the Ivory Coast* (Princeton, N.J., 1964).

Ghana, for example, the CPP government has stimulated the revival of many public festivals and ritual occasions that had long lapsed. The Traditional Area Councils receive funds from the government or from the CPP district branches to cover the costs of such festivals, including in some instances stimulating drinks. Party representatives appear at these events and make speeches about the need to be loyal to the President, the party, and the government. Even the formal political rallies held in Accra and other urban centers increasingly entail the format of a traditional public occasion, with local Chiefs and their entourage participating. Their appearance at such rallies, always in regal splendor, is often taken as a cue by the crowd for merrymaking; the result is the blunting of the serious side of political gatherings and the political perception of the masses. In short, the traditional context of popular political participation long utilized by caucus-type parties like the SLPP is increasingly being adopted throughout African party systems in order politically to rout the masses.

A final facet of the leader-follower relationship that should be mentioned is the mode of communicating party aims and policies. The SLPP, which is the only party discussed here, reaches its supporters through the same intermediary bodies that secure most of its backing in the first place. The Chiefs and Native Administrations play the most important role in this regard, and during elections the SLPP works almost exclusively through Chiefs. In the local government elections in 1959 the SLPP Propaganda Secretary in Kenema District recorded in his report how he organized campaign rallies through the Native Administration; at one such rally in the Gorama Mende Chiefdom, he lectured the people and Chiefs "on the importance of the local election and why a PNP member should not be given any chance." The selection of candidates was also done through the Native Administration, and local sentiment on the choice of candidates was given great weight. In Wando Chiefdom, for example, the Propaganda Secretary recorded that he "held a meeting in the Chief's barri with the tribal authority. I read out the names of the applicants for the election. They unanimously declared that they would not allow a man staying outside the chiefdom to represent them in the [district] council . . . Section Chief Alfred Pekawa was unanimously appointed . . ."[9]

The national leaders of the party communicate with the masses in the same manner. Sir Milton Margai was particularly keen on this method of conducting his contact with the rural populace; a typical newspaper account of one of Sir Milton's innumerable political tours of the provinces observed: "The Premier, Sir Milton Margai, has met the tribal authority of the Jong Chiefdom (Bonthe District) at Mattru . . . Tomorrow, Sir Milton will visit Gbap, after meeting the Chiefs and tribal authorities of Sitia and Bendu-Cha Chiefdoms."[10] Occasionally Sir Milton summoned Paramount Chiefs to his office in Freetown to discuss party policies and to give them directives on how to disseminate it. In December 1960, for example, he met with twenty-five leading Paramount Chiefs to inform them of the party's plans for attaining independence from Britain and instructed them how to communicate the information to the masses. "Their duty," he directed, "was to tell all the section chiefs about independence; the section chiefs in turn should educate the town headmen who should explain to the people."[11]

Thus the SLPP's method of informing the rural populace of its policies may be described as a primary communication network; it rests upon the face-to-face contact, inherently coercive, that characterizes traditional relationships between Chiefs and peasants. Moreover, this method of political communication is congruent with, and a direct function of, the SLPP's conservative view of modernization—a view which considers as desirable and necessary the integration of as much as possible of traditional authority patterns into the modern socio-political system.

The SLPP, however, was required, like other African parties, to adopt more explicitly modern channels of communicating its aims and policies to the literate and semi-literate urban population. Here the party relied to some extent upon its formal

[9] Kone, *SLPP Propaganda Secretary's Report on Kenema Election*, October, *1959.*
[10] *Sierra Leone Daily Mail,* October 8, 1959, p. 9.
[11] *Shekpendeh,* December 2, 1960, p. 4.

branches; in 1960–61 the SLPP had twenty-one organized branches, and those situated in coastal urban centers of Free-town and Bonthe, and in the leading provincial towns like Moy-amba, Makeni, Bo, and Kenema, were of some use in channeling party policies.[12] More important than the party branches, how-ever, were its ties to voluntary associations like the Sierra Leone Women's Movement, the Youth Movement, the Cooperative So-cieties, and the Ex-Servicemen's Association, all of which were bound to the SLPP through interlocking leadership and invari-ably influenced their thousands of members on behalf of the party. Thus Dr. Karefa-Smart, President of the Ex-Servicemen's Association, was Minister of External Affairs in the SLPP govern-ment; Paramount Chief R. B. S. Koker, Secretary of the influential Old Bo School Boys' Association, was Minister without Portfolio; M. S. Mustapha, a leading figure in the Muslim Congress, was Minister of Finance and treasurer of the SLPP; Mrs. Constance Cummings-John, founder and Organizing Secretary of the Sierra Leone Women's Movement, was a Vice President of the SLPP; Madame Nancy Koroma, Mende Tribal Headman in Freetown and head of the Mende Tribal Committee, was a member of the SLPP Executive Committee; and Kandeh Bureh, Temne Tribal Headman in Freetown and founder of several Temne tribal associ-ations, was a member of the SLPP's Executive Committee and Minister of Public Works.

At election time, though on other occasions as well, the inter-locking tie between the SLPP and voluntary associations was a crucial factor in the popular backing the party received. The voluntary associations also gave the articulate supporters of the SLPP much more opportunity to initiate lines of action and policy for the party than did the party branches. And as long as they are not fully absorbed into the party structure—which has been the plight of voluntary associations in the single-party states, especially those with the mass-type party—the voluntary associ-ations in Sierra Leone will provide some democratic initiation at the grass roots. Neither the largely inactive party branches nor the

[12] Interview with R. G. O. King, General Secretary of SLPP, January 1961.

Native Administrations approximates the voluntary associations in this regard.

It should be noted, finally, that the mass media are also of some importance in channeling the party's aims and policies. Since its formation the SLPP has had two newspapers—the *Sierra Leone Observer* and the *African Vanguard*. The former was founded by Sir Milton Margai two years before the founding of the party, and in 1958, the year the *Sierra Leone Observer* folded, it had a circulation of 1,500 copies weekly. The *African Vanguard*, founded by the liberal Creole politician Laminah Sankoh in 1948 and turned over to the SLPP in 1951, is now the party's only newspaper; it has a biweekly circulation of 3,000. The SLPP also depends upon the British-owned *Sierra Leone Daily Mail* for favorable coverage; it has the largest circulation in Sierra Leone. The total newspaper readership in Sierra Leone was estimated at 40,000 in 1961. It should also be mentioned that the SLPP has access to the government-owned and controlled radio station for political purposes. In 1961 there were 23,000 radio receivers and between 150,000 to 200,000 listeners in Sierra Leone, most of whom were literate and resided in the coastal urban centers and in the provincial towns.

B. DISTRIBUTION OF POWER WITHIN PARTIES

1. Party Machinery

The three parties which predominated in Sierra Leone during the 1950's—the SLPP, UPP, and PNP—resemble one another in their structure. Each provides for an Annual Conference or Convention to act as the primary governing or policy-formulating body. The constitution of the PNP, for example, provides that "the supreme government of the party shall be in the hands of the National Annual Convention [whose function is] to formulate policy and draw up a programme of the party for the following year."[13] The SLPP constitution requires that "the work of the Party shall be under the direction and control of the Party Con-

[13] *Constitution of the People's National Party* (1959), clause 3.

243

ference [which] shall consider and lay down the broad principles of the Party [and] determine the programme to be adopted by the Party."[14] The Annual Conference of the parties also elects all national party officers, though this function was modified for the UPP and the SLPP in 1958 when these parties instituted the office of Life President.

Representation at the Annual Conference is formally a democratic arrangement. Party constituency organizations, party members who held elective office, and party officials, are the main categories constituting the Annual Conference. But insofar as most Sierra Leonean parties have very little in the way of constituency organization, the legislators and national party officers invariably dominate the Annual Conferences. The SLPP's Annual Conference, however, has been an exception to this pattern since 1958, at which time some 159 representatives of local-government bodies (143 of them chosen by Native Administrations) were seated as delegates at the Annual Conference.[15] This arrangement was the outcome of the struggle for control of the SLPP leadership between Sir Milton Margai and Albert Margai; after the latter's defeat Sir Milton sought to guarantee his position against any future threats. Packing the Annual Conference with representatives of Native Administrations was as good a guarantee as any, for Sir Milton, in his capacity as Minister of the Interior, exercised tremendous authority over Native Administrations.

Another important executive body in Sierra Leonean parties is the Central Committee, whose actual role in determining party policy is superior to that of the Annual Conference. The size of the Central Committee is seldom more than a dozen representatives who are normally the ranking party officials. Its function is the same for all parties—namely, to serve as the executive arm of the Annual Conference and the National Executive Committee,

[14] *Constitution of the Sierra Leone People's Party* (1958), clause IV. I read this document in a typescript produced in Freetown in 1958. The original version was published as the *Constitution and Standing Orders of the Sierra Leone People's Party* (Freetown, 1956).

[15] The 1956 version of the SLPP constitution had given the formal advantage in representation at the Annual Conference to the constituency branches. Cf. *Constitution of the Sierra Leone People's Party* (1956), clause 5, and *Constitution of the Sierra Leone People's Party* (1958), clause 4.

the latter chosen by the Annual Conference. Thus, the SLPP constitution provides that the Central Committee, composed of the
party's national officers, shall "execute the decisions of the Executive Committee in closest collaboration with the Parliamentary
Council."[16] In practice, however, the SLPP's Central Committee
has never played an important role in decision making, and in
view of the fact that the party's constitution does not state what
constitutes a quorum of the Committee, it is doubtful that it was
ever meant to be of any importance.

It has rather been the Cabinet of the SLPP government that has
dominated the formulation of party policy. This has come about
for a variety of reasons. For one thing, the membership of the
Cabinet and the SLPP Central Committee are partly coterminous;
in 1961 some 37 per cent of the national officers who comprise the
Central Committee were members of the Cabinet. For another
thing, the SLPP Cabinet is reasonably well representative of the
major interest groups within the party. Chiefs, businessmen,
Creoles, Mende, and other interests are all able to obtain a fair
measure of influence in the Cabinet; in 1961, for example, some
38 per cent of the members of the SLPP Parliamentary Council or
Party were in the Cabinet, and they constituted a nearly perfect
cross section of the major interests represented in Parliament.

Even more important, perhaps, than either of the foregoing
reasons for the hegemony of the Cabinet in policy making has
been the personal influence of the Prime Minister, Sir Milton
Margai. Until his death in 1964—following which he was succeeded in the premiership by his brother, Albert Margai—Sir
Milton was the only SLPP leader who could claim a wide support
among the major interest groups in the country. He was particularly strong among the Chiefs who, in the last analysis, held the
political influence of the rural masses in their hands. Sir Milton
also claimed a certain natural legitimacy or authority owing to his
leading role in the Sierra Leone movement for self-government.
When combined with Sir Milton's own conception of political
leadership, a conception rooted in traditional authority patterns,
these situations led him to assert a rather autocratic influence over

[16] *Ibid.*

245

the definition of party policy, thereby elevating the Cabinet to its leading role. Though Sir Milton had the choice of exercising his autocratic influence within the Central Committee rather than the Cabinet, he did not do so simply because the SLPP was not, as a party, a crucial constituent of his political influence. His direct, personal relationships with Chiefs and traditional institutions generally, combined with the authority that accrued to him by virtue of his office, were far more important constituents of Sir Milton's influence. Consequently the Central Committee of the SLPP has never had an active part in policy making, in which respect it has differed markedly from its counterparts in Ghana or Guinea—though in the past two years the Central Committee of the CPP has been progressively eclipsed by President Nkrumah and his Cabinet, or rather certain selected members thereof.

There is some likelihood, however, that since Albert Margai's succession to the leadership of the SLPP, the Central Committee might very well replace the Cabinet as the main policy-making body. The style of Albert Margai's leadership, highly militant, is likely to compel him to develop the party into a bona fide political machine, which it has never been. There are certainly elements within the Cabinet who might recoil from certain consequences of his militant leadership (e.g., the Creoles, the Chiefs, and the business interests), in which case Albert Margai's response could be to strengthen the Central Committee and the party generally as a counterweight. It is not insignificant in this connection that he has revived the Annual Convention which, until the time of his succession to the premiership in April 1964, had not been convened for several years. Following his ascendancy to the premiership, which entailed a serious though momentary split between the leading Mende and Temne personalities in the SLPP, Albert Margai convened the Annual Convention in order to legitimize his rather stormy succession. In the following year a large effort was put into reorganizing the party, for which purpose an extraordinary Annual Convention was held. And at the regular Annual Convention in June 1965, the party reported that its membership had expanded from around 100,000 in 1961 to nearly 1,000,000. Though this figure seems rather dubious, there is no doubt that some reorganization of the SLPP has accompanied Albert Margai's take over of the party's leadership. This is further indicated by the announcement at the 1965 Convention that the party would be housed in large, permanent headquarters, a luxury it has never had.

It is, however, rather unique to Sierra Leonean politics that the governing party should now find itself activating party organs. For the post-colonial tendency throughout most of Africa has been to de-emphasize party machinery and activity as a bona fide outlet for political participation, replacing them with a highly centralized, leader-dominated, authoritarian single party which has little more than a contrived relationship with the masses (e.g., in Ghana the masses participate in the single-party regime merely as a "captive audience"; they are herded together for party purposes at their places of work, in government offices or government industries, faced with the threat of dismissal for failure to comply). This relationship is characterized by callous or indifferent lines of communication between leaders and followers, the latter invariably on the receiving end, the object of party-government directives and constantly watched by party-government activists for dissident elements.

It may well be, of course, that the tendency of the SLPP under Albert Margai to activate the popular forces is little more than a tactical move, common elsewhere in Africa during the mature stage of the anti-colonial nationalist movement, whereby the leaders prone to the militant style of politics sought to legitimize their style—and thus their power—through activistic party organization. Once legitimized, however, power is usurped; the leader and the inner political elite entrench themselves and tend toward a self-perpetuating oligarchy. Under these circumstances the masses, as a positive category, are looked upon askance. They must be deactivated, put in a state of organizational disarray (that is, as regards their measure of organizational autonomy within the dominant party), and forestalled from exerting an independent influence. This has occurred in its most radical form in Ghana,

247

where left-wing symbols, methods, and the language of mass politics are utilized to rout the masses.[17] Elsewhere in Africa (e.g., Ivory Coast, Kenya, Uganda) other methods are employed to undercut the masses in the post-colonial regimes. It may well be, then, that once the militant political style of a leader like Albert Margai in Sierra Leone has been legitimized, in the sense that it is reinforced by effective party organization, this organization will be usurped. It will, in short, cease to function as a mode of bona fide mass participation and will become an agency for perpetuating the power monopoly of the leader and the political elite in general.

2. Party Finance

Although the nature of a political party's financial arrangements provides some understanding of political influence in a party, it is by no means a sufficient guide to such influence. There are many areas of political influence in an African party which are quite impervious to financial considerations. The conditions under which popular forces might exert significant influence upon party policy, for example, are rarely coincident with financial considerations; at least not in the sense that popular forces have a major responsibility for party finance and to that extent exercise a significant bargaining position. Few African parties have ever had their popular following effectively organized for financial purposes.

Sierra Leonean parties are no exception to this generalization. Since its foundation the SLPP has required a fee of 1s. plus a monthly subscription of 6d. from its members; but the income

---

[17] It is curious and unfortunate that so many observers of African politics have accepted at face value the symbols and other attributes of the formal ideological garb, including programs of "African socialism," used by African parties and ruling elites. Effective political analysis requires that the ideological and related attributes of politics be seen in the context of actual social and political relations, and in the way these attributes affect the structures and processes governing the allocation of benefits or resources among the competing segments of society. Unless this is done, no viable analytical sense can be made of, say, the role of "Nkrumaism" (a crude variant of Marxism-Leninism) in the Ghanaian political system. Cf. Martin Kilson, "Politics of African Socialism," *African Forum* (Winter 1966) pp. 17–26. See also my review article on Dennis Austin's book, *Politics in Ghana 1946–1960, ibid.*, pp. 131–134.

accruing from this source has been of little significance to the party's finances. As a result, the party leaders became the main source of finance. In the SLPP Sir Milton Margai was a major contributor to the cost of election campaigns, along with another leading figure, M. S. Mustapha, a wealthy businessman who was elected Treasurer of the SLPP in 1956 and was Minister of Finance in Sir Milton's second Cabinet. Sir Milton Margai, as mentioned before, was also responsible for financing the SLPP's first news-paper, the *Sierra Leone Observer,* which he founded at Bo in 1950. Other party leaders likewise financed their party's news-papers. Dr. Bankole-Bright was founder and owner of the NCSL's organ, the *Evening Dispatch;* C. Rogers-Wright financed the UPP's organ, *Shekpendeh;* and Albert Margai met a large part of the costs of the PNP's rather short-lived newspaper, *Liberty.*

The SLPP, however, claims a decided advantage over the op-position parties in matters of party finance by virtue of being the governing party. One such advantage is the salaries of its legis-lators which, as shown in Table 18, are comparatively large and readily accessible to the party. Before 1957 the SLPP tapped this source of finance only when the legislators themselves volunteered donations; thereafter each SLPP legislator contributed, by formal

TABLE 18

Salaries and Allowances of Legislators, 1960

Position	Salary (£)	Allowances (£)[a]
Prime Minister	4,000	480
Ministers	3,000	420
Ministers without Portfolio	2,000	300
Junior Ministers	1,500	240
Speaker	2,500	380
Deputy Speaker	1,250	180
Chief Whip	1,200	180
Leader of Opposition	1,500	380
Members	920	180

Source: Data supplied by Ministry of Finance.
[a] Excluding automobile allowances.

249

arrangement, at least £6 per month to the party fund, and Ministers, Junior Ministers, the Deputy Speaker, and Chief Whip contributed a larger amount. This contribution to the party fund was guaranteed through a check-off system whereby the legislators empowered the Auditor-General to deduct an agreed amount from their monthly salaries.

Another source of income accruing to the SLPP by virtue of its governing position comes from expatriate business groups. A large European firm helped Sir Milton Margai launch the *Sierra Leone Observer,* and the same firm has always had a lenient credit policy toward the party when it requires goods.[18] European banks have also granted the party favorable loans; one such loan amounting to £12,000 was granted to the SLPP during the 1962 General Election campaign. Some SLPP candidates obtain financial contributions from expatriate businesses, and in some areas Native Administrations solicit funds for SLPP candidates from Lebanese merchants. Although it is difficult to weigh the political significance of financial contributions to the SLPP by expatriates, it is reasonable to presume that some consideration is reciprocated by the SLPP government.

Unlike many other governing African parties, the SLPP has not, to my knowledge, utilized government funds for explicitly party purposes. In Ghana, for example, a commission of inquiry in 1956 revealed that the CPP employed funds of the Cocoa Purchasing Corporation for party purposes, and since 1960 hardly any distinction at all has been made between government and party funds.[19] Party newspapers and pamphlets galore, party vans, party buildings, salaries of party officers, and the like are all paid in whole or part from the government budget. Similarly, in Eastern

[18] Interview with Sir Milton Margai, April 1960.

[19] O. Jibowu, *Report of the Commission of Enquiry into the Affairs of the Cocoa Purchasing Company* (Accra, 1956), pp. 28–29, and *passim.* Cf. P. T. Bauer, *West African Trade* (Cambridge, 1954), pp. 315–316. Bauer was one of the few observers of African politics during the early 1950's who predicted that the parties would exploit the large funds of marketing boards for political ends. The CPP in Ghana, incidentally, also obtains funds through a 10 per cent kickback from most government contracts. Since no accounting is made of these funds, it is likely, on basis of other evidence, that they are used for other than party purposes, thus being a part of a much wider process of bureaucratic corruption that is rather widespread in Ghana and other African states.

and Western Nigeria commissions of inquiries revealed in 1956 and 1962, respectively, that a major part of the finances of the National Convention of Nigerian Citizens, the governing party in Eastern Nigeria, and the Action Group, formerly the governing party in the West, were financed largely through illicit uses of public funds. In the latter instance, some £4,000,000 of government funds reached the party coffers by way of prearranged kickbacks from loans to Nigerian businessmen.[20] It should be noted, however, that the SLPP government has granted funds to sundry voluntary associations, most of which have never faltered in their support of the party's candidates at election time. But this pattern of government financial aid to party activities, though important to the SLPP's support, is not precisely of the same order as that which has prevailed in Nigeria and Ghana and elsewhere. The SLPP remains a voluntary political body supported largely by the funds of those who have a stake in it, whereas the CPP in Ghana is an integral part of an authoritarian government.

[20] See *Report of Coker Commission of Inquiry into the Affairs of Certain Statutory Corporations in Western Nigeria, 1962* (Lagos, 1962). For similar material on Eastern Nigeria, see *Proceedings of the Tribunal Appointed To Inquire into Allegations of Improper Conduct by the Premier of the Eastern Region of Nigeria in Connection with the Affairs of the African Continental Bank and other Relevant Matters* (Lagos, 1957), Vol. II.

CHAPTER 16 -

Dynamics of Party Politics

A. POLITICAL IDEAS, VALUES, AND METHODS

1. Nationalism and Traditionalism

The competing ideas, values, and methods in Sierra Leone party politics are readily classifiable under the terms nationalism and traditionalism. The former term refers to those types of political perceptions, values, and modes of action that resulted primarily from European domination of Sierra Leonean society. The latter term embraces those socio-political values and methods that are essentially indigenous to the society or that resulted from a qualified fusion of indigenous and expatriate modes.

In general, the militant anti-colonial nationalism found elsewhere in Africa was not a prominent feature of party operations in Sierra Leone, either at the time I observed them in 1960–61 or prior to this period. This was especially the case for the SLPP, the dominant party since the commencement of bona fide party politics in 1951. Neither in the SLPP's constitution nor in its first election manifesto (1951) do the favored words in the vocabulary of militant African nationalism like "colonialism" and "imperialism" appear. They do appear twice in the SLPP's 1957 election manifesto, but in the rather obscure and diffident context of a "Message" written by Albert Margai, then party chairman, and appended to the main body of the manifesto.[1]

The relatively small role of the nationalist outlook in the politics of the SLPP was apparent as well from its leaders' view of the process by which colonial peoples gain independence. Militant

[1] *The S.L.P.P. Road: Statement of Policy Issued by the Executive of the Sierra Leone People's Party* (Freetown, 1951); *Election Manifesto of the Sierra Leone People's Party* (Freetown, 1957).

252

nationalist parties like the Convention People's Party (CPP) in Ghana and the *Parti Démocratique de Guinée* (PDG) conceived this process as a struggle by colonial peoples to wrest power from expatriate authorities. SLPP leaders, however, saw it largely as an operation through which power was granted by, not wrested from, the colonial authorities when the subject peoples proved their ability properly to handle power. This conception was quite evident in a political broadcast by Sir Milton Margai during the 1957 general election. "We [SLPP leaders] were the first Ministers ever in Sierra Leone," he said. "We were pioneers. The evidence of how well we have done our jobs is seen in the readiness with which Her Majesty's Government has agreed for us to take another step towards self-government."[2]

Inevitably, this outlook influenced specific policy issues like the role of expatriate personnel during the decolonization period. Whereas the rather more militant opposition parties in Sierra Leone like the PNP were suspicious of the expatriate official, believing he would not "pursue with any degree of fervour lines of policy which he knows to be against the interest of himself or his class," as Siaka Stevens, the PNP deputy leader, put it, the SLPP leaders claimed publicly, as Sir Milton did on one occasion, that expatriate officials were desirable and "seek the interest of the country very, very keenly."[3] Nor did the SLPP affect the suspicious stance toward private capital, foreign or African, that was so characteristic of the militantly anti-colonial nationalists in much of Africa. The SLPP Minister of Trade and Commerce, I. B. Taylor Kamara, remarked in the Legislature in 1957 that "it is Governments' policy to encourage private enterprise," and ever since the late 1950's the SLPP government has done just that.[4] Much assistance has been given to African businessmen, including the pur-

---

[2] *Sierra Leone Daily Mail*, May 3, 1957, pp. 4–5. See also *Daily Mail*, May 30, 1957, p. 1.

[3] Siaka Stevens, "The People's National Party and Expatriatism," *Liberty*, July 25, 1959, p. 5; *ibid.*, July 18, 1959, p. 8. Sir Milton Margai's remarks and others by SLPP leaders are in *Legislative Council Debates, No. 1 of Session 1951–52* (Freetown, 1953), pp. 120–121; *Election Manifesto of the Sierra Leone People's Party*, p. 12; *Legislative Council Debates, No. 9 of Fifth Session 1955–57* (Freetown, 1958), pp. 77–78.

[4] *House of Representatives Debates, First Session 1957–58* (Freetown, 1958), p. 81.

chase by government of manufacturing machinery for sale to
African entrepreneurs at less than market costs.[5] Foreign firms
have received an array of government support under the Development Ordinance of 1960, which provided, *inter alia,* for a "tax
holiday" and the privilege to import free of duty the articles or
materials required for the establishment of mining industries,
plantations, and other enterprises.

The absence of a militant nationalist approach by the SLPP reflected both the circumstances of the party's rise to power and
the conscious preference of its leadership, especially Sir Milton
Margai. As we have seen in the preceding chapter, the SLPP did
not pursue mobilization of the rural masses as a means of gaining
their support at elections. Rather, it relied upon, and articulated
its political structure to, the traditional institutions controlled by
Chiefs, who held legitimate—though not uncontested—claim
upon political allegiance of the rural populace. The Chiefs, as
shown earlier in this study, were themselves transformed significantly enough under colonial institutions to lend their status and
role to the modern party process.

Circumstances and preferences reinforced each other. Sir Milton
Margai in particular had little understanding of or sympathy for
the kind of expedient democratic outlook required of a political
leadership whose claim for power rested upon an organized mass
basis. Sir Milton's thought was alien to the kind of political outlook that admitted a measure of autonomous, self-interested ra-
tionality to the political needs and orientation of the masses. It
was, for instance, inconceivable to Sir Milton that the peasantry
should harbor doubts regarding chiefly rule; on one occasion he
warned that the SLPP government would not permit such doubts.
"I don't know what has brought this idea of 'loss of confidence'
[in Chiefs]," he declared during a debate on Chiefdom affairs in
1955. "To depose someone because of loss of confidence, I say it
is a myth . . . That idea of loss of confidence should be wiped out.
It is only in European countries where the people feel in their
constitutional powers the term is applicable. But to come here

[5] *Ibid.,* pp. 81–82.

and say that a chief has lost confidence is absolutely nonsense: the sooner we do away with that the better . . . I know how this 'loss of confidence' business goes about," he continued, "and it should not be allowed to ruin the Protectorate. If anybody is found causing trouble, we ought to take the most vindictive steps in dealing with that one."[6] Similarly, Paramount Chief Yumkella II, a leading SLPP figure in the Northern Province and a member of the House of Representatives for Kambia District, gave vent to the same type of political values during a debate in 1960 on an opposition motion that incapacitated Chiefs be retired on government pension. Uncompromisingly opposed to the motion, Chief Yumkella charged that "by bringing the motion to the House the mover was abusing the privilege of democracy."[7]

There were, of course, other leading figures in the SLPP during its formative period—notably Albert Margai and Siaka Stevens, respectively Minister of Local Government and Minister of Lands, Mines, and Labour 1953–1957—who personally inclined toward allowing the rural populace political expression outside traditional institutions and values. But the circumstances were so favorable to the kind of approach espoused by Sir Milton Margai, combined with his large personal influence in the SLPP, that these figures followed suit. "I assure the chiefs that we are very confident that the position of chieftaincy is very necessary and must continue," Albert Margai declared during the crucial debate on the 1955–56 tax riots. And he was seconded by Stevens: "Chieftaincy is an office which is very useful and which we will need for a very long time."[8] Even when Albert Margai and Stevens formed the opposition PNP in 1958, they paid deference to chiefly rule. "The People's National Party strongly maintains that chieftaincy has and will continue to have a most important place in our National development for a very long time," said a policy statement of the PNP Executive Committee in August 1959.[9]

[6] *Eleventh Assembly Proceedings* (Freetown, 1955), esp. pp. 13–14.
[7] *Summary of Proceedings of the House of Representatives, 29th November, 1960* (Freetown, 1960), p. 2.
[8] *Legislative Council Debates, No. 8 of Session 1955–56* (Freetown, 1958), pp. 448, 426.
[9] *Liberty,* August 8, 1959, p. 4.

2. *Political Uses of Secret Societies*

Given the significance of the leader in modern African politics, we cannot overemphasize the seminal role of Sir Milton Margai in fitting the SLPP's behavior to traditional patterns. His social origins and status as the son of a chiefly family, and the fact that his father's brother was an influential Mende Chief in Bonthe District throughout his political career, certainly predisposed Sir Milton toward this method. Moreover, during two decades of service (1932–50) as a medical officer in the hinterland prior to entering party politics, he had himself experimented with the use of Mende tribal associations like the Sande Society, an initiation order for females, in disseminating modern health and household practices and in training a corps of midwives.[10]

Indeed, in a certain sense Sir Milton inherited a predisposition toward the synthesis of traditional and modern forms from Mende society itself. The Mende, more than other Sierra Leonean tribes but not unlike tribes elsewhere in Africa, initially experimented with the use of traditional cultural associations to cope with aspects of the Western intrusion as early as the turn of the twentieth century. As Kenneth Little points out, during the Hut Tax War of 1898 (also known as the Mende War, since the Mende carried a major share of it), the Mende Chiefs "called warriors to arms over a wide area by sending round the Poro sign of war—a burned palm-leaf."[11] Ever since this event the Poro Society has been used variously by Chiefs and peasants for political purposes connected with the colonial situation. Throughout the twentieth century educated Mende—and also Temne, to whom Poro had spread—never hesitated to join Poro Society, and, according to Little, even when well established in modern professions or trades,

[10] See the fascinating article by Sir Milton Margai on his experiences, "Welfare Work in a Secret Society," *African Affairs* (March 1948), pp. 227–230. Interviews with Sir Milton in 1960 gave me a keen sense of the role of traditional institutions and values in his political method.

[11] Kenneth Little, "Mende Political Institutions in Transition," *Africa* (January 1947), p. 12, n. 1. For a detailed account of the role of Poro in the Hut Tax War of 1898, see Sir David Chalmers, *Report by Her Majesty's Commissioner and Correspondence on the Subject of the Insurrection in the Sierra Leone Protectorate, 1898*, Cmd. 9391 (London, 1899), Pt. II, pp. 34–35, 382 ff.

they were likely to "continue to play a part in Poro activities."[12]

It is no surprise, then, that the modern elite in the Protectorate who founded the SLPP in 1951 adopted the traditional Poro symbol, the palm leaf, as the party symbol. Incidentally, a not implausible alternative explanation of this act might run as follows: If the conservative nationalist method of SLPP leaders is viewed psychologically as a function of a Caliban-like personality trait—otherwise called an Uncle Tom personality or the Sambo syndrome—in the context of a colonial situation, then the adoption of the palm leaf as a party symbol may be a subliminal form of radical or revolutionary expression. This is especially so when it is noted that the most symbolically significant use of the Poro palm leaf in the context of the colonial situation was at the time of the Hut Tax War. Further credence is lent to this type of psychological explanation of the symbolic side of SLPP political behavior by the fact that the SLPP chose the date of April 27 as Independence Day, which was the same date on which the Mende War broke out. Whatever the limitations of this type of explanation, there are certainly many features of African political behavior under colonial rule—and equally in the post-colonial period, given the persistence of neo-colonial relations—that are illuminated by it.

Besides the palm leaf, the SLPP exploited other features of Poro for political purposes. Sir Milton Margai was most astute at manipulating Poro obligations in his relations with Chiefs and other traditional notables; and throughout Sierra Leone, individual candidates drew upon Poro obligations at every opportunity. A known instance of the latter occurred in the Bo Town constituency during the 1957 general election. There was a dispute between the local branch and the party headquarters over the nominees for candidate. The SLPP headquarters, cognizant of the fact that the constituency concerned was basically urban, not rural, backed Prince J. William, a popular businessman (druggist and real estate owner) who was Creole on his paternal side but of a Mende mother and who spoke Mende, while the local branch inclined

[12] K. L. Little, "Social Change and Social Class in the Sierra Leone Protectorate," *American Journal of Sociology* (July 1948), pp. 20–21.

toward Kamanda Bongay, also a businessman (hotel owner) but the son of a late and powerful Paramount Chief of Bo Town.[13] The nominee of the central headquarters prevailed; but Bongay stood as an Independent, and, being a full-blooded Mende of high rank, he called upon Poro obligations and won the election by a sizable majority.

This event, incidentally, points up an important feature of the utilization of Poro obligations for modern political purposes: persons exploiting these obligations were invariably of high traditional status, mainly sons of Chiefs. This conformed to traditional uses of Poro authority and influence, for traditionally Chiefs virtually claimed ascriptive right to exercise this authority. As shown in an earlier chapter, this pattern of Poro authority was weakened under colonial change, with the result that the peasant disturbances of the 1930's and the postwar period saw the rebellious exercise of Poro obligations by commoners. But within the structure of the SLPP's nationalist politics, such perversion of traditional authority patterns and values was *verboten,* and the few SLPP politicians of commoner origin were keen to recognize this.

3. Ritualistic Flattery: Personalism and Leadership

The personal style of SLPP politicians in their relations with each other, and especially with the party leader, was equally governed at many points by traditional patterns. Ritualistic flattery,

[13] It was not unique for the SLPP to put up a desirable Creole candidate in an urban constituency. Ever since 1951 the party reserved all but two of the constituencies in the Freetown urban area for Creole candidates. At the same time, the party invariably campaigned in the hinterland constituencies as an anti-Creole party. Kamanda Bongay, in fact, exploited this contradiction in the party's handling of the Creole issue in his own campaign. He was strengthened in this by the fact that his father was the powerful Paramount Chief at Bo who expropriated the property of hundreds of Creole merchants in 1929 (see chapter 7). On the role of anti-Creole propaganda in the 1957 election campaign, one observer remarked that "Distrust of the Colony Creoles is deeply entrenched and shows every sign of having been discreetly stimulated by S.L.P.P. organizers. It is noticeable that the accepted translation of the name U.P.P. into any of the Protectorate languages seems to be something like 'Creole Party' or 'Creole Government.' Such conditions make it extremely difficult for any party other than one of Protectorate origin to establish a solid footing there." Derek J. R. Scott, "Protectorate Politics in Sierra Leone," *West Africa* (May 25, 1957), p. 487. See also, Scott, "The Sierra Leone Election, May 1957," in W. J. M. Mackenzie and K. Robinson, eds., *Five Elections in Africa* (Oxford, 1960), pp. 202–215, 223–228.

widely used traditionally as a means of gaining influence with Mende and Temne Chiefs, was common in interpersonal relations among politicians. SLPP legislators and ministers were particularly keen in using ritualistic flattery when confronting Sir Milton Margai. This not infrequently entailed a minister or party official indulging in self-negation, all to the end of symbolizing one's dependence upon the leader as well as the leader's own omnipotent sagacity.

Institutionally speaking, ritualistic flattery creates a symbolic relationship of dependence between the persons concerned. Among the Mende in particular such a bond is highly valued, reinforced as it is by the transfer of benefits or prestige.[14] This style of interpersonal relations among politicians is prevalent elsewhere in Africa and has been a factor in the rise of a highly personalistic dictatorial leadership under single-party rule, as in the case of the Nkrumah regime in Ghana and the Houphouet-Boigny regime in the Ivory Coast.[15] Although dictatorial rule has not yet occurred in Sierra Leone, the prevalence of ritualistic flattery in interpersonal political relationship is a facilitating factor, emanating from, and reinforced by, traditional society, where the life cycle of the average man is still imbedded.

4. Voluntary Associations in the SLPP: A Reciprocity Model of African Politics

The SLPP's adherence to traditional norms of socio-political relations affected nearly every aspect of its behavior. This may be illustrated by an account of the party's relationship with modern and quasi-modern (or neo-traditional) voluntary associations.

The SLPP had a distinct preference for voluntary associations that were formed through a fusion of modern and traditional elements. Thus the party's initial ties with voluntary associations were with the Mende Tribal Committee and the Temne Tribal Union in Freetown. Both grew out of the system of tribal headmen

[14] Cf. Marion D. de B. Kilson, "Social Relationships in Mende Dɔmɛisia," *Sierra Leone Studies* (December 1961), pp. 170–171.

[15] In Ghana ritualistic flattery is not only an institutionalized relationship among politicians and the leader but is imbedded within the party and governmental apparatus as well and often carried to ridiculous extremes.

administration employed by the colonial government in Freetown, beginning with the statutory establishment of a Mende tribal headman in 1905. These associations invariably touched the lives of a major segment of the urban population; throughout the post-war period, during which they grew, they performed, quasi-legally, an array of basic administrative functions under their tribal headmen, like the registration of births and deaths, settling disputes of a traditional nature, performing marriages, registering migrants from the hinterland. Community development functions were also performed, such as the collection of £20,000 by the Temne Tribal Union to build two mosques in the late 1940's and the raising of a comparable sum by the Mende Tribal Committee to build in 1960–61, an additional church of the United Brethren in Christ Mission, which was erected within a stone's throw of the Tribal Committee's headquarters.[16]

Within the Mende Tribal Committee and the Temne Tribal Union, the political process was in some measure traditional. For example, the home of the Mende tribal headman (or rather headwoman—Madame Nancy Koroma—when I observed the institution in 1960–61) was also the headquarters of the Tribal Committee. This kind of personalization of roles and functions is ubiquitous in traditional society, and, like the setting of the chiefly role in hinterland areas of Sierra Leone, the home office of Nancy Koroma was a beehive of activity where modern, traditional, and ritual functions intertwined and overlapped. In a sense, then, the political process within these tribal associations centered more around the charismatic position or attributes of the headman than around the functions of the office.[17] It was not, however, a situation

[16] See *Report of the Committee Appointed to Examine the Working of the Tribal Administration (Colony) Ordinance, Cap. 244* (Freetown, 1955), esp. pp. 4–6, 13–20. See also M. P. Banton, "Tribal Headmen in Freetown," *Journal of African Administration* (July 1954), esp. pp. 141–142, where he observes: "In most of the tribes represented in Freetown the institution of chiefship plays a central role. The natives look to their chief or headman for a variety of services and it will be a long time before other institutions can take over all his functions."

[17] The notion of "charisma" used here is borrowed from Max Weber—namely, "a relationship between leader and follower entailing devotion to the specific and exceptional sanctity, heroism or exemplary character of an individual person, and of the normative patterns or order revealed or ordained by him." *The Theory of Social and Economic Organization* (New York, 1947), p. 328.

of either the one or the other, for the charismatic (or ritual) role gained credence in the non-traditional, urban environment through the secular role ordained by colonial government.

The combination of the ritual and secular roles within the tribal associations naturally rendered them attractive to the SLPP as bases for spreading its influence in the urban areas and towns. The associations were, among other things, capable of maintaining traditional relationships between leaders and followers even in the non-traditional urban environment—a goal central to the SLPP's political values. The SLPP always preferred linkage with associations headed by persons who had both Western education and high rank in traditional society. Nancy Koroma and Kandeh Bureh, the heads of the Mende and Temne tribal associations respectively, both claimed the latter attribute. Madame Koroma was of a chiefly Mende family in Moyamba District, and her father was the first Mende tribal headman in Freetown, appointed by the colonial government partly because he possessed high traditional rank. Kandeh Bureh was a member of a Temne ruling family in Mange Bure Chiefdom, Port Loko District. Both were also comparatively well-educated, at the upper primary level, and Kandeh Bureh was a schoolteacher for many years. Both were experienced, too, in the running of modern organizations. Madame Koroma, for example, was a leading and long-standing member of the United Brethren in Christ Church in the Mende Community of Freetown, as well as a member of other welfare bodies. Likewise, Kandeh Bureh, besides his teaching career, organized a group of recreational associations of young Temne males in Freetown called "dancing compins," established a night school for literacy training, and founded an agricultural settlement for unemployed Temne males.[18]

This combination of traditional and modern attributes of leadership appeared as well among the leaders of the other, more modern, voluntary associations that contributed to the SLPP's in-

[18] Banton, "Tribal Headmen in Freetown," p. 143. See also Michael Banton, "The Dancing Compin," *West Africa* (November 7, 1953), pp. 1041–1042; L. Proudfoot, "Towards Muslim Solidarity in Freetown," *Africa* (April 1961), pp. 147–156.

fluence in the urban areas and towns. For instance, John Karefa-Smart, President of the Sierra Leone Ex-Servicemen's Association (membership of 3,000 in 1960–61), was of a Mende chiefly family on his mother's side and a Temne chiefly family on his father's side. He was trained in medicine in the United States and Canada, joined the Royal Air Force during World War II, and after the war practiced medicine in Sierra Leone and spent several years with the World Health Organization before entering politics in 1956. Similarly, A. H. Kabia, President of the Sierra Leone Youth Clubs and Assistant General Secretary of the Old Bo Boys' Association (an organization of graduates of the prestigious Bo Government School), belonged to a chiefly family in Port Loko District and attained secondary school education. A final example worth noting here is that of Paramount Chief R. B. S. Koker, President of the Old Bo Boys' Association and Secretary of the Sierra Leone National Association (a pressure group organized by Chiefs), who was an educated member of an influential chiefly family in Bo District.

Traditionally in African society, a person contracts ties beyond his primary unit more as a member of the primary collectivity than as an individual, thereby continuing basic allegiance to the primary unit and its needs and obligations. In other words, the primary collectivity itself mediates one's wider social relations. Something like this principle of traditional social relations was evinced in much of the SLPP's relations with voluntary associations. Few members of voluntary associations held outright membership in the SLPP; they were linked to the party through the intermediary of the associations and their leaders. Even if the individual member of a voluntary association held outright membership in the SLPP, it was understood that the act of membership intimately embraced his relations with the voluntary association. And the voluntary associations themselves were linked to the SLPP less through outright membership (in fact, the constitution of the SLPP made no provision for such membership) than through a pattern of interlocking leadership. Invariably the leaders of the major voluntary associations—who were themselves possessed of both high traditional status and modern-leadership attributes—simultaneously held posts in the formal structure of the SLPP.

Thus, the SLPP both integrated the masses, after a fashion, into modern politics and preserved the efficacy of traditional modes of mediating socio-political relations. The party, moreover, reinforced this arrangement by dispensing finance and general patronage in a traditional manner. Wealth in traditional society as Marcel Mauss brilliantly showed in his *Essai sur le don* (1925), circulated in a manner congruent with the prerequisites of the maintenance of kinship and general social obligations.[19] Seldom was wealth used, as in modern society where production and exchange of goods and services revolve around the cash nexus and the impersonal market system, to subdue or overcome primordial social relations. When it was so used, it became politically (and socially) redundant through conspicuous consumption by authorities or was flushed off through warfare.

This traditional principle of circulating wealth can be detected in the SLPP's use of finance to bind voluntary associations to it. A variety of voluntary associations received a major part of their operating finance from the SLPP government. The Ex-Servicemen's Association, for example, received annual grants during 1957–60 which totaled £4,433; the Sierra Leone Football Association shared in the £6,725 government grant to the Sierra Leone Sports Council, a quasi-government body, over the same period; the Sierra Leone Students' Union in London received a £500 grant in 1959–60; and, also in 1959–60, some 283 Producers' Cooperative Societies with a membership of 15,624 obtained a variety of government assistance valued at £68,605, plus a government-

[19] The following analysis of African socio-political relations in terms of exchange and reciprocity relies heavily upon the writings of Marcel Mauss. (See the translation of his 1925 study by Ian Cunnison, in Marcel Mauss, *The Gift—Forms and Functions of Exchange in Archaic Societies* [Glencoe, Ill., 1954].) It also draws upon the works of other anthropologists, especially E. E. Evans-Pritchard, *The Nuer* (Oxford, 1940); M. Fortes and E. E. Evans-Pritchard, eds., *African Political Systems* (London, 1940); J. M. Middleton and David Tait, eds., *Tribes Without Rulers* (London, 1958); Max Gluckman, *Culture and Conflict in Africa* (London, 1955); Lucy Mair, *Primitive Government* (London, 1962).

guaranteed loan of £120,000, and influential members of the societies received "advances . . . to buy building materials to improve their houses."[20]

The recipients recognized, above all, the principle of reciprocity implicit in the exchange (gift) between themselves and the SLPP.[21] Primitive exchange binds the individual and his social unit. This lent the SLPP a convenient political lever: Lacking adequate political machinery for the manifold purposes of modern politics, it could, through reciprocity, leave to voluntary associations the matter of ensuring that their members supported the party when required. Related matters of political discipline and sanction could, within certain limits, also be left to voluntary associations. The members, cognizant of the fact that they *and* their kinship unit were bound, were not inclined to falter when the party needed support. The system, then, was, in a certain sociological sense, rather oppressive—and worked partly because of this. It worked also because it met certain needs of individuals and groups. But in the context of a developing society this type of political process also had its drawbacks, some consequences of which are noted presently.

A number of interesting political consequences emerge from the type of relationship the SLPP established with voluntary associations. When compared to the direct mode of integrating an individual *qua* individual into the party politics of developing African societies, the method adopted by the SLPP may be less conducive to the growth of politically alert citizens. Nevertheless, the political experience acquired within voluntary associations—at a sub-governmental level, so to speak—may eventually foster the organizational pluralism that seems to be a precondition of viable competitive politics. But in the short run at least, the type of political relationship established by the SLPP between the new elite

[20] The information on grants to veterans' groups and sports organizations and cooperatives is found in *Sierra Leone Government Estimates of Expenditure and Revenue, 1959–60* (Freetown, 1959), pp. 48–50, 124; *House of Representative Debates, No. 1 of Session 1958–59* (Freetown, 1959), p. 126. Figures on support of students appear in *Legislative Council Debates, No. 9 of Fifth Session 1955–57*, p. 115.

[21] Interview with Nancy Koroma and members of the Mende Tribal Committee, January 1960.

and the masses is unlikely to advance the average voter much beyond the traditional authority system.

For the ruling elite this has obvious advantages when they wish to stabilize socio-political relations in the course of modernization. African voluntary associations, rooted as they are in traditional relations, reduce the tension and cleavage that stem from a change in the individual's primary social loyalties, obligations, and expectations. But from the viewpoint of the masses, the stability produced by this socio-political pattern may well hinder their advance. This is especially so when it is recognized that the new elite in Africa incline toward a pattern of resource allocation or use that is basically Western, in the sense that it is governed more by individual preference than by obligations of traditional kinship—particularly where such allocation concerns the share claimed by the elite groups themselves. Yet these same elite groups, cognizant of the persistence of traditional perceptions of social relations among the population, formally infuse the modern political process with as many traditional norms or evaluations as they can. Hence an interesting and far-reaching contradiction.

Much of post-colonial politics centers around this contradiction between the elite's self-serving approach to the allocation of scarce resources, on the one hand, and their political espousal, on the other hand, of traditional norms and obligations as guideposts for political behavior. The single-party tendency so widespread in post-colonial Africa is not, for instance, unrelated to this contradiction; through the single party the elite endeavor to curb political groups likely to question this contradiction and exploit it for political purposes. Thus many facets of politics within the elite and between the elite and the masses may be expected to revolve around the contradiction I have delineated.

B. THE PARTY PROCESS

1. Coalition

The Sierra Leone party process took the form mainly of alliances, coalitions, and mergers between contending groups. The SLPP's hegemony emerged and was maintained in this manner. In the 1951 general election the SLPP won only two of the seven seats that were directly contested and four of the indirectly contested seats; the NCSL gained five of the former, and the remaining ten indirectly contested seats were gained by Independents. The election thus resulted in an impasse as far as party government was concerned: the new Legislative Council provided for an unofficial African majority, but no party gained a majority of the seats in the election. This situation impelled the Governor, Sir Georges Beresford-Stooke, to delay the installation of party government until further developments took place in the party system. "Where there is a well developed 'party system,' it is the practice ... to send for the leader of the party which commands a majority and invite him to form a government," declared the Governor at the first meeting of the new Legislature. "Here in Sierra Leone today I am not sure that the party system is yet quite sufficiently developed for me to introduce a procedure modelled, *mutatis mutandis*, on that which I have described."[22]

But, though the colonial government seemed unaware of it, the 1951 Legislature did have a majority of Protectorate representatives, and this fact proved to be of far-reaching significance in the future course of party politics. The Protectorate representatives were all indirectly elected—two by the Protectorate Assembly and twelve by District Councils, and eight of those chosen by the Councils were Paramount Chiefs. Sir Milton Margai, who was elected to the 1951 Legislature by the Bonthe District Council, applied his keen understanding of the political behavior of Protectorate Chiefs and, through a series of consultations with them, produced a majority for the SLPP. The Governor recognized the SLPP majority, and Sir Milton was called upon to form the first Executive Council with an African majority.

The subsequent SLPP governing majorities in the Legislature were formed through virtually the same maneuvers after both the 1957 and the 1962 general elections. The 1957 election results gave the SLPP eighteen of the thirty-nine directly contested seats, against nine for the UPP and twelve for Independents, while

[22] *Legislative Council Debates, No. 1 of Session 1951–52* (Freetown, 1952), p. 271.

eleven seats were reserved to Paramount Chiefs. The SLPP again fashioned a coalition within the Legislature with the Chiefs and the Independents, all but two of whom represented Protectorate constituencies, gaining thereby forty-one seats to nine for the UPP. The 1962 election results gave the Independents thirteen seats, twelve reserved for Chiefs, twenty for the opposition All People's Congress, and twenty-nine seats went to the SLPP. The Independents and Chiefs again allied with the SLPP, giving it a governing majority.[23]

2. Elaboration of the Reciprocity Model

The seemingly symbiotic relationship in the Legislature between the SLPP, Independents, and Chiefs rested upon a set of traditional values these Protectorate elements held in common. It was reinforced by competition between Colony and Protectorate interests and the political understanding that evolved among the Protectorate elite after World War II to meet this situation. The Chiefs, for instance, were for all practical purposes an integral part of the SLPP ever since its inception, and this fact virtually ensured that they would barter their twelve reserved seats in the Legislature in behalf of the SLPP. But it is notable that on each occasion when the Chiefs' seats were up for barter, it was clearly understood by all concerned that the SLPP had no ascriptive right to them. To the extent that the SLPP could gain these seats, it did so in full awareness that Chiefs did not divest themselves of their obligations to the chiefly elite—and thus of their autonomous vantage point of political action—upon legislative alliance with the SLPP.[24] The significance of this principle was

[23] A. G. Simpson, *Report on the Sierra Leone General Election, 1957* (Freetown, 1957), pp. 1–6; Electoral Commission, *Sierra Leone General Election, 1962, Score Sheet* (Freetown, 1962), pp. 1–12. As regards the voting strength of the SLPP, the situation was as follows in 1957 and 1962. In the 1957 election the SLPP gained 75,575 out of 165,479 votes, or 46 per cent, as against 89,904 votes for all other parties, or 54 per cent. Furthermore, the UPP and the Independents together gained 84,666 votes, or 51 per cent. In the 1962 general election the SLPP gained only 35 per cent of the total of 671,995 votes (this total represents 52 per cent of the qualified voters), whereas the opposition APC (in alliance with the SLPIM in Kono District) gained 23 per cent, and the Independents gained 42 per cent.

[24] Interview with Sir Milton Margai, March 1960.

267

underscored in 1957 when, faced with a threat to their autonomous political vantage point as a result of the contest for leadership between Sir Milton Margai and his brother, the Chiefs endeavored to guarantee their party position by founding their own pressure group within it, the Sierra Leone National Association. By the same token, the SLPP itself accepted the institutionalization of traditional political relationships by supporting the statutory reservation of chiefly representation in the Legislature. Sir Milton Margai played a large role in establishing this arrangement in all of the postwar constitutions.

Thus, the principle of reciprocity used in our analysis of the SLPP's relationship with voluntary associations is equally applicable to its other political relations. It enables us, in fact, to penetrate the complexity of the group basis of African politics, which I have emphasized throughout this study in contrast to or rather as a necessary complement of, the charismatic analysis of African political behavior used by some observers but which renders a much less intimate, less empirically valid, and less dialectically intricate comprehension of this behavior.[25]

Cognizant of the principle of reciprocity in African social relations, most Africans feel bound to seek a traditional or neo-traditional basis of political action. Among other things, it is the most effective way to maximize material *and* prestige benefits derived from politics, as well as to minimize the losses. The latter, in fact, may be more significant than the former goal, insofar as political losses within the assumptions of traditional society affect a network of persons beyond the individual actor; and given the general conditions of underdevelopment or backwardness, such persons are much less capable of individually recouping political losses through alternative outlets. Thus, in a certain sense African politics entails people acting from a kind of defensive or protectionist viewpoint, concerned more with conserving their

[25] Cf. David Apter, *The Gold Coast in Transition* (Princeton, 1955). For a more modified use of the charismatic model of African political behavior, see David Apter, *The Political Kingdom in Uganda* (Princeton, 1961). Cf. Lloyd Fallers and Audrey Richard, eds., *The King's Men* (London, 1963).

own or their group's needs and interests as they exist at any given moment than with advancing them in time and space.

Apart from utilizing a strategy of alliances, coalitions, and mergers in relation to the Chiefs and Independents within the Legislature, the SLPP employed this approach to reduce its organized opponents. This occurred most dramatically in March 1960 when, following a series of All-Party Roundtable Talks preparatory to the London Constitutional Conference scheduled for April, the opposition parties accepted a bid from the SLPP to join it in a coalition arrangement. The coalition, called the United National Front (UNF), endeavored "to bring the resources of all parties, sections and organizations to bear on the immediate problems which will be discussed at the Constitutional Conference . . . and other problems thereafter . . . including . . . the implementation of Independence and the efficient administration of Government. . . ."[26] Like most coalitions in African politics, the UNF tended toward a merger or fusion. In traditional society the surrender of autonomy by one group to a wider socio-political unit was effected through a measure of charismatic authority, insofar as a particular leader was endowed with that measure of authority implicit in the surrender of autonomy. The groups entering the UNF likewise placed themselves "under the leadership of Sir Milton Margai . . . our Premier."[27] But the loss of autonomy through charismatic authority is traditionally redressed under the assumptions of reciprocity. Thus after the completion of the Constitutional Conference the opposition party leaders were named members of the SLPP Cabinet. Albert Margai, the most important opposition leader, became Minister of Natural Resources and later Minister of Finance; C. Rogers-Wright of the UPP became Minister of Housing and Country Planning and later Minister of External Affairs; G. Dickinson-Thomas of the Independent Progressive Party became Minister of Social Welfare; and John Nelson-Williams, also of the Independent Progressive Party, became Minister of Information and Broadcasting.

[26] *Sierra Leone Daily Mail*, March 26, 1960, p. 1.
[27] *Ibid.*

Traditionally, when the principle of reciprocity applies to coalitions, it is reinforced by further surrender of autonomy of one group to the other through formal acts of deference, this being a concomitant feature of the role of charismatic (personal) authority in group interaction. Thus, within a year of joining the UNF "under the leadership of Sir Milton Margai," the opposition parties agreed to dissolve their formal structures in favor of merger with the SLPP. Even this act, however, did not destroy their traditional autonomy, which any of the coalescing groups remained free to assert if they could. Hence the role of feuds, intratribal wars, etc., in traditional African society.

At mid-1965 the merger of the opposition parties with the SLPP showed no sign of fragmentation. Nevertheless, in view of the rather militant leadership style of Albert Margai, who succeeded to the premiership of the SLPP following Sir Milton Margai's death in April 1964, there is a tendency for him to rely too heavily upon charismatic forms of authority in order to strengthen his own position. Traditionally, such overextension of charisma without structural reinforcements (i.e., the further institutional elaboration of reciprocity) frequently sparked political conflict. It is equally a source of conflict in the present Sierra Leonean government, as it is in most new African governments. Moreover, the conflict resulting from the breakdown of charisma under these circumstances tends to be rectified, by one party or another, mainly through tyrannical authority—a prospect faced by not a few African states.

The relations between opposition parties have equally centered around alliances, coalitions, and merger; and, as in the case of their relations with the SLPP, this has reflected a certain traditional inspiration. Within less than a year of its formation by Albert Margai and Siaka Stevens in September 1958, the PNP benefited from the accession to it of three leading SLPP legislators (Maigore Kallon, a Ministerial Secretary; S. T. Navo, Chief Whip; and A. J. Massally, Deputy Speaker) who were ideologically dissatisfied with the governing party. The PNP further expanded its position in the Legislature when, in November 1959, the venerable nationalist I. T. A. Wallace-Johnson brought his Radical Democratic Party (which he had created in July 1958 as a party cover for himself within the Legislature) into alliance with it. At the same time the members of the Legislature for Kono District, Tamba S. Mbriwa and A. A. Mani (leaders of the Kono Progressive Movement which was formed in the mid-1950's) allied with the PNP to form the PNP-Alliance. A final opposition party that gained much of its legislative standing through realignments within the Legislature was the Independent Progressive Party (IPP). It emerged during the months of December 1959 and January 1960 when five UPP legislators, disgruntled over what they called the "autocratic rule" of the party's leader, Cyril Rogers-Wright, regrouped under a new party cover—the IPP. The UPP, in fact, had started to disintegrate in February 1958 when two of its executive members who were Protectorate Africans joined the SLPP, and the formation of the IPP merely marked the culmination of this process.

Outside the Legislature, two parties of some significance have resulted from the same realignment process. The lesser of these was the Sierra Leone Progressive Independence Movement (SLPIM), which was organized in September 1959 when Tamba S. Mbriwa's KPM and Edward W. Blyden's Sierra Leone Independence Movement (SLIM) merged. The SLIM, led by a university lecturer, had suffered a devastating defeat in the 1957 general election, gaining no seats and defaulting the deposits of its four candidates, including Mr. Blyden. It thus had little choice but to join a more viable party structure if it wished some form of survival. The KPM, on the other hand, had long sought an opportunity to gain support outside the Kono District; it accordingly took on the flimsy structure of the SLIM and its verbally active but small membership, most of which was limited to Freetown. Tamba Mbriwa assumed the presidency of the new party, the SLPIM, and all SLIM members automatically registered as members of the new combined Movement.

The All People's Congress (APC) was the other party that emerged by way of realignments outside the Legislature. Within a year of its formation in August–September 1960, the APC became the most vigorous competitor the SLPP had encountered

271

since 1951. The circumstances surrounding the formation of the APC provide an illuminating example of the breakdown of traditional political values.

Siaka Stevens, the leader of the APC and a Protectorate African, was deputy leader of the PNP when it joined the SLPP-instigated United National Front in April 1960. But the leading elements in the UNF failed to satisfy his expectations from the application of the principle of reciprocity in the functioning of the coalition, partly owing to ideological differences but equally to Stevens' own political ambitions, which the SLPP component within the UNF firmly opposed. It was, of course, no matter of surprise that Stevens' ambitions were opposed; the UNF, as an articulation of competing authorities (hence a coalition), was contingent upon the charismatic (personal) authority of the SLPP's leader, Sir Milton Margai, and inevitably charisma fails as a stabilizing force in the political process when, as is usually the case in African politics, there is conflict or competition regarding its possessor.

The result was preordained: the breakdown of the principle of reciprocity as a binding factor in Stevens' relationship to the UNF. Traditionally, the breakdown of the reciprocity principle was a grave matter, which individuals and groups did their utmost to avert. Marion Kilson, analyzing Mende social relationships through folklore told to her by Mende males, has underscored the significance of reciprocity in Mende society, finding that "Of the stories in which male friendship was the pivotal relationship, 80 per cent revolved about the abrogation of the norms of reciprocity and mutuality . . . Reciprocity in terms of service and respect is the primary norm governing male friendship. It is assumed that friends will give one another trustworthy advice which should be followed. Nevertheless, it is expected that circumspectness will characterize these relationships and that a man will not shame his friend. When friendships are broken, it is because one of the pair has failed to heed the other's advice, has broken their agreement by failing to fulfill his obligations, insulted the other by being overtly frank, or has displayed excessive greed."[28]

[28] Marion Kilson, "Social Relationships in Mende Domɛisia," p. 170.

Whereas traditionally the breakdown of the reciprocity principle, especially between groups, was a prelude to feuding, vendetta, or warfare, under modern African politics the result is party or group factionalism and perpetual realignment. Certain features of feuding or related behavior, including violence between parties, also occur. Stevens, for instance, chose the occasion of the ceremony for signing the independence agreement between the Sierra Leone delegation and the British government to assert his withdrawal. To the utter surprise of both the British and African participants at the conference, he, with no prior announcement, refused to sign the documents embodying the independence agreement when it was passed to him at the ceremony—an act akin to feuding behavior. He also returned to Sierra Leone after the Constitutional Conference two weeks before the rest of the delegation and proceeded immediately to give his feud with the UNF organization expression in the form of the Elections-Before-Independence Movement, formed by Stevens at the end of May 1960.[29]

Stevens' action attracted disaffected groups within his opponent's camp. These included Wallace-Johnson's rather insignificant Radical Democratic Party, some equally insignificant Creole elements who never accepted the National Council of Sierra Leone's decision to join the UNF, and the rather more significant rump PNP elements in the hinterland towns (mainly young clerks and skilled workers who were ideologically uncomfortable in alliance with the SLPP), and a motley category of urban and town-dwelling poor who, though normally backing the SLPP, were open to alternative political outlets. Although Stevens failed in his goal of forcing a general election before the advent of independence in April 1961, it was the potential support to be gained among these groups that enabled him to reorganize the Elections-Before-Independence Movement into a full-fledged party, the

[29] The political propaganda of Stevens' elections movement and APC reflected the feuding quality in Stevens' behavior. See, e.g., Siaka Stevens, *Why I Did Not Sign the Conference Papers* (Freetown, 1960); *Resolutions Passed by a Mass Meeting of the Elections-Before-Independence Movement, 17th July, 1960* (Freetown, 1960); *Resolutions Passed by a Mass Meeting of the All People's Congress, 11th September, 1960* (Freetown, 1960).

APC, which took place in September 1960. Two months later the APC won the annual elections to the Freetown City Council, has won each such election since then, and in the 1962 general election it gained one-third of the directly contested seats—the first such success by an opposition party since the rise of party politics in 1951.

3. Political Degeneration and the Erosion of Democracy

We can deduce from the preceding analysis—which is, I think, applicable within limits to other African states—several important consequences for the future development of the party process in Sierra Leone. For one thing, although parties or groups coalesce to form more effective political units, they persist in holding a certain sub-identity within the new structure. This sub-identity is a function of the transfer of traditional perceptions of the guideposts of political behavior into the modern, democratic party process inherited from colonial rule. Its assertion in Sierra Leonean politics produced a high measure of fluidity in the constellation of groups that lent the SLPP a governing majority, though it has not destroyed this majority despite the close call of the 1962 general election following upon the APC's breakaway from the UNF. This assertion of group sub-identity has, however, been the Achilles' heel of Sierra Leone opposition parties ever since 1951; and this same experience has, in fact, plagued opposition groups elsewhere in Africa.

Thus a seemingly inherent instability pervades a democratic party process in which the participating groups fail to arrive at a pattern of consensus capable of surmounting the assertion of group sub-identity whenever major differences arise between them.[30] Moreover, before such a consensus can be achieved in new African political systems, the political perceptions and norms emanating from traditional society must be modified or replaced by more appropriate ones. Meanwhile it is likely that democratic political arrangements bequeathed to Africa by colonialism will degenerate into dictatorial arrangements, for only such arrange-

[30] Dankwart A. Rustow, *The Politics of Compromise: A Study of Parties and Cabinet Government in Sweden* (Princeton, 1955), esp. pp. 226–237.

ments are likely to hold the political system in some state of equilibrium—albeit unstable—while new political norms or values are being forged. This kind of political degeneration has already set in throughout much of post-colonial Africa, and there are not many conceivable alternatives to it in the foreseeable future.[31]

It is also possible to locate sources of future party trends by considering their sociological context. The relevant features of this context relate to the rural masses and the town-dwelling wage-laborers. Both segments of the population have, throughout the postwar years, variously displayed antagonism to the SLPP government. Their bursts of hostility, though sporadic and short-lived, have not been without political effect. The 1955 railway workers' strike, for example, sparked the formation of the Sierra Leonean Labor Party and stimulated the UPP to become a full-fledged party. Other outbursts by the masses also influenced opposition parties and the SLPP as well.

Mass discontent is rooted in the lack of opportunity for agricultural development in the hinterland and the drab life in dilapidated quarters in the towns. A social survey of Freetown in 1960 revealed that 40 per cent of the 5,656 persons studied in a total of 1,357 households earned under £10 per month; 37.2 per cent earned £10–19 per month, and 61.6 per cent of all families had only one earning member. Some 36.9 per cent of all households had three or more persons per room, four families out of every ten lived in one room, and only one family in six had approximately four rooms for living. Furthermore, four in ten families lived in houses built of corrugated iron sheets, and of these families 82 per cent used kerosene or candles for light. In the hinterland towns, living conditions were and are worse.[32]

Such conditions, especially now that the masses are taking

[31] Cf. Samuel P. Huntington, "Political Development and Political Decay," *World Politics* (April 1965), pp. 415–417. Huntington's discovery (or rediscovery) of the theory of "political degeneration" is very relevant to post-colonial African regimes.

[32] Sierra Leone Department of Labor, *Results of a Population Survey taken in Connection with the Revision of the Consumer Price Index for Freetown, September 1960* (mimeographed; Freetown, 1960), pp. 3, 56. On conditions in provincial towns, see A. Raymond Mills, *The Effect of Urbanisation on Health in a Mining Area of Sierra Leone* (mimeographed; Edinburgh, 1962).

greater notice of the difference between their standard of living and that of the elite, are relevant to the future of party politics. Election data provide a good gauge of what this relevance has been thus far, especially as regards the potential for opposition party development. The 1957 general election showed that, despite its Creole origin, the UPP had a measure of success as the first opposition party to contest Protectorate constituencies. It gained one seat in Kambia, two in Port Loko, and one in Moyamba; these districts were centers of the tax riots in 1955–56. With the exception of Moyamba, these same districts, plus Tonkolili and Bombali —also involved in the tax riots—gave the opposition APC a large share of the twenty seats it won out of the sixty-two directly contested in the 1962 general election. The APC won all three constituencies in Kambia, three of the four Bombali constituencies, three of the four Tonkolili constituencies, and three of the five Port Loko constituencies. Two constituencies in Kambia were won by more than 3,000 majority over the SLPP, one Bombali constituency by nearly 3,000 majority. Similarly, in the Freetown urban area constituencies, the APC won four out of twelve contests, and its defeat in the remaining constituencies was in no way as decisive as the defeat it inflicted on the SLPP in the Northern Province. Likewise in the Kono District, where the APC was in alliance with the SLPIM, it gained a striking victory in all four constituencies, piling up the largest over-all majority won anywhere in the election. It had nearly 8,000 majority in Kono North constituency, 3,029 in Kono South, nearly 6,000 in Kono East, and 4,153 in Kono West.[33]

The Kono victory was, of course, impossible without the alliance the APC had with the SLPIM, formerly the KPM, which carried the main burden of the victory. Formed in the mid-1950's when the Kono area was experiencing immense social change and political unrest consequent upon the diamond-mining industry, the KPM built itself a thoroughgoing political monopoly in Kono District. It astutely capitalized upon the unwillingness of the British mining firm, the Sierra Leone Selection Trust, to grant African

[33] Election figures are found in, *Sierra Leone General Election, 1962, Score Sheet.*

diggers areas not effectively mined by it—a policy which led to rampant illicit mining and smuggling.[34] The KPM also capitalized on the failure of the SLPP government to return to Kono District by way of adequate local government services (water supply, roads, education—all sadly neglected in Kono) a fair share of the sizable contribution to national revenue made by Kono District.[35] In organizing in behalf of these neglected needs of the Kono populace, the KPM affected a political style rather akin to the militant anti-colonial nationalism found in places like Ghana. Its election poster for the 1960 local election was a rare piece of militant nationalist propaganda for Sierra Leonean politics. It proclaimed: "To Save your Diamonds—to Revive and Protect Your Trade— for the Prosperity, Peace and Progress of Your Country and for Freedom and Plenty—Vote Solidly in the Great Freedom Pot and FREE SIERRA LEONE PEOPLE FROM IMPERIALIST EXPLOITATION." The 1960 local election was, incidentally, the first major encounter between the SLPP and the KPM; the latter won decisively, gaining twenty-four of the thirty seats in the District Council.

Faced with growing opposition among some peasants and wage-laborers combined with the increasing capacity of opposition parties to capitalize on this tendency, the SLPP responded largely by strengthening the traditional sources of its influence. This reac-

[34] See *Kono Mannda Weekly Bulletin,* October 27, 1958, p. 1. This organ of the KPM firmly backed the demands of African diggers for access to diamond fields. In 1960 a government source reported that smuggling and illicit digging involved £10,000,000 worth of diamonds. It is difficult to escape the conclusion that the British mining firm shared much of the responsibility for the chaotic state that smuggling and illicit digging brought to the industry and Kono District. During a closed investigation of illicit mining in 1957, the Provincial Commissioner, J. W. Malcom, expressed a similar view. "I understand," he said, the whole situation of Kono is that they have . . . [more] diamonds than any other area in the country but they have the least chance to dig them. This is the whole trouble about Kono, and it will continue as long as the Company has taken all the rich land." In response to the Commissioner's remarks, one of the commissioners of inquiry, R. T. Russel, declared: "That really has nothing to do with our inquiry; but after all it is the Company that has developed the thing." See "Proceedings of Commission of Inquiry into the Issue of Alluvial Diamond Mining Licenses at Gbambaiadu, Sando Chiefdom, Kono District, 1957" (unpublished MS; Sierra Leone Government Archives), pp. 313–314.

[35] See Ministry of Internal Affairs, *Plan for the Development of the Kono District, 1960–1964* (mimeographed; Freetown, 1959).

tion has been both conservative and incipiently authoritarian in character and portent. As already intimated, any other response by the SLPP was unlikely, given the intimate tie between the breakdown of the reciprocity principle and the spread of more developed opposition tendencies under the APC.

Politically, the breakdown of the reciprocity principle cuts two ways. For one thing, the post-colonial equilibrium of the elite, as a ruling group, is put in doubt. To avert this, the elite resort to authoritarian measures that seek to discourage factionalism within the ranks and to put the wider populace on notice that attempts to take advantage of the disarray within the elite will not be tolerated. But this reaction, in turn, merely complicates further the problem of the breakdown of the reciprocity principle and of its restoration as a governing force in political life. In reinforcing the position of the elite groups, authoritarian measures necessarily restrict the masses' access to the political process, thereby downgrading in the eyes of the masses the value of the reciprocity principle as a legitimate guide to political behavior. Increasingly, therefore, the elite rule not with the aid of a common set of political values held by themselves and the masses alike but by sheer monopoly of power.

Nevertheless, it is interesting that despite the weakening of the reciprocity principle (and of related traditional norms), the elite persist in using tradition to strengthen their rule. When faced with the breakdown of the reciprocity principle in its relations with the APC, the SLPP endeavored, *inter alia*, to shore up the traditional basis of its influence. It first sought to ensure that the Chiefs remained firm in their support of the party; in particular, the SLPP backed the election of the more conservative Chiefs to the twelve seats reserved for Chiefs in the Legislature. The SLPP assumed that such Chiefs were less inclined, in the face of modernizing forces, to discard the influence of traditional values in their relationship with the party. It also assumed that as the masses grew skeptical of the efficacy of traditional values as applied to the elite-mass political relationship, they would revert to the Chiefs as the only leadership they could trust. (Another response by the masses, of course, could be sheer alienation from all current leadership.)

Thus in 1961 the SLPP, in anticipation of the 1962 general election, expanded the representation of Tribal Authorities in the District Councils, the bodies that elect Chiefs to the Legislature.[36] Such packing of the District Councils was necessary to ensure the selection of more conservative Chiefs, because since the mid-1950's the Councils had attracted an increasingly more educated and modernized membership that preferred to send progressive Chiefs to the Legislature. For instance, in 1960–61 the influential Bo District Council had thirty-five middle-class persons among its sixty-two councillors (viz., three teachers, one retired senior civil servant, one clergyman, two druggists, one clerk in a European firm, three cash-crop farmers, and twenty-four traders and businessmen), only five of whom were illiterate. Moreover, twenty-seven of the councillors were traditional officeholders (viz., fifteen Paramount Chiefs, three Section Chiefs, one Town Chief, four Native Court Presidents, one Native Court Speaker, three Chiefdom Clerks).[37]

There was thus a clear need to reconstitute the politically relevant local elites.[38] The purpose of the SLPP policy of packing the District Councils with more representatives of Tribal Authorities was partly realized at the 1962 general election. The election resulted in the defeat of several rather advanced Chiefs, among whom was the well-educated and urbane Paramount Chief Bai Koblo of Marampa Chiefdom, Port Loko District. His successor was the rather poorly educated Paramount Chief Alkali Modu II, whose oppressive leadership in the Maforki Chiefdom, Port Loko District, was roundly criticized by the British commissioner of inquiry into the 1955–56 peasant tax riots. "In my opinion," concluded the commissioner, "the proved misconduct of the Paramount Chief on these complaints [viz., forced labor on his private farm, imposition of various illegal levies, cruelty to tardy taxpayers, and hindrance of right of petition to District Commissioners] amounts to conduct subversive of good government. I

---

[36] The Franchise and Electoral Registration Act, 1961, sec. 7.

[37] I am indebted to R. B. Kowa, former Secretary to the Bo District Council, for these data on the composition of the Bo Council.

[38] See Professor Huntington's discussion of what he calls "slowing mobilization" in order to stabilize developing political systems and modernization in general. Huntington, "Political Development and Political Decay," pp. 418 ff.

can find no extenuating circumstances in favour of the Paramount Chief; his misconduct is unworthy of a Paramount Chief."[39]

The SLPP's method of backing the efficacy of traditional values in the modern political process readily lends itself to authoritarian practices. Indeed, I see no feasible democratic alternative to this problem in the form in which it manifests itself in Sierra Leone and elsewhere in Africa. In 1960 the SLPP government, through the Minister of Internal Affairs, Sir Milton Margai, granted wide latitude to Native Administration Courts in controlling political activities of opposition groups. These activities fall within jurisdiction of Native Courts under the Tribal Authorities Ordinance of 1946, and in mid-1960 the Chiefs in Kono District—where the strain is greatest—exercised authority under the ordinance against the SLPIM. The party leader, Tamba Mbriwa, was tried and convicted by a Native Court of conspiring against a Paramount Chief's authority, and the Chief concerned was a member of the Court.[40]

Besides the more active use of their powers under the 1946 ordinance, Native Administrations have had their police powers strengthened through the provision of modern Chiefdom Police Forces. Established in 1959–60 by the SLPP government and elaborated in 1961, the new Chiefdom Police Forces were ensured a high measure of local autonomy through the formation of Watch Committees whose membership was drawn from Native Administrations.[41] Although at mid-1965 there was no evidence of undue use of local police power by Native Administrations, it is apparent that such could readily occur if the measures thus far taken by the SLPP to shore up traditional values in the party process prove of little avail.

---

[39] *Reports of the Commissioner of Enquiry into the Conduct of Certain Chiefs* (Freetown, 1957), p. 7. It is noteworthy that Paramount Chief Bai Koblo, a founding and influential member of the SLPP, did not take his defeat lightly. He showed signs of moving into open opposition to the SLPP after the 1962 general election, with the result that the SLPP government conducted an inquiry into the administration of his Chiefdom and temporarily banned him from functioning as a Paramount Chief.

[40] *Sierra Leone Daily News*, November 11, 1960, p. 1.

[41] *Report of the Sierra Leone Police Force*, 1959 (Freetown, 1960), pp. 45–46; *Chiefdom Police Ordinance, No. 195 of 1961*.

CHAPTER 17

Conclusion: The Nature of African Political Change

In this study the term "political change" has been used in its broadest sense, to include alteration in the ideas, values, procedures, and institutions concerned with the role of authority, power, influence, and government in a modernizing colonial system. The primary hypothesis used to analyze such political change was simple enough, namely, that fundamental political innovations occur in response to the endeavor of the colonial oligarchy of officials, technicians, and entrepreneurs, to create and maintain the framework of a market or money economy as the basic means for introducing the natural and human resources of an African territory into the world market system.[1] No doubt a stage is reached when the process of change in colonial political institutions takes on a logic of its own, untraceable in any mechanical way to some specific requirement of expanding the market economic and social systems. But even this stage of, as it were, built-in political change functions in the generalized context of the rationalizing norms and ethos of a developing colonial-type market economy; for as Weber, Marx, and other social theorists of modernization have been well aware, rationalization (by which I mean the effectuation of specialized structures or procedures appropriate to the performance of the major needs of a social system) is fundamental to the modern socio-economic system.[2]

[1] Cf. J. S. Furnivall, *Colonial Policy and Practice* (Cambridge, 1948), pp. 5 ff.; Kathleen Stahl, *The Metropolitan Organization of British Colonial Trade* (London, 1951), pp. xii-xiii (Margery Perham's Preface), 3–8, and *passim*.

[2] Cf. Max Weber, "Politics as a Vocation," in H. Gerth and C. Wright Mills,

As already intimated, the political change we speak of may be described as "modern" insofar as the sum total of the interplay of forces involved in introducing pre-literate or primitive societies into the world market system is tantamount to "modernizing" such societies. If the terms "modernization" or "modernization process" mean anything in this context, they refer at least to the transition of social systems from the stage of subsistence economic organization and method to that mode of economy centered upon the cash-nexus and the impersonal market system.[3] Politically, however, the term "modernization" also means something more than this. It means, especially, what S. N. Eisenstadt has called the spread or dispersal of power—that is, the widening of the sphere of access on the part of a given populace to the institutions of authority, decision making, command, administration, force and coercion in a social system.[4] This spread of power is the crucially distinctive feature of political modernization, setting off modern political systems from their historical antecedents. Throughout our study the analysis of the kinds of political change consequent upon colonial rule was governed by this kind of conception of the distinctive nature of political modernization.

A. LOCAL COLONIAL ADMINISTRATION

The problems of rural or local administration are an effective starting point for the analysis of African political change. This is so not only because we know rather little about them but

eds., *From Max Weber—Essays in Sociology* (New York, 1946); Karl Marx, "The British Rule in India," in *K. Marx and F. Engels on Colonialism* (Moscow, n.d.), pp. 23–81.

[3] Our notion of a money economy as a stage of development is taken from M. M. Postan who sees it as something "wider and more general than that of a mere currency inflation . . . A money economy in the true sense of the term depended for its development not so much on a general increase in production as on those subtler historical changes which led men away from domestic self-sufficiency and directed them towards shops and market places." Postan, "The Rise of a Money Economy," in E. M. Carus-Wilson, ed., *Essays in Economic History* (London, 1954), p. 8. Cf. Reinhard Bendix, *Nation-Building and Citizenship* (New York, 1964), pp. 4–9.

[4] S. N. Eisenstadt, "Modernization and Conditions of Sustained Growth," *World Politics* (July 1964), pp. 576–594.

because they provide the best opportunity for approaching political modernization in colonial Africa from the vantage point of the majority of the indigenous population and its native institutions and political values. Whatever experiences most Africans have with colonial modernization and however these experiences alter their political values, perceptions, and behavior, it is in rural society rather than the urban headquarters of colonial rule that these experiences take place.

Viewed from this perspective, one asks a set of questions about how and why modern political change occurs in colonial African societies rather different from those asked when the vantage point is the urban headquarters of government and of that much smaller segment of Africans, the new elite, that interacts more immediately with the central machinery of government. Besides enriching the analytical and theoretical aspects of the study of African political change, this perspective simultaneously lends such study a more practical bent, facilitating awareness of specific institutional and behaviorial problems of what Hicks has called "development from below."[5] Above all else, African development or modernization is, I think, fundamentally a matter of transformation of rural or local society, much more than it is a matter of large-scale industrialization, which cannot possibly occur in the foreseeable future. Finally, the perspective on the analysis of African political change that we suggest attunes the observer to the ways in which colonial political institutions and procedures are shaped by the pre-existing African institutions and the norms or values that inspire them. Our account of the foundation of the Native Administration system has shown the kind of interplay that occurred in Sierra Leone between the needs of local administration and the inherent characteristics of the traditional authority structures. The outcome of this interplay was no doubt modern in certain concrete respects, despite the lag of the traditional arrangements. For instance, the colonial political changes entailed the spread of power on a scale hitherto inconceivable; for the first time the rural populace had the opportunity to become citizens of the political institutions that governed their lives. For another

[5] Ursula Hicks, *Development from Below* (Oxford, 1961).

thing, there was a rationalization, after a fashion, of the uses of traditional authority and power along lines conducive to the processes contingent upon the rise of a market economy and related institutions.

Yet neither the spread of power nor the measure of institutional or procedural rationalization approximated a form of political modernization comparable to that found in Western societies. And this for good reasons, among which was the capacity of the traditional authority structures to assert some measure of their own mode of political organization and evaluation upon the colonial administrative system. They were equally capable of absorbing some degree of the socio-economic changes wrought by colonialism. Consequently, the traditional elite attained a framework of modernization—or rather something approximating such —coexistent with the mainstream of modernization controlled by the colonial oligarchy. This rather aberrant framework of modernization in the hands of traditional elite was found widely in colonial Africa and it facilitated the important role they played at all levels of colonial change. Accordingly, a major part of our analysis of political change in Sierra Leone has concerned the forces enabling the traditional authority structures to tilt colonial change in their behalf; it has also concerned the consequences of this traditionalist tilting of the colonial modernization process.

B. THE "MASS FACTOR" IN POLITICAL CHANGE

By grasping the way in which traditional authority structures interacted with the institutions of colonial change, it is possible to discern a rather special role played by the rural populace in political change. Insofar as the traditional authority structures were utilized to mediate change in local African society, the rural masses experience much of colonial change through these structures. Quite unwittingly, this method of colonial administration stimulated the masses to become a not inconsequential political force.

The role played by the masses in political change stemmed from the contradictions inherent in a method of colonial administration

which utilized traditional authority structures to mediate modernization in local society. It was doubtful that these structures could
avert the disintegration and weakening of at least a facet of their
legitimacy while mediating colonial change. The rural populace's
reaction to this contradiction normally followed anomic lines, entailing violent, riotous political expression. Although such anomic
behavior lacked the kind of sustained, articulated political action
capable of basically altering the traditional structures utilized to
mediate colonial change, it did have the effect of stimulating a
broader receptivity for political change in the colonial system. In
particular, it created situations of political instability with which
the colonial oligarchy had to contend, lest the requirements of
colonial efficiency be impaired. In attending to these situations,
the British colonial oligarchy, imbibed with the democratic-type
political heritage of the metropolitan society, responded to the
anomic behavior of the masses by facilitating the "spread of
power" in rural society. The establishment of Native Administrations in the late 1930's was an initial step to this end, but serious
steps to institutionalize a form of citizenship for the masses do
not occur until after World War II.

Linked to the colonial government's search for means to institutionalize the spread of power in rural society were changes in
the constitutional structures and principles of central colonial
government. Here it was less a question of rationalizing the masses'
relationship to colonial modernization—though this was partly involved—than a matter of rationalizing the institutional setting in
which the new elite endeavored to generalize its mode of politics
to the African masses. Such rationalization was the essence of
colonial constitutional change in Sierra Leone and elsewhere in
Africa, and the result was the assimilation of the masses' mode of
political evolution, essentially dysfunctional to the requirements
of colonial modernization, to the basically Western-type political
behavior of the new elite.

As this assimilation of the political patterns of the masses and
the elite groups developed, the elite were capable of exacting
further constitutional concessions from the colonial oligarchy.
The new elite and the colonial oligarchy had common interests in

facilitating constitutional change: the elite required such change to advance their own socio-economic standing; the colonial masters obtained greater efficiency through the advancement of the new elite. The colonial oligarchy also expected greater stability in local society as the new elite, abetted by constitutional change (including ultimately the mass franchise), spread their political influence and leadership to rural society.

It was ultimately this curious identity of interest between the new elite and the colonial oligarchy that facilitated the peaceful transfer of power to African regimes in most of colonial Africa. Although an array of international forces in the postwar world also influenced this transfer, it would seem almost unlikely without the perception on the part of the new elite and the colonial oligarchy of a set of mutual interests. The impact of this mode of the transfer of power should be evident at many levels of the postcolonial African regimes.

C. THE ROLE OF TRADITION AND
THE EROSION OF DEMOCRACY

When viewed from the perspective of local society, the role of tradition stands out in the evolution of the elite-mass relationship in African political change. In Sierra Leone, for example, the attempt of the new elite to obtain mass support for its bid to rule was contingent upon a variety of ties with the traditional ruling strata. It was also contingent upon the new elite's infusion of its political relationship with the masses with traditional perceptions and evaluations of political behavior.

We have demonstrated the variety of ways in which traditional perceptions permeated Sierra Leonean politics through an analysis of the SLPP's relationship with voluntary associations and the role of alliances and coalitions in the party process. In delineating these features of Sierra Leonean politics we utilized a reciprocity model of traditional socio-political relations, emphasizing those features of the principle of reciprocity that seemed unique—or rather that we projected conceptually as being unique—to African societies. The value of such a model is that it brings the analysis of contemporary politics closer to the primordial texture of African social and political behavior. It was of particular value in helping us cast our account of the tendency toward the breakdown or degeneration of the competitive party process in terms of a crisis of traditional African political perceptions in a modernizing context.

For example, when transposed to the modern context without prior modification, the principle of reciprocity is difficult to assimilate politically because of the sizable material wealth (gift) required for its functioning. In traditional society the number of persons with viable access to the political process was decidedly smaller than that in the modern political system; it is, after all, precisely the fact that larger numbers have access to structures of authority and power that make a socio-political system *modern*. Thus, to persist in the modern context in utilizing traditional African guideposts to political relations or behavior like the reciprocity principle is, I suggest, inevitably to court basic sociopolitical breakdown or disequilibrium, especially in view of the sizable wealth required for these guideposts to function in a modern system.

Reference to the role of charismatic (personal) authority illustrates the problem well. African political leaders, for example, treat the personal aspects of their authority in the modern context as if they were actually functioning in a traditional setting. Traditionally, any overextension of charismatic authority—that is, asserting it beyond its "natural" limits—usually entailed a further institutional elaboration of the reciprocity principle, which meant the establishment of an arrangement for a new flow or exchange of wealth to the group or person affected by the overasserted charisma. But such application of charismatic authority in a modern setting—as has occurred under Nkrumah in Ghana and in many other states as well, although at a lower level of charismatic appeal, as in Nigeria—entails so much more in the way of supportive wealth. To obtain this wealth, however, requires an exceptionally effective program of economic development, which is rare in post-colonial Africa. The political elite thus have resort to bureaucratic corruption—a process the African elite have proved extraordinarily astute in perfecting—in order to support their unqualified application of traditional norms like the reciprocity principle to the modernizing systems inherited from colonialism.[6]

Confronted with such difficulties of assimilating traditional African political norms or perceptions to the modernizing systems, the new elite invariably resort to authoritarian political methods, many of which border on tyrannical uses of power. There is, then, some sense in which such methods may be seen as necessary for the maintenance of the political integrity of a given regime, though few things can be held as absolutely necessary in the realm of politics, for alternative political methods are infinite. Equally significant, however, is the fact that the new elite resort to authoritarian methods especially to maintain their own favored status in the post-colonial regimes; such methods enable them either to prevent or to regulate on their own terms the claims by the masses for more equitable access to the available spheres of modernization. The new elite are, after all, largely parasitic; they bring mainly bureaucratic or political (manipulative) skills to the modernizing process but depend upon the economically productive role of either the cash-cropping peasantry or expatriate capital and entrepreneurs for the revenues without which their bureaucratic role goes for naught. Indeed, short of the productive role of cash-cropping peasants and expatriate capitalists most of the new elite in Africa approximate the emperor with no clothes. Thus, there is a range in which the new elite are impelled to reinforce their status through authoritarian and/or tyrannical means, much as what Marx meant when he remarked that "during the very first storms of the [French] revolution, the French bourgeoisie dared to take away from the workers the right of association but just acquired."[7]

Presently, such means have become established features of

[6] For a good study of the bureaucratically corrupt and economically distorting search for the wealth (gift) required to underwrite the kind of political process I have delineated, see Charles V. Brown, *Government and Banking in Western Nigeria* (Ibadan, 1964). This phenomenon can also be discerned by the discriminating observer from the data on state-owned corporations in Ghana, published in *The Budget 1965* (Accra, 1965).

[7] Karl Marx, *Capital* (New York, 1936), p. 813.

many post-colonial regimes in Africa. Sierra Leone, however, has been almost unique in maintaining a fair measure of the democratic polity it inherited from colonial rule, and one would hope it can persist in this. But our analysis of the post-colonial party process in Sierra Leone leaves few grounds for optimism, and a movement toward full-fledged authoritarian rule in the near future would be no surprise.[8]

[8] In January, 1966, the SLPP introduced in Parliament a motion calling for the establishment of a one-party regime. In support of the motion, Sir Albert Margai, the Prime Minister, invited its opponents to visit Ghana in order to see the presumed effectiveness of the one-party system. He considered the system "in the interest of political stability and solidarity" of Sierra Leone. *West Africa,* February 5, 1966, p. 160.

Selected Bibliography

Index

Selected Bibliography

BOOKS AND ARTICLES

General

Balandier, Georges. *Sociologie actuelle de l'Afrique noire*. Paris: Presses Universitaires de France, 1955.

Buell, Raymond L. *Native Problems in Africa*. New York: Macmillan, 1928.

Cowan, L. Gray. *Local Government in West Africa*. New York: Columbia University Press, 1958.

————. "Local Politics and Democracy in Nigeria," in W. O. Brown and G. Carter, eds. *Transition in Africa*. Boston: Boston University Press, 1958.

Emerson, Rupert. *Malaysia: A Study in Direct and Indirect Rule*. New York: Macmillan, 1937.

Furnivall, J. S. *Colonial Policy and Practice*. Cambridge: Cambridge University Press, 1948.

Hailey, Lord Malcolm. *An African Survey*. London: Oxford University Press, 1938.

————. *Native Administration in British African Territories*. Vols. III–IV. London: HMSO, 1951.

Hodgkin, Thomas. *Nationalism in Colonial Africa*. London: Frederick Muller, 1957.

————. *African Political Parties*. London: Penguin, 1961.

Lugard, Sir Frederick D. *The Dual Mandate in British Tropical Africa*. Edinburgh: William Blackwood and Sons, 1922.

Perham, Margery. *Native Administration in Nigeria*. London: Oxford University Press, 1937.

Sierra Leone

Alldridge, T. J. *The Sherbro and Its Hinterland*. London: Macmillan, 1901.

————. *A Transformed Colony*. London: Seeley and Co., 1910.

Austin, Dennis. "People and Constitution in Sierra Leone," *West Africa* (September 13, 20, 27, October 4, 11, 1952).

Banton, Michael. *West African City*. London: Oxford University Press, 1957.

SELECTED BIBLIOGRAPHY

Cox-George, N. A. *Finance and Development in West Africa: The Sierra Leone Experiment.* London: Dobson, 1961.

Easmon, M. C. F. "Sierra Leone Doctors," *Sierra Leone Studies* (June 1956).

Fyfe, Christopher. *A History of Sierra Leone.* London: Oxford University Press, 1962.

————. "The Life and Times of John Ezzidio," *Sierra Leone Studies* (June 1955).

————. "The Sierra Leone Press in the Nineteenth Century," *Sierra Leone Studies* (June 1957).

Hair, P. E. H. "An Analysis of the Register of Fourah Bay College, 1827–1950," *Sierra Leone Studies* (December 1956).

Hargreaves, J. D. *A Life of Sir Samuel Lewis.* London: Oxford University Press, 1958.

Hedges, D. M. "Progress of Kambia District Council, Sierra Leone," *Journal of African Administration,* V (January 1953).

Keith-Lucas, Bryan. "Electoral Reform in Sierra Leone," *Political Studies,* III (June 1955).

Kilson, Martin. "Sierra Leone Politics," *West Africa* (June 22, 29, July 2, 9, 1960).

————. "Sierra Leone," in Helen Kitchen, ed. *Educated Africans.* New York: Frederick Praeger, 1962.

————. "Grass-Roots Politics in Africa," *Political Studies,* XII (February 1964).

————. "Sierra Leone," in James S. Coleman and Carl G. Rosberg, Jr., eds. *Political Parties and National Integration in Tropical Africa.* Berkeley: University of California Press, 1964.

Kirby, D. "Ballots in the Bush: A Case Study on Local Elections in the Bo District of Sierra Leone," *Journal of African Administration,* IX (October 1957).

Lewis, Roy. *Sierra Leone.* London: HMSO, 1954.

Little, K. L. *The Mende of Sierra Leone.* London: Routledge and Kegan Paul, 1951.

————. "Social Change and Social Class in the Sierra Leone Protectorate," *American Journal of Sociology,* LIV (July 1948).

————. "The Role of Voluntary Associations in West African Urbanization," *American Anthropologist,* LIX (August 1957).

McCullough, Meran. *Peoples of the Sierra Leone Protectorate.* London: International African Institute, 1950.

Ndanema, I. M. "The Martha Davies Confidential Benevolent Association," *Sierra Leone Bulletin of Religion,* III (December 1961).

Porter, A. T. *Creoledom.* London: Oxford University Press, 1963.

————. "The Social Background of Political Decision-Makers in Sierra Leone," *Sierra Leone Studies* (June 1960).

Proudfoot, L. "Towards Muslim Solidarity in Freetown," *Africa,* XXXI (April 1961).

Scott, D. J. R. "Sierra Leone General Election, May 1957," in W. J. M. Mackenzie and Kenneth Robinson, eds. *Five Elections in Africa.* Oxford: Clarendon Press, 1960.

SELECTED BIBLIOGRAPHY

OFFICIAL REPORTS, 1898–1960

Sierra Leone Report for 1898. Cmd. 9498. London: HMSO, 1899.

Chalmers, Sir David. *Report by Her Majesty's Commissioner and Correspondence on the Subject of the Insurrection in the Sierra Leone Protectorate 1898.* I–II. Cmd. 9388, 9391. London: HMSO, 1899.

Annual Report of the Southern Province for the Year 1921. Freetown: Government Printer, 1922.

Sierra Leone Blue Book, 1926. Freetown: Government Printer, 1927.

Trade Report for the Year 1926. Freetown: Government Printer, 1927.

Despatches in Connexion with the Estimates for 1927, Sessional Paper No. 3 of 1927. Freetown: Government Printer, 1927.

Administrative Sub-Divisions of the Colony and of the Protectorate. Freetown: Government Printer, 1930.

Report of Census for the Year 1931. Freetown: Government Printer, n.d.

Fenton, J. S. *Report on a Visit to Nigeria and on the Application of the Principles of Native Administration to the Protectorate of Sierra Leone.* Freetown: Government Printer, 1935.

Annual Report of the Provincial Administration for the Year 1936. Freetown: Government Printer, 1937.

Annual Report of the Provincial Administration for the Year 1937. Freetown: Government Printer, 1938.

Annual Report of the Provincial Administration for the Year 1938. Freetown: Government Printer, 1939.

Correspondence Relating to the Reorganisation of Protectorate Administration, Sessional Paper No. 5 of 1939. Freetown: Government Printer, 1939.

A Scheme for the Reorganisation of the Court Messenger Force, Sessional Paper No. 7 of 1939. Freetown: Government Printer, 1939.

Despatches in Connexion with the Estimates for 1939, Sessional Paper No. 4 of 1939. Freetown: Government Printer, 1939.

Report of the Slum Clearance Committee, Sessional Paper No. 9 of 1939. Freetown: Government Printer, 1939.

Report on the Tribal Administration in Freetown, Sessional Paper No. 4 of 1940. Freetown: Government Printer, 1940.

Sierra Leone Labour Report, 1939–1940. Freetown: Government Printer, 1941.

Report on the Labour Department, 1943. Freetown: Government Printer, 1944.

Childs, Hubert. *An Outline of the Ten-Year Plan for the Development of Sierra Leone, Sessional Paper No. 4 of 1946.* Freetown: Government Printer, 1946.

Proposals for the Reconstitution of the Legislative Council in Sierra Leone, Sessional Paper No. 2 of 1948. Freetown: Government Printer, 1948.

Report of the Select Committee Appointed by His Excellency . . . to Consider Proposals for a Reconstituted Legislative Council in Sierra Leone, Sessional Paper No. 7 of 1948. Freetown: Government Printer, 1948.

Annual Report on the Sierra Leone Protectorate for the Year 1947. Freetown: Government Printer, 1949.

SELECTED BIBLIOGRAPHY

Annual Report on the Sierra Leone Protectorate for the Year 1948. Freetown: Government Printer, 1950.

Reconstitution of the Legislative Council of Sierra Leone, 1950, Sessional Paper No. 2 of 1950. Freetown: Government Printer, 1950.

Annual Report on the Sierra Leone Protectorate for the Years 1949–1950. Freetown: Government Printer, 1952.

Annual Report on the Sierra Leone Protectorate for the Year 1951. Freetown: Government Printer, 1953.

Annual Report on the Provincial Administration for the Year 1952. Freetown: Government Printer, 1953.

Brooke, N. J. *Report on the Native Court System in Sierra Leone.* Freetown: Government Printer, 1953.

Assumption of Ministerial Portfolios, Sessional Paper No. 1 of 1953. Freetown: Government Printer, 1953.

Davidson, H. W. *Report on the Function and Finance of District Councils in Sierra Leone.* Freetown: Government Printer, 1953.

Keith-Lucas, Bryan. *Report of the Electoral Reform Commission.* Freetown: Government Printer, 1954.

Annual Report on the Administration of the Provinces for the Year 1953. Freetown: Government Printer, 1955.

Report on Progress of Africanisation, 1954. Freetown: Government Printer, 1955.

Collected Statements of Constitutional Proposals, September 1955. Freetown: Government Printer, 1955.

Report of the Committee Appointed to Examine the Working of the Tribal Administration (Colony) Ordinance, Cap. 244. Freetown: Government Printer, 1955.

Report on the Administration of the Provinces for the Year 1954. Freetown: Government Printer, 1956.

Cox, Sir Herbert. *Report of Commission of Inquiry into Disturbances in the Provinces, November 1955–March 1956.* Freetown: Government Printer, 1956.

1955 Report on the Administration of the Provinces. Freetown: Government Printer, 1957.

Reports of the Commissioners of Enquiry into the Conduct of Certain Chiefs. Freetown: Government Printer, 1957.

Further Reports of the Commissioners of Enquiry into the Conduct of Certain Chiefs. Freetown: Government Printer, 1957.

Marke, R. B. *Report of the Commission of Inquiry into the Issue of Alluvial Diamond Mining Licences in the Gbambaiadu Area, Kono District.* Freetown: Government Printer, 1957.

Report on the Administration of the Provinces, 1956. Freetown: Government Printer, 1958.

Exchange of Despatches on Further Constitutional Change, Sessional Paper No. 2 of 1958. Freetown: Government Printer, 1958.

Cox-George, N. A. *Report on African Participation in the Commerce of Sierra Leone.* Freetown: Government Printer, 1958.

Report of the Sierra Leone Constitutional Conference, 1960. Freetown: Government Printer, 1960.

Index

PUBLICATIONS WRITTEN UNDER THE AUSPICES OF THE CENTER FOR INTERNATIONAL AFFAIRS HARVARD UNIVERSITY

BOOKS

The Soviet Bloc, by Zbigniew K. Brzezinski (jointly with the Russian Research Center), 1960. Harvard University Press.

The Necessity for Choice, by Henry A. Kissinger, 1961. Harper & Bros.

Strategy and Arms Control, by Thomas C. Schelling and Morton H. Halperin, 1961. Twentieth Century Fund.

Rift and Revolt in Hungary, by Ferenc A. Váli, 1961. Harvard University Press.

United States Manufacturing Investment in Brazil, by Lincoln Gordon and Engelburt L. Grommers, 1962. Harvard Business School.

The Economy of Cyprus, by A. J. Meyer, with Simos Vassiliou (jointly with the Center for Middle Eastern Studies), 1962. Harvard University Press.

Entrepreneurs of Lebanon, by Yusif A. Sayigh (jointly with the Center for Middle Eastern Studies), 1962. Harvard University Press.

Communist China 1955–1959: Policy Documents with Analysis, with a Foreword by Robert R. Bowie and John K. Fairbank (jointly with the East Asian Research Center), 1962. Harvard University Press.

In Search of France, by Stanley Hoffman, Charles P. Kindleberger, Laurence Wylie, Jesse R. Pitts, Jean-Baptiste Duroselle, and François Goguel, 1963. Harvard University Press.

Somali Nationalism, by Saadia Touval, 1963. Harvard University Press.

The Dilemma of Mexico's Development, by Raymond Vernon, 1963. Harvard University Press.

Limited War in the Nuclear Age, by Morton H. Halperin, 1963. John Wiley & Sons.

The Arms Debate, by Robert A. Levine, 1963. Harvard University Press.

Africans on the Land, by Montague Yudelman, 1964. Harvard University Press.

Counterinsurgency Warfare, by David Galula, 1964. Frederick A. Praeger, Inc.

People and Policy in the Middle East, by Max Weston Thornburg, 1964. W. W. Norton & Co.

Shaping the Future, by Robert R. Bowie, 1964. Columbia University Press.

Foreign Aid and Foreign Policy, by Edward S. Mason (jointly with the Council on Foreign Relations), 1964. Harper & Row.

Public Policy and Private Enterprise in Mexico, by M. S. Wionczek, D. H. Shelton, C. P. Blair, and R. Izquierdo, ed. Raymond Vernon, 1964. Harvard University Press.

How Nations Negotiate, by Fred C. Iklé, 1964. Harper & Row.

China and the Bomb, by Morton H. Halperin (jointly with the East Asian Research Center), 1965. Frederick A. Praeger, Inc.

Democracy in Germany, by Fritz Erler (Jodidi Lectures), 1965. Harvard University Press.

The Troubled Partnership, by Henry A. Kissinger (jointly with the Council on Foreign Relations), 1965. McGraw-Hill Book Co.

The Rise of Nationalism in Central Africa, by Robert I. Rotberg, 1965. Harvard University Press.

Pan-Africanism and East African Integration, by Joseph S. Nye, Jr., 1965. Harvard University Press.

Communist China and Arms Control, by Morton H. Halperin and Dwight H. Perkins (jointly with the East Asian Research Center), 1965. Frederick A. Praeger, Inc.

Problems of National Strategy, ed. Henry Kissinger, 1965. Frederick A. Praeger, Inc.

Deterrence before Hiroshima: The Airpower Background of Modern Strategy, by George H. Quester, 1966. John Wiley & Sons.

Containing the Arms Race, by Jeremy J. Stone, 1966. M.I.T. Press.

Germany and the Atlantic Alliance: The Interaction of Strategy and Politics, by James L. Richardson, 1966. Harvard University Press.

Arms and Influence, by Thomas C. Schelling, 1966. Yale University Press.

Export Instability and Economic Development, by Alasdair MacBean, 1966. Harvard University Press.

Planning without Facts, by Wolfgang F. Stolper, 1966. Harvard University Press.

Political Change in a West African State, by Martin L. Kilson, 1966. Harvard University Press.

OCCASIONAL PAPERS, PUBLISHED BY THE
CENTER FOR INTERNATIONAL AFFAIRS

1. *A Plan for Planning: The Need for a Better Method of Assisting Underdeveloped Countries on Their Economic Policies*, by Gustav F. Papanek, 1961.
2. *The Flow of Resources from Rich to Poor*, by Alan D. Neale, 1961.
3. *Limited War: An Essay on the Development of the Theory and an Annotated Bibliography*, by Morton H. Halperin, 1962.
4. *Reflections on the Failure of the First West Indian Federation*, by Hugh W. Springer, 1962.
5. *On the Interaction of Opposing Forces under Possible Arms Agreements*, by Glenn A. Kent, 1963.
6. *Europe's Northern Cap and the Soviet Union*, by Nils Örvik, 1963.
7. *Civil Administration in the Punjab: An Analysis of a State Government in India*, by E. N. Mangat Rai, 1963.
8. *On the Appropriate Size of a Development Program*, by Edward S. Mason, 1964.
9. *Self-Determination Revisited in the Era of Decolonization*, by Rupert Emerson, 1964.
10. *The Planning and Execution of Economic Development in Southeast Asia*, by Clair Wilcox, 1965.
11. *Pan-Africanism in Action*, by Albert Tevoedjre, 1965.
12. *Is China Turning In?* by Morton H. Halperin, 1965.
13. *Economic Development in India and Pakistan*, by Edward S. Mason, 1966.